T0320110

State and Local Financial Instruments

STUDIES IN FISCAL FEDERALISM AND STATE–LOCAL FINANCE

Series Editor: Wallace E. Oates, *Professor of Economics, University of Maryland, College Park and University Fellow, Resources for the Future, USA*

This important series is designed to make a significant contribution to the development of the principles and practices of state–local finance. It includes both theoretical and empirical work. International in scope, it addresses issues of current and future concern in both East and West and in developed and developing countries.

The main purpose of the series is to create a forum for the publication of high quality work and to show how economic analysis can make a contribution to understanding the role of local finance in fiscal federalism in the twenty-first century.

Titles in the series include:

State and Local Financial Instruments

Policy Changes and Management

Craig L. Johnson
Indiana University, Bloomington, USA

Martin J. Luby
DePaul University, USA

Tima T. Moldogaziev
University of Georgia, USA

STUDIES IN FISCAL FEDERALISM AND STATE–LOCAL
FINANCE

Edward Elgar
Cheltenham, UK • Northampton, MA, USA

Published by
Edward Elgar Publishing Limited
The Lypiatts
15 Lansdown Road
Cheltenham
Glos GL50 2JA
UK

Edward Elgar Publishing, Inc.
William Pratt House
9 Dewey Court
Northampton
Massachusetts 01060
USA

A catalogue record for this book
is available from the British Library

Library of Congress Control Number: 2014938813

This book is available electronically in the ElgarOnline.com
Social and Political Science Subject Collection, E-ISBN 978 1 78347 617 6

ISBN 978 1 78347 616 9

Typeset by Servis Filmsetting Ltd, Stockport, Cheshire
Printed and bound in Great Britain by T.J. International Ltd, Padstow

To the Elders: Larry, Willie Mae, Frank and Dorothy, who led all others by word, deed and heart.
To the memory of William F. Luby, who from my earliest age inspired my passion for politics and public policy.
To the memory of my parents: Gülbübü and Tilek Moldogaziev, who showed me how to embrace the world with an open mind and heart.

Contents

1. Introduction

Why is understanding the financial instruments sold by state and local governments in the United States of America important?

The 2007–09 Financial Crisis and Great Recession tested financial institutions and markets like nothing else since the depression of the 1920s and 1930s, changing them in fundamental ways. The municipal securities market and its institutions were no exception. The municipal market was placed under extreme stress and several of its practices and institutions did not stand up to the challenge. The municipal market is a changed market, and our understanding of the market must evolve as well.

The scope of this book is the market that state and local (subnational)[1] governments have used to meet their capital needs since the seventeenth century.[2] The municipal market is essential to the well-being of American society and our book provides an analytical treatment of the essentials of the market. Our book contributes to the understanding of the municipal securities market in the post-Financial Crisis era. The focus of the book is on subnational debt issuers and their constituents. The aim of the book is to assist scholars and students, policymakers and practitioners, develop policies and implement practices that help the municipal securities market serve its vital role in society. Throughout the book we stress the importance of understanding how the role and function of the municipal market operates alongside the unique structure of American fiscal federalism. It has become almost customary to refer to United States state governments as 'fiscal sovereigns'. While we recognize and appreciate the constitutional undergirding providing states with the 'right' of fiscal independence from the United States federal government, we also focus on the 'responsibilities' that states have regarding their own fiscal affairs and that of the local governments they create.

Moreover, fiscal federalism lies at the heart of the ability of subnational governments to maintain access to the market for capital at reasonable prices in a free market system where economic resources are allocated by private decision makers, not coerced from or by a higher level of government. In the post-Financial Crisis world, a basic fiscal federalism question must be asked: what is the role of the federal (central) government in the financial market of state and local (decentralized) debt issuers?

Our perspective on this question is that state–local (subnational) capital financing decision making is more likely to optimize social welfare than centralized decision making. We follow the view articulated by Oates that: 'an outcome with local outputs tailored to the demands (and particular conditions) of each jurisdiction will clearly provide a higher level of social welfare than one in which a central government provides a single, uniform level of public output in all jurisdictions.' (Oates, 2005, p. 351).[3]

Subnational governments should have the fiscal freedom to finance the particular capital needs of their constituents without undue federal interference. Otherwise, local capital output will provide a level of social welfare that is less than optimal. For many generations the municipal market flourished largely as a decentralized market left to its own devices. Federal laws governing the market started to change with the Revenue and Control Act of 1968 (Public Law 90-364). Since then, the federal government has passed a series of municipal market reform laws, the most pivotal being the Tax Reform Act of 1986 (Public Law 99-514), designed to limit the federal tax expenditure and regulate the intermediaries that provide services to municipal issuers. Problems leading up to and during the Financial Crisis led federal authorities to investigate any segment of the market that was not under federal regulation.

Our book is intended to help inform current public policy debates on the future of municipal issuers and their intermediaries. Our approach utilizes modern financial economics, and is a part of those ideas and methodologies described by Oates (2005) as the 'second-generation theory of fiscal federalism'. We use modern financial economics, information economics, public choice and principal–agent theories to analyze how the market operates, how the market should operate, the role and practice of financial intermediaries, and the appropriate level and type of state–local and federal regulation. The book should help policymakers, public administrators and practitioners make informed decisions in the post-Financial Crisis world.

1. OVERVIEW OF THE MUNICIPAL SECURITIES MARKET

In the federalist system in the United States of America much of the responsibility for building, operating and maintaining the nation's basic physical infrastructure (roads, bridges, airports, educational and health facilities, etc.) rests with state and local (municipal) governments and their public benefit organizations. General governments, along with special districts, public authorities, non-profit organizations and other entities have a demand for funds to finance the primary capital facilities the nation needs for the economy to run and society to function.

Yet the supply of available funds for the physical infrastructure provided by municipal governments has always been limited. Unlike the federal government, subnational governments cannot print money. They also have no constitutional right to share in federal revenues or to require the federal government to meet their capital financing needs. While municipal governments do receive funds from the federal government in the form of intergovernmental grants and loans, such funds do not, nor are they intended to, fulfill the basic capital financing needs of subnational governments. Good debt issuance and management practices are required for state and local governments to meet the capital needs of their citizens at reasonable cost.

In 2012 there were 89 054 state and local governments in the United States.[4] Table 1.1 shows the indebtedness by level and type of subnational government. The total amount of subnational outstanding debt is substantial, $2.9 trillion in 2011, 61 percent the responsibility of local governments, and reaching $3.7 trillion in 2013.[5] City and county general governments account for over 50 percent of local debt, and they include a diverse array of governmental units, townships, school districts and special districts that are responsible for issuing and repaying a large amount of debt issued in the municipal securities market.

Subnational governments must raise money for capital projects from private sector funds. The private suppliers of financial capital, which are mostly households, mutual funds, commercial banks and property and casualty insurance companies, must agree to supply the government with funds in the form of a loan contract or bond. They are not legally required to buy government debt obligations. Subnational governments must compete in the marketplace with other investments for a share of investor funds. This means that in order to meet their constituents' capital needs, state and local government officials must work to put their government in a position to obtain sufficient funds at lowest cost. Moreover, subnational governments must operate within the legal constraints imposed by fiscal rules and institutions such as balanced budget requirements, revenue and expenditure limitations, and debt requirements and limitations. This book is written to help issuers meet the needs of their constituents within a constrained financial and legal environment.

The municipal securities market, also referred to fondly as the 'muni' market or more matter-of-factly as the 'tax-exempt' market, since interest payments on most debt instruments sold in the market are not subject to income taxation, is not typically viewed as a leader in financial innovation. But its transformation over the years demonstrates financial and political

Table 1.1 *Indebtedness and debt transactions of state and local*
governments, in millions of dollars

Panel A

Year	Total Debt State and Local	State Debt	State Share of Total Debt	Local Debt	Local Share of Total Debt
1961	$75024	$19993	26.65%	$55031	73.35%
1976	$240086	$84379	35.15%	$155707	64.85%
1991	$915711	$345554	37.74%	$570157	62.26%
1997	$1224509	$456657	37.29%	$767852	62.71%
2003	$1812666	$697929	38.50%	$1114737	61.50%
2011	$2907756	$1132814	38.96%	$1774942	61.04%

Panel B

Year	Local Share of Debt Total	County	County Share of Local Debt	Municipality	Municipality Share of Local Debt
1961	$55031	$4949	8.99%	$25108	46%
1976	$155707	$20372	13.08%	$68785	44%
1991	$570157	$121755	21.35%	$226554	40%
1997	$767852	$166652	21.70%	$293380	38%
2003	$1114737	$210893	18.92%	$433307	39%
2007	$1468691	$258131	17.58%	$568379	39%

Panel C

Year	Township	Township Share of Local Debt	School District	School District Share of Total Debt	Special District	Special District Share of Total Debt
1961	$1171	2.13%	$12963	23.56%	$10840	19.70%
1976	$4034	2.59%	$34862	22.39%	$27654	17.76%
1991	$11111	1.95%	$56755	9.95%	$153982	27.01%
1997	$15261	1.99%	$107659	14.02%	$184900	24.08%
2003	$23341	2.09%	$221888	19.90%	$225308	20.21%
2007	$30027	2.04%	$292573	19.92%	$319582	21.76%

Source: US Bureau of Census, Governmental Finances, various years.

ingenuity. Funds flow into the municipal market through loans made directly by large institutions and individuals or indirectly through money market and mutual funds. Funds finance facilities that are used in everyday activities: government buildings, convention centers, schools, roads, bridges, airports, hospitals, water and wastewater treatment facilities, and others.

While sharing the basic characteristics of any modern fixed income market, the 'muni' market, however, is different from other markets in more than just name. The 'muni' market has developed uniquely because of the nature of the US federalist system which gave birth to it and helped it develop the institutional arrangements and practices that support it to this day. The unique nature of the municipal securities market has spawned institutional arrangements and practices that while not always efficient, did and do enable state and local governments to raise sufficient capital in a timely manner at an affordable price.

The soundness of the municipal security comes from the strength of the federalist system that created it. State governments in the United States of America are not merely fiscal 'creatures' of the national government. Because each state has its own power to raise revenue, spend money, borrow and take on debt, they are viewed as fiscal sovereigns. Moreover, the fiscal federalism relationship also covers the relationship between state governments and their local governments. Local governments are created by their state governments, and they are fiscally constrained by state laws. State governments have fiscal control over their local governments, including control over debt finance. Mikesell (2011) puts it this way: 'In state–local relationships, state government holds all powers. That is a critical limitation on local government fiscal activity.'[6]

He notes that some states have conferred home-rule powers on certain local governments, but such empowered local governments are often constrained by the state government in their fiscal activities.

The nature of the states' fiscal sovereignty extends to the centuries' old hands-off posture of the federal government when it comes to directly regulating municipal debt issuers. While the federalist system has created a secure municipal bond, it has also produced a disjointed regulatory framework for municipal bond issuers and the intermediaries that are their primary financial service providers: underwriters, financial advisors, rating agencies and bond insurers. Strengthening the federal regulation of financial service providers has been the impetus behind many important legislative initiatives over the recent years, including the Dodd–Frank Wall Street Reform and Consumer Protection Act (Public Law 111-203), enacted on 21 July 2010.

Debt obligations are large, long-term, expensive contractual obligations.

The willingness and ability of any government to meet its debt obligations is tested during times of national financial crises and economic distress. Many local and state governments found themselves in deep financial trouble partly as a result of the Financial Crisis in 2007–09 and the resulting economic recession, but also because of bad decisions they made regarding their debt obligations. The financial and economic turmoil merely laid bare the weaknesses in several financial management practices. Prior to discussing the intricacies of the municipal market, it is useful to provide more background on the fundamental characteristics of municipal financial instruments.

2. THE BASIC CHARACTERISTICS OF MUNICIPAL FINANCIAL INSTRUMENTS

Debt securities are financial instruments that represent a pledge to fulfill a contractual obligation; the borrower promises to repay to the lender the amount borrowed plus interest over some specified period of time. A municipal debt instrument is a financial instrument that is sold and bought on the municipal securities market. Municipal debt represents a financial asset that is designed to produce funds to support the production of real goods and services (roads, bridges, buildings, etc.). Municipal debt is commonly sold in denominations of $5000. This is the principal value, also known as the face or par value, which is to be repaid to debtholders on the maturity date. Debt instruments selling above the face or par value are selling at a premium; debt selling below par value is priced at a discount. Traditionally, most municipal debt consists of long-term bonds that pay interest at a fixed coupon interest rate. We continue our discussion by describing municipal securities in terms of maturity, coupon interest rate and security.

3. TERM-TO-MATURITY

The term-to-maturity represents the life of the security, and the amount of time before the principal amount becomes due. State and local governments issue both long- and short-term securities. Most debt is long-term, but short-term securities provide an important option for municipal issuers. From 1990–2011, 14 percent of all municipal securities issued were short-term and 86 percent were long-term securities. This contrasts to the period from 1969–75 when 50 percent or more of the annual issuance was short-term. This was a period of historically high interest rates, high inflation, and preceded the use of variable rate and derivative securities. Short-term issuance peaked at 55 percent in 1974, dropped to a low of 8 percent in 1985, and stabilized at the current rate of issuance of 14 percent by 1992.

3.1 Short-Term Notes

Traditional short-term debt instruments, or notes, have a stated maturity of 13 months or less, have a fixed interest rate, are sold at a discount, and are usually issued to meet cash flow needs in anticipation of future revenues. Short-term notes are defined by the source of funds used to repay the obligation at maturity and can be divided into two major categories based on the general purpose for which they are issued: (1) to smooth cash flows; and (2) to provide temporary or bridge financing.

Notes are named after the revenue source(s) the issuer expects to receive in the future to repay the notes, which include tax anticipation notes (TANS), revenue anticipation notes (RANS), tax and revenue anticipation notes (TRANS), and grant anticipation notes (GANS). GANS and bond anticipation notes (BANS) may be issued as a form of bridge financing for construction projects. Notes are referred to as GONS when they are backed by the general obligation of the issuer rather than a specific source of revenue.

Also, a recent innovation in the market is the floating rate note (FRN). FRNs are often sold directly to money market funds and are variable rate notes that pay a floating rate at a spread to the Securities Industry Financial Market Index (SIFMA), or the London Interbank Offered Rate (LIBOR).[7] The benefit of FRNs is that they are not expected to have to rely on secondary market demand for liquidity, and thus, do not require a liquidity facility or remarketing agent (Wallace, 2011).

3.2 Commercial Paper Programs

Municipalities also issue commercial paper (CP) to meet short-term working capital or interim financing needs. CP is an unsecured short- to intermediate-term promissory note that may contain a wide variety of interest rates and maturities for 270 days or less. Tax-exempt commercial paper programs are run by remarketing agents that structure the interest rates and maturities of the CP program to meet the specific cash flow needs of investors. Despite being sold mostly by highly-rated issuers, CP issuers commonly purchase a bank letter of credit (LOC) or a revolving line of credit to provide enhanced liquidity protection against cash flow problems at maturity.

3.3 Long-Term Debt

Long-term debt instruments, or bonds, have maturities greater than 13 months and are most often sold to finance capital improvements, although they may also be sold to augment the operating positions of state and local governments. The sale of long-term bonds to finance short-term operating problems is not viewed as a sound use of debt financing. While it may seem like an immediate solution to officials faced with an operating budget deficit, it is likely to lead to more and greater problems in the future.

4. THE INTEREST RATE: FIXED RATE DEBT

Most bonds pay interest at a fixed coupon interest rate. While the bond is outstanding, borrowers make semi-annual payments of coupon interest (the rate stated on the face of the bond) at a specified percentage of the face value (for example, a 5 percent interest rate). Usually, the coupon interest rate is the same, or fixed, over the life of the bond. A bond with a fixed coupon interest rate is called a fixed rate bond. Some bonds are sold that do not pay interest. They are called 'zero' coupon or capital appreciation bonds. These bonds are sold at a deep discount to par value and their value grows, or accretes, to the principal payment at maturity. The only cash flow the bondholder receives is the principal payment at maturity.

Most fixed rate municipal bonds with a final maturity greater than 10 years have a call option.[8] The call option gives the issuer the right, but not the obligation, to 'call' and redeem the bond prior to final maturity at the call date. The call option is effectively 'sold' by investors to borrowers at the initial sale, therefore a callable bond sells at a lower price (higher yield) than a non-callable bond. For the additional cost issuers buy the right to redeem their bonds prior to the final maturity. This benefits issuers if they want to terminate the bond contract early, restructure the terms of the bond contract, or as in most cases, if they would like to realize savings from a lower interest rate environment. If interest rates decrease significantly, issuers can sell a new, low interest rate bond and 'buy back' the old, higher interest rate bond, and benefit from the interest expense savings.

5. VARIABLE RATE DEBT

A debt instrument with an interest rate that changes at intervals according to an index, formula or auction is floating, or variable, rate debt. Variable

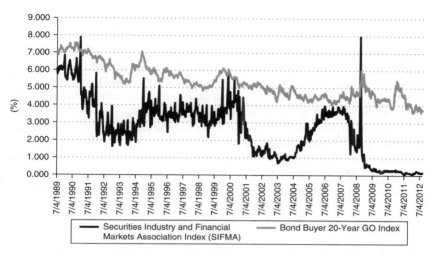

Source: Board of Governors of the Federal Reserve System, selected interest rates, state and local bonds. Thomson Reuters.

Figure 1.1   *Historical trends in interest rates: long-term vs. short-term municipal bond interest rates 1989–2012*

rate bonds have a long-term final maturity date, but their interest rate is reset at scheduled intervals. If the interest rate is tied to a formula or market index it is usually the yield on an index of high-quality, variable rate tax-exempt securities such as the SIFMA index.

Variable rate bonds potentially enable issuers to reduce borrowing costs by selling long-term bonds priced at the shorter maturity, and lower cost, end of the yield curve. Since the municipal yield curve normally slopes steeply upward, selling long-term bonds pegged to short-term interest rates can potentially result in significant interest-cost savings. The potential borrowing cost advantage is shown in Figure 1.1.

Between March 1990 and March 2012, the SIFMA index of high-grade variable rate municipal debt has produced lower interest rates in almost all periods compared to the Bond Buyer 20-Year GO Index (BBI 20 GO),[9] an index of high-grade 20-year fixed rate general obligation municipal bonds. The average interest rate for the SIFMA index for this period was 3.11 percent compared to 5.45 percent for the BBI 20 GO, a 233 basis point advantage for short-term floating rate securities.[10]

Recognizing the potential advantages of variable rate debt, the Government Finance Officers Association advocated the use of variable rate debt in certain circumstances for some issuers, stating that 'variable rate debt can be an important tool in managing a government's debt program and can help lower the cost of borrowing and provide a hedge against interest rate risk' (GFOA, 1997). The advantages of an expected lower interest expense and increased flexibility, however, must be weighed against the uncertainty of future debt service payments and additional issuance costs for the standard remarketing agreements and liquidity facilities. To protect issuers and bondholders against extreme fluctuations in market interest rates, early variable rate bonds sometimes contained an upper (cap) and lower (floor) bound on interest rates. The cap is designed to reduce the risk of higher-than-expected interest costs to issuers by placing a ceiling on the interest rate. The floor is to reduce the risk of lower-than-expected returns for bondholders if interest rates decrease.

5.1   Variable Rate Demand Obligations

Variable rate bonds were first issued in 1980. Most variable rate bonds issued now are variable rate demand obligations (VRDOs). VRDOs are issued with long-dated final maturities of 20 to 40 years, but their yield may be reset on a daily, weekly or monthly basis. VRDOs contain a put option, referred to as a demand or tender option, that gives bondholders the right to demand payment from the issuer at regular scheduled intervals prior to the stated maturity date (possibly even daily), at a price specified in the bond contract, often par plus accrued interest.

A put option, in direct contrast to a call option, is effectively 'sold' by issuers to investors in the form of a lower required yield on the bonds. Put options protect investors from being locked into a security with a yield lower than that available in the current market, effectively giving investors the right to turn a long-term bond into a shorter investment, but it can place a large and unexpected demand on the issuer's revenues. To ensure that sufficient funds are available if investors choose to exercise their put option and tender their securities for payment before final maturity, variable rate securities are backed by liquidity support facilities such as bank letters of credit or standby bond purchase agreements. The trade-off is that at the initial sale, variable rate put-option bonds have significantly lower yields than fixed-rate bonds, which should produce lower all-in costs for the issuer.

Many variable rate bonds have provisions enabling the issuer to convert the interest rate to a fixed rate. This conversion feature is of benefit to the issuer if long-term interest rates fall significantly and the issuer would like to lock in a low, fixed interest rate (Peng, 2003). There have been two major peaks in VRDO issuance. First, on the heels of historically high and volatile interest rates from 1978 to 1982, variable rate bond issuance peaked at 25 percent of total municipal debt in 1985. The peak in 1985 came as issuers began to seek hedges against potential opportunity losses if interest rates declined in the future, as they did from 1982 to 1986. In a decreasing interest rate environment, the sale of variable rate debt, rather than fixed rate debt, enabled issuers to raise money, but at a rate that would decrease in the future if interest rates decreased, thus potentially producing significant savings over fixed rate debt.

Second, VRDO issuance peaked to almost 30 percent of total issuance in 2008 during the tumult of the Financial Crisis. This was due to interest rate and supply and demand factors. For the second time in modern municipal market history, short-term interest rates briefly went above longer term rates (an inverted yield curve).[11] In such an interest rate scenario, issuers have an incentive to try to lock in lower long-term rates, but there are unlikely to be substantial buyers for fixed long-term debt. Indeed, in the midst of a collapsing banking industry, investors had no appetite for locking in long-term interest rates, much less low long-term rates. As the financial collapse rippled through the economy, municipal budgets began feeling the pinch of the recession, but they still needed debt financing. Total debt issuance dropped only 7 percent from 2007–08, because issuers rushed to market in the second half of 2007 as the extent of the Financial Crisis began to unfold.

5.2 Municipal Auction Rate Securities[12]

The most recent innovation in variable rate debt instruments is the Municipal Auction Rate Security (MARS), which has its interest rates reset via an auction process. Auction rate securities emerged in the mid-1980s as another way for corporations, mutual funds, and state and local governments and authorities to issue long-term debt instruments at short-term interest rates. The interest rate on auction rate securities is tied to short-term interest rates with the rate reset through a Dutch auction process at predetermined and frequent intervals, commonly 7, 28 or 35 days. Owners of MARS have the option to hold their securities at each auction regardless of the new rate, bid to hold an existing position at a specified rate, or request to sell at the rate set by the auction. Therefore, provided an auction does not fail, investors viewed MARS as short-term securities and bid on them as such. Consequently, MARS enjoyed similar pricing advantages as VRDOs since they were also able to take advantage of the historical interest rate benefit of the short end of the yield curve.

Auction rate securities, however, were viewed as more liquid (i.e. could be sold more quickly without a loss in principal value) than traditional variable rate debt instruments since the interest rate was reset at auction, and investors had historically been able to liquidate their positions at par value if needed. They were also viewed as having lower transaction costs since they could be sold without a put option and the liquidity supports typically required for VRDOs.

In 1990, five MARS debt issues were sold for a total of $283 million, representing 2.1 percent of variable rate debt, and only 0.17 percent of the entire market. By 2004 the sale of $42 billion in MARS represented the peak of the market at 85 percent of variable rate debt issuance and 10 percent of the total market, evidencing a dramatic shift in the process of setting interest rates on variable rate securities in the municipal market. The years 2005, 2006 and even 2007 saw significant MARS sales where almost half the total size of the auction rate securities market (both municipal and corporate) was accounted for by MARS (Han and Li, 2008). By late 2007 the MARS market was in free-fall, and in 2008 zero MARS were issued, and no new issues have been sold since. In the brief span of 21 years we have actually seen the birth, growth and death of the MARS primary market. MARS presents an interesting case on the diffusion of a financial innovation. In Chapter 11 we analyze the curious rise and fall of the MARS market, and its implications for subnational government finance.

6.   REPAYMENT PLEDGES

Municipal debt instruments vary according to the type of revenue security pledged as the source of debt service repayment. Until the mid-1970s municipal debt mostly consisted of general obligation bonds repaid with general tax revenues. Now, the repayment structure of today's municipal bond market is more diverse, more complex, and much less dependent on general governmental tax revenues. Today, there is relatively more debt sold with a limited liability repayment promise, and fewer debt issues sold with a full faith and credit unlimited liability repayment pledge. Unlimited liability debt is called general obligation (GO) debt. Limited liability debt has two basic forms: appropriation-backed and revenue debt. One of the most significant transformations in the municipal market over the past 40 years is the decline in the amount of GO debt issued and the corresponding increase in the amount of revenue debt. In 1969, 84 percent of new issue dollar volume was GO debt; by 1985, revenue debt accounted for 70 percent of new debt. In 2012, revenue debt has declined to only 56 percent of new debt issue volume. Figure 1.2 shows the historic shares of revenue vs. general obligation debt in the US municipal market.

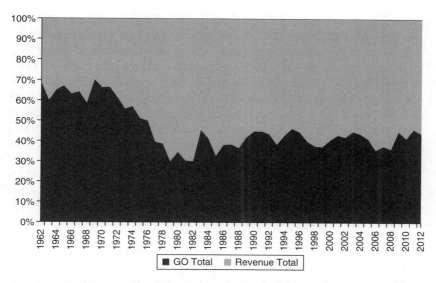

Source: Board of Governors of the Federal Reserve System, new security issues, state and local governments.

Figure 1.2   General obligation (GO) vs. revenue bonds, 1962–2012

6.1   Unlimited and Limited Tax-Supported Debt

There are two basic types of tax-supported bonds: unlimited tax (GO) bonds and limited tax bonds. GO bonds have traditionally financed general governmental operations and are backed by the full faith and credit (or, in other words, the general taxing power) of the debt issuer. Because of the unconditional repayment pledge, voter approval is often required by state law for the issuance of GO debt. Unlimited tax-supported bonds have traditionally been viewed as the most secure of all municipal bond investments and therefore the least costly to municipal issuers. Other tax-supported bonds are backed by a limited, dedicated or special tax obligation. For example, bonds sold to construct a convention center may be repaid from hotel receipt surtaxes. Limited tax obligation bonds are also sold by special taxing districts, such as (property) tax increment districts.

6.2   Revenue Debt

One of the most important transformations in municipal debt is the establishment of revenue debt as a preferred security pledge. The greatly expanded use of municipal bond proceeds to finance projects previously financed through the private sector (for example, single-family home mortgages) primarily account for this shift, combined with new legal constraints (many arising directly from taxpayer revolts) on the issuance of GO debt. Revenue bonds are primarily secured by the revenue generated from a project – usually one intended to be self-sustaining – not the taxing power of government. They are commonly issued by public authorities, which are associated with (but for debt issuance purposes are not a legal part of) an affiliated general government unit. Therefore, the revenue bonds they issue are not included under constitutional or statutory debt limits, often do not require voter approval, and promote economic efficiency (to the extent that user charges, rather than general tax revenues, are used to repay the debt). However, because of the narrower repayment pledge, revenue bonds typically incur higher interest costs and exhibit higher issuance costs than comparable GO debt.

Revenue bonds consist of three broad categories: enterprise, conduit and asset-backed. Enterprise bonds are payable from the revenues, usually user charges, of a government-owned enterprise, such as a water, sewer or electric utility. Conduit revenue bonds are payable from the income or revenues of private entities or individuals, such as private hospitals, for-profit businesses or homeowners. These bond issues are referred to as conduit bonds because the sponsoring government provides the private entity with access to the municipal market but provides no commitment to pay or guarantee debt service on the bonds. The issuance of conduit bonds was severely curtailed by the federal Tax Reform Act of 1986. Municipalities may provide additional security for their revenue bonds by including a 'moral obligation' or 'double-barrel' pledge. Moral obligation bonds are revenue bonds, typically issued by a state authority, that bear the state legislature's moral commitment to meet any shortfall in debt service payments by the authority.[13] A double-barrel repayment pledge may have the revenues from the project as the primary source of repayment, but may also carry a tax or general obligation pledge.

6.3   Appropriation-Backed or Lease Rental Obligations

Municipalities regularly issue securities that are repaid from lease rental payments. The lease rental payments are not secured by a specific revenue stream or tax pledge. In the leasing arrangement, the lessee contracts to include in the budget an annual appropriation to cover rental payments. Therefore, these securities are supported only by the anticipated annual appropriation. The lessee, however, has the legal right not to make the annual appropriation. That is, the lessee has the right to 'non-appropriate', not make an appropriation to pay the rental, and it is not legally a default. Certificates of participation (COPs) have become the preferred leased-backed security beginning in the 1980s. Since COPs, like other lease-backed securities, are not legally classified as 'debt' in most states, they are commonly used to circumvent state debt limitations and voter requirements.

Appropriation-backed securities enable issuers to tap the general fund to increase debt capacity beyond formal debt limits. Several high-profile cases occurred in the 1990s where the issuer demonstrated the willingness to 'non-appropriate', resulting in investors reaffirming the view that the issuers' commitment to service their COPs is just as morally binding as the issuers' pledge on traditional bonds.[14] Therefore, issuers should consult with their constituents prior to obligating future general fund revenues in the form of future lease rental payments, even though they may not be legally required to do so.

6.4 Asset-Backed or Securitized Debt

Asset-backed securities have a cash flow structure similar to other debt instruments, but the debt service payments come directly from the asset(s) being securitized. In a typical revenue bond financing, the revenue generated from the project or enterprise is dedicated to repay the bond issue.[15] A fundamental difference between a revenue bond issue and a securitized bond issue is who 'owns' the cash flows. On a typical revenue bond, the issuer pledges revenue for repayment, but retains ownership of the revenue. In a securitization, the subnational government no longer owns the cash flows expected to pay debt service.[16] The expected cash flows (assets) are in effect put into a 'trust' and the cash flows from the trust are 'sold' to investors in return for the net proceeds from the sale of the securitization debt issue.

For years subnational governments attempted to securitize several receivables, such as property tax liens, with limited success. Then in 1998 the major United States tobacco companies[17] and 46 state governments, the District of Columbia, and five United States territories agreed to settle all legal claims brought by the signatories against the major tobacco companies and signed the 'Master Settlement Agreement' (MSA).[18] The MSA is the largest civil settlement in United States history. At the time the agreement was signed, payments from the tobacco companies to the subnational governments and territories were estimated to amount to $229 billion (nominal dollars) between 1998 and 2025.[19] Annual settlement payments are structured in a similar way to an annuity, with roughly equal payments to be paid by the tobacco companies annually, *in perpetuity*.

Several governments decided to cash-in all or a portion of their expected

MSA payments by securitizing their expected revenue stream and creating asset-backed securities for sale to investors.[20] Tobacco securitization bonds are created through the securitization process by transferring, irrevocably, the rights to the expected MSA payments to a trust organization (commonly a public authority) established by the subnational government but that is legally a separate and distinct entity from the government. The public authority then uses the trust assets, the expected MSA payments, as collateral to support the repayment of the asset-backed securities. The sale of tobacco asset-backed debt produces net proceeds, thereby transforming the stream of illiquid, expected MSA payments into up-front cash.

Tobacco securitization debt has become one of the most enduring forms of securitization by subnational governments, with state governments alone reportedly selling over $46 billion in tobacco securitization bonds (TSBs) from 2000–11.[21] When the government sells a TSB, it is selling its right to all or some of their future MSA settlement payments, but the proceeds can come with high costs. TSBs are an expensive form of financing, they exhibit high transaction costs and low realized net proceeds.[22] Finally, there are also other public policy implications associated with TSBs. The agreement did not place any legal restrictions (earmarks) on the use of MSA funds, and research shows that state governments that securitize their settlement payments spend less, not more, money on anti-tobacco spending (Johnson et al., 2013).

The remainder of the book is divided into three parts. The first part contains four chapters and is titled "What makes the 'muni' market different?" Part I provides the structural backbone of our book and the 'muni' market. In this part we discuss why the 'muni' market is a special, uniquely American financial institution, and why it works despite its being diverse, complex, decentralized and segmented.[23] Part I has chapters on the nature of the tax exemption of municipal debt (Chapter 2), and the essential importance of the idea of the 'state' as 'fiscal sovereign' in debt finance (Chapter 3). Chapter 4 concludes the fiscal federalist discussion by describing the multi-layered, disjointed regulatory structure, and the growing federal regulatory requirements. Despite the shrinking discretionary space over the governance of their financial market, subnational government issuers still retain ultimate control over their debt financing affairs. With fiscal rights, come fiscal responsibilities.

Part II describes the business and technical side of how subnational governments, financial intermediaries and investors create value. The part details how subnational governments create financial instruments that non-coerced investors are willing to buy and subnational governments can and do repay. Chapters 5 and 6 cover technical, yet fundamental, subnational government debt financial management principles, policies and practices. Chapter 5 describes basic principles and provides examples of essential policies. Chapter 6 walks the reader through the process of bringing a debt issue to market, using the frameworks of network analysis and principal–agent theory.

The municipal securities market is a developed and sophisticated capital market. Understanding the market requires a technical sophistication of fixed income mathematics and investments. Chapter 7 covers the basic serial bond structure of debt issues in the municipal securities market. It should be read in conjunction with Appendix A: Review of time value of money, and Appendix B: Basic principles of valuing debt instruments. The technical appendices can be read through in their entirety, or by topic as needed. They are in the book because we believe understanding and effectively participating in the municipal market requires a basic understanding of time value of money principles and fixed income mathematics. Chapter 8 concludes this part of the book with an analysis of secondary market disclosure. Secondary municipal market research has blossomed in recent years, with the creation of new data sources available for empirical research. Our focus is for general readers and primary market participants to develop an understanding of the secondary market that was heretofore unavailable; for issuers to appreciate how the secondary market affects their primary market debt issues; and to underscore the fiscal federalist issues involved in the federal regulation of the secondary market.

Part III covers the risks and rewards of structuring municipal debt instruments. The first three chapters in Part III describe several sophisticated financial instruments used by subnational governments; they analyze their risks and rewards, and provide analytical frameworks for evaluating the appropriate use of such instruments. Chapter 9 covers engineering financial derivatives; Chapter 10 covers debt refinancing; and Chapter 11 analyzes the birth, growth and collapse of the municipal auction rate securities (MARS) market. Chapter 12 discusses credit enhancement and analyzes the supply and demand of municipal bond insurance, before and after the Financial Crisis. Chapter 13 concludes the part by discussing 'non-traditional' capital financing mechanisms, focusing on public–private partnerships and federal credit support and loan programs. Chapter 14 provides the book's concluding remarks.

NOTES

1. Throughout the book we use the terms 'municipal', 'subnational' and 'state' and 'local' interchangeably, unless otherwise indicated.

2. Johnson and Rubin (1998) describe the beginnings of municipal debt in the United States.
3. Oates (2005).
4. US Bureau of Census, Census of Governments.
5. US Bureau of Census, Government Finances and the Municipal Securities Rulemaking Board.
6. Mikesell (2011, 8th edn, p. 32).
7. The SIFMA Municipal Swap Index is an often used index which consists of seven-day maturity high quality tax-exempt VRDOs. It was formerly The Bond Market Association/PSA Municipal Swap Index. LIBOR is the wholesale money market rate of interest at which banks lend money to each other in London.
8. The time period before a bond with a call option can be called by the issuer is referred to as the call deferment period.
9. The BB 20-Bond GO Index consists of 20 GO Bonds that mature in 20 years with an average rating of Aa2 from Moody's Investors Service and AA from Standard & Poor's.
10. Peng (2003) simulates the annual interest rate difference between the average short-term rate and the annual 20-Bond Index from 1970–2000 for a 20-year bond. He finds that for all years except three the average short-term rate was lower. The three exceptional years were in 1971, 1972 and 1973. He concludes that: 'barring a revisit of . . . hyperinflationary times, the average short-term rate should generally be lower than a 20-year fixed rate'.
11. The municipal yield curve was inverted for the first time on 26 December 1990, the SIFMA Index was 7.89 percent and the BBI 20 GO Index was 7.14 percent.
12. Much of the discussion on MARS is adapted from the unpublished paper by Johnson and Luby (2009).
13. The government has no legal obligation, however, to honor its moral commitment.
14. See Johnson and Mikesell (1994) for a discussion of the Richmond Unified School District default in California and the post-sale voter referendum in Brevard County, Florida.
15. Nova Edwards, Cal. Debt & Investment Advisory Commission, Issue Brief, www.treasurer.ca.gov/cdiac/reports/tobacco.pdf.
16. Johnson (2004).
17. The MSA was signed by companies representing almost all of the tobacco industry's United States sales: Brown & Williamson, Lorillard, Phillip Morris USA (now Altria), R.J. Reynolds, Commonwealth Tobacco, and Liggert & Myers.
18. Master Settlement Agreement (1998), http://www.naag.org/backpages/naag/tobacco/msa/msa-pdf.
19. US Government and Accountability Office, GAO-01-851, Tobacco Settlement: States' Use of Master Settlement Agreement Payments 14 (2001).
20. Johnson (2004).
21. Johnson et al. (2013).
22. Johnson and Kioko (2005).
23. Martell and Kravchuk (2012).

PART I

What makes the 'muni' market different?

The municipal market has a long, elaborate and complicated history. Municipal debt is issued within layers of constitutional and statutory legal prescriptions and prohibitions. The US federalist system creates a legal framework that makes the market different and special. Traditional municipal practices are not 'fly-by-night', or speculative, but lie at the heart of the legal ability of governments to raise funds in America. They are intrinsically woven into the fabric of American finance. The tax exemption of municipal securities interest income is deeply rooted in the nation's legal framework. The tax exemption creates a persistent, yet narrow demand by investors seeking tax-free income. Fiscal rules and institutions – debt limits and other restrictions, balanced budget rules, tax and expenditure limits – provide additional layers of repayment security on municipal securities, and the tax pledge supporting general obligation debt and user charges from monopoly providers generally creates a very secure repayment stream on revenue debt.

Yet the market contains a large number of issuers across all levels of government and regions and a cross-section of local communities across the country. There are a multitude of debt issues with various levels and types of repayment securities and pledges. Also, the federal and state regulatory environment is ever changing and the fiscal sovereignty of state governments adds uniqueness to the debt issues coming out of the states and United States territories. The result is a non-uniform, disjointed regulatory framework responsible for overseeing a diverse, complex, decentralized and segmented marketplace.

2. The tax exemption of municipal debt

A defining characteristic of the municipal securities market is the tax-exempt status of most municipal bonds. The interest paid on most municipal debt is not taxable.[1] While increases in the principal value of the municipal bond are taxable as capital gains income, the interest income to the bondholder is not taxed as federal gross income.[2] Section 103(a) of the Internal Revenue Code of 1954 specifically exempts municipal bond interest from the federal income tax unless otherwise indicated in law.[3] The tax-exempt feature found on most municipal debt separates the municipal market from all other debt markets. In 2011, over 90 percent of new debt was tax-exempt. We know of no other public financial market in the world where the national government securities are taxable and those of the subnational governments are tax-exempt. The tax-exempt feature has historically been a source of continuing controversy at the federal level. The legal basis of the tax exemption is now widely recognized as solely one of federal privilege. Thus, Congress could pass and the President could sign a bill taking away the federal tax exemption on future debt issues, and state and local governments would have no judicial redress.

This chapter reviews the constitutional, judicial and legislative underpinnings of the tax exemption of municipal debt. The chapter then covers the demand for municipal securities, and highlights the market segmentation that results from different state income tax systems. It continues with a discussion of taxable debt sold in the market, focusing on the use of tax credit bonds as a federal policy device, and highlighting the federalism implications of the Build America Bonds (BABs) program.

1. TAX EXEMPTION: THE US CONSTITUTION AND SUPREME COURT RULINGS

The origin of the tax exemption on subnational securities is traced backed to the 1819 McCulloch v. Maryland decision by the US Supreme Court under Chief Justice Marshall which struck down a tax levied by the State of Maryland on the Bank of the United States (Johnson and Rubin, 1998).

The decision by Justice Marshall's court protected the national government from the taxing powers of the states. It is the origin of the exemption of federal activities from state taxation and is also cited as the genesis of the exemption of interest on state and local government securities from federal taxation (Johnson and Rubin, 1998).

The first federal income tax was enacted during the Civil War in 1862. It had provisions institutionalizing the taxation of subnational government salaries, and interest payments on bonds sold by subnational governments. In Collector v. Day (1871), however, the Supreme Court ruled it unconstitutional for the federal government to tax the salary of a state judge, establishing the doctrine of 'reciprocal intergovernmental immunity', and protecting the federal government and state and local governments from taxing each another (Johnson and Rubin, 1998). The US Supreme Court reinforced the reciprocal immunity doctrine in Pollack v. Farmer's Loan and Trust Company (157 US 492 (1895)), by holding that the 'federal government had no power to tax the interest on state securities, nor any state property' (Johnson and Rubin, 1998).

The Sixteenth Amendment to the US constitution was ratified in 1913 establishing the modern income tax system and directly overturning the 1895 Pollack decision. The Sixteenth Amendment states: 'The Congress shall have power to lay and collect taxes on incomes, from whatever source derived, without apportionment among the several States, and without regard to any census enumeration.'

Read literally, the Sixteenth Amendment clearly gives the federal government the right to tax the interest income on state and local bonds. During the ratification debate policymakers opposed to ratification argued that the language of the Amendment was a violation of states' rights and would severely limit the ability of state and local governments to borrow and would place them at the mercy of the federal government. Following ratification of the Sixteenth Amendment, the Congress passed the Revenue Act of 1913, which explicitly exempted interest on state and local debt that was 'issued with a guaranty that the interest payable thereon shall be free from taxation' (Sixty-Third Congress. Sess. I. Ch. 16. 1913).

Although several attempts to eliminate the tax exemption were not successful, including a proposed constitutional amendment in 1922, the scope of the exemption was narrowed by the courts over the years. In 1939 the US Supreme Court overturned Collector v. Day (1871) and sustained a state tax on a federal salary, effectively eliminating the intergovernmental exemption on taxing state salaries (Johnson and Rubin, 1998).

The notion that the tax exemption of interest income on municipal debt had a constitutional basis was unequivocally put to rest in the historic 1988 US Supreme Court decision in South Carolina v. Baker (108 Sup. Ct. 1355).

In two sentences the Court overruled 103 years of intergovernmental tax immunity, writing: 'the owners of state bonds have no constitutional entitlement not to pay taxes on income they earn from (municipal) bonds, and States have no constitutional entitlement to issue bonds paying lower interest rates than other issuers'. Moreover, '. . .states must find their protection from Congressional regulation through the national political process, not through judicially defined spheres of unregulated state activities'.

According to the Court, the taxation of state and local interest payments was a matter of legislative prerogative and not a constitutional right. If Congress wanted to pass a law eliminating the state and local interest exemption, it could (Johnson and Rubin, 1998).

2.   THE LEGISLATIVE PREROGATIVE

Before the South Carolina v. Baker (1988) ruling the federal legislative basis for the tax exemption was weakened by a series of legislative actions in the 1980s. The 1982 Tax Equity and Fiscal Responsibility Act (TEFRA) limited tax-exempt status to what are called registered bonds, that is, those bonds for which the owner's name is recorded by a transfer agent. The interest on newly issued bearer bonds which were owned by whoever holds (or bears) them, was to be taxed.[4] In 1983 amendments to the Social Security Act imposed a tax on social security benefits on income above a specified level, and income was defined to include municipal bond interest. By refusing to hear cases regarding the constitutionality of the amendments, the Supreme Court permitted the continuation of the indirect taxation of municipal interest. The 1986 Tax Reform Act further narrowed the tax exemption by legally distinguishing two types of municipal debt: (1) governmental; and (2) private activity.

The interest on governmental bonds remained exempt from federal income taxation. Governmental bonds are intended to finance basic governmental functions for which there is a clear public purpose, like elementary schools, and from which the debt service is being paid from governmental funds. Private activity bonds involve financing arrangements where the government serves as a conduit providing financing to a non-governmental entity (i.e. private business or individuals).[5] The basic rationale for distinguishing and limiting the tax exemption of private activity bonds is that their proceeds are used to primarily benefit private entities, not the general public, and such entities should not be indirectly subsidized by the federal government. The interest on most private activity bonds is subject to federal income taxation, which reduces the loss of federal revenue on municipal bonds sold for what are now defined as 'private' activities. Some private activity debt may be 'qualified' and retain its tax-exempt status when the governmental issuer acts as a conduit and issues debt on behalf of the 'qualified' issue.[6] In 2005, approximately one-quarter of all municipal bonds were private activity bonds.[7]

3.   THE DEMAND FOR MUNICIPAL SECURITIES

The municipal market has a unique demand structure. Its securities have been carefully crafted over the years to meet the demands of specific groups of investors that value the tax exemption. The tax-exempt feature is one of the primary factors that influence the demand for municipal securities. Typically, state and local debt sells for lower yields than comparable securities subject to taxation. Investors calculate their return on investment on an after-tax basis, and investments that reduce an investor's after-tax liability are attractive to investors. However, many federal government economists view the tax exemption as merely an inefficient and expensive tax expenditure to be curtailed. Related to its inefficiency, these economists argue that the tax shield benefit provided to investors exceeds the interest cost reduction to state and local government issuers. With respect to federal budgetary expense, the Joint Committee on Taxation estimates that the interest exemption of municipal securities income will cost the federal government $177.6 billion between 2011 and 2015 (DePaul, 2012).

Tax-exempt bonds have the advantage of being a legal, tax shelter investment alternative. Moreover, the higher the investor's federal marginal income tax rate, the greater the tax shelter advantage. Therefore, the demand for tax-exempt securities is greater among taxpayers in higher marginal tax brackets. As a consequence, municipal market investors were historically limited to commercial banks, property and casualty insurance companies, and households – taxpayers with high marginal tax rates. However, changes in income tax laws that impact these taxpayers have affected the distribution of ownership of municipal bonds over time.

Until 1982 commercial banks and other depository institutions were permitted by law to deduct interest payments to depositors when calculating taxable income, even if these deposits were invested in tax-exempt bonds. The Tax Equity and Fiscal Responsibility Act of 1982 (TEFRA) restricted this tax arbitrage by limiting bank deductions to 85 percent of their interest payments on liabilities backed by tax-exempt assets, and the limit was further reduced in 1984 to 80 percent. The 1986 Tax Reform Act allowed the 80 percent deduction only on bonds issued by governments that did not expect to issue more than $10 million of new debt in the issue

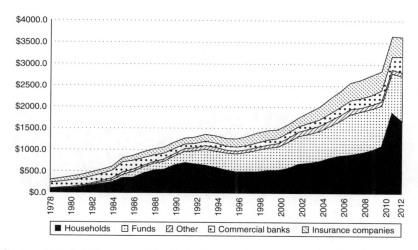

Source: Board of Governors of the Federal Reserve System, new security issues, state and local governments, various years.

Figure 2.1   Holders of municipal debt, 1978–2012, in billions of dollars

year, so-called 'bank qualified' bonds. The 1986 limits applied only to debt acquired after August 1986. Banks have had little incentive to expand their holdings of municipal debt since then and the household sector has emerged as the primary sector purchasing municipal debt.

Figures 2.1 and 2.2 show from 1978 to 2012 the groups holding municipal debt in terms of dollar amount and percentage shares. Commercial banks steadily reduced their holdings of municipal securities, from 40 percent of the outstanding total in 1980 to 7 percent in 1995, remaining at that level even today. The reduction in bank holdings of municipal securities was offset by the substantial increase in household purchases, especially mutual fund holdings which increased from 1 percent to 16 percent over the same period. For short-term maturities, tax-exempt money market funds, which had no recorded holdings prior to 1980, replaced commercial banks as the market clearing investor. Mutual and money market funds expanded the retail reach of municipal securities beyond wealthy individuals. But demand for tax-exempt securities remained restricted since their yields are lower than alternative fixed income investments and because one group of major potential buyers, pension funds, have no substantial demand for tax-exempt securities as they are exempt from income taxes.

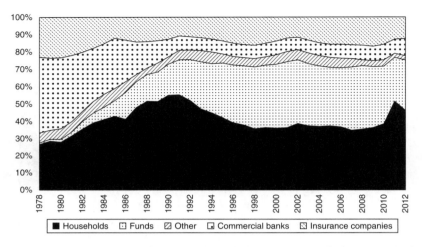

Source: Board of Governors of the Federal Reserve System, new security issues, state and local governments, various years.

Figure 2.2 Holders of municipal debt, 1978–2012, shares of total

4. STATE INCOME TAXATION AND MARKET SEGMENTATION

Another important characteristic that makes the muni market different from other capital markets is the variation in state income tax rates and exemptions. Each of the 50 states and US territories act as fiscal sovereigns and attempt to create greater capital access for their in-state jurisdictions and may arguably be involved in tax 'competition' to some degree. This tendency of asymmetric tax treatment in the states results in state-level market segmentation (Leonard, 1998; Pirinsky and Wang, 2011). In most cases, interest on municipal bonds issued from municipalities within an investor's state of residence is exempt from state income taxation. This asymmetric treatment steers investor preferences away from out-of-state toward in-state debt obligations.

Empirical evidence shows that market segmentation due to tax asymmetries results in an inefficient allocation of capital. A study by Pirinsky and Wang (2011, p. 456) provides a very concise summary of the effect of market segmentation on municipal market outcomes.

> We present strong evidence for state level segmentation of the municipal bond market and demonstrate that this segmentation results in a significant valuation discount of municipal bonds. Additionally, we find that by limiting inves-

tor ability to diversify across state borders, tax-induced segmentation creates an incentive for insurance in the market, a cost borne largely by the issuers. Moreover, we confirm that segmented markets are characterized with higher costs of financial intermediation, as measured by underwriting fees and mutual fund expense ratios. Our overall conclusion is that segmentation imposes significant costs in capital markets and these costs could take many forms, only one of which is yields.

Therefore, state tax asymmetry-induced market segmentation in the USA is a direct result of fiscal federalism. Capital market participants should be aware of the supply and demand implications created by market segmentation. For issuers and underwriters, market segmentation narrows the pool of municipal investors. On the flip side, municipal investors may have to choose from a limited supply of fully tax-exempt securities.

5. TAXABLE DEBT

Not all municipal bonds are exempt from federal taxation. In 2008 slightly over 5 percent of all securities sold in the municipal market were taxable. By 2010, this number had increased to 30 percent with the advent of the federal Build America Bond (BAB) program started in 2009. The BAB program was allowed to expire at the end of 2010 and as a result taxable bond issuance dropped to 9 percent in 2011, which is generally consistent with its 1986–2008 pre-BAB taxable amount average of 6 percent.

There are three types of taxable debt. The first is debt that is fully federally taxable. That is, the interest on such debt is not excludable from gross federal income nor may it be credited against federal income tax liability. Second is debt sold as potentially subject to the 'alternative minimum tax' (AMT) which may be ultimately federally taxable to taxpayers subject to the AMT. Third is tax credit debt where interest income may be credited against the federal income tax liability of the bondholder, or where the credit amount is paid directly to the issuer, as in the BAB program.

6. TAX CREDIT BONDS AS A FEDERAL POLICY DEVICE

Some analysts have offered taxable tax credit bonds as a policy alternative related to the decades-long debate about the most effective way the federal government can subsidize subnational capital-raising. Taxable tax credit bonds represent a direct subsidy to state and local governments either in the form of a specific tax credit amount provided to investors or as a specific subsidy amount paid directly to the state or local government. Contrast this with tax exemption, which represents an indirect subsidy to state and local governments in which the federal government allows interest income on municipal bonds to be exempt from a bondholder's earnings for income tax purposes. Such tax exemption should be reflected in lower returns demanded by investors in municipal bonds, which should translate into lower interest costs paid by state and local governments on such tax-exempt debt. The lower interest rates represent the indirect subsidy by the federal government to subnational governments.

The lack of efficiency in the tax exemption approach, according to some economists including some at the Congressional Budget Office (Congressional Budget Office, 2004), comes from the fact that investors in municipal bonds are diverse with different: (1) preferences for types of state and local government bonds; (2) marginal tax rates; and (3) views on future expected tax rates. With respect to different marginal tax rates among municipal bond buyers, critics of tax exemption argue that lower income bracket buyers set the bond-clearing price, costing the federal government more in lost tax revenues than the benefits received by state and local government issuers as measured by reduced interest cost. For these critics of tax exemption, providing a direct subsidy to offset the borrowing cost of state and local governments on their financings would be a more effective way of subsidizing subnational capital activities.

An example will help clarify this theoretical efficiency problem. Assume 50 percent of the buyers of a municipal bond are in the 25 percent income tax bracket and 50 percent of the buyers are in the 35 percent income tax bracket and the comparable interest rate on a $1000 par amount taxable bond is 5 percent. Investors would be indifferent between the taxable bond or a tax-exempt bond if the tax-exempt bond carried an interest rate of 3.75 percent since the after-tax interest rate on the taxable bond would be $(1-0.25) \times 5$ percent, or 3.75 percent. Thus, assuming the 25 percent marginal tax bracket investor sets the bond clearing, the state or local government would pay an annual interest of $37.50 (3.75 percent $\times$ $1000), which would represent a reduction in borrowing cost of $12.50 ($50 taxable interest payment compared to $37.50 tax-exempt interest rate) compared to what they would pay without the federal government granting tax exemption. However, the cost of the subsidy for the federal government would be $1500 (35 percent interest tax shield on the $25 taxable interest payment and 25 percent interest tax shield on the $25 taxable interest payment) since half the buyers were in the 35 percent tax bracket and half were in the 25 percent bracket. This difference between the borrowing cost savings from tax exemption of $1250 and the cost to the federal government in lost tax revenues for providing tax exemption of $15 theoretically provides evidence of an inefficient use of federal resources.

Expanding the universe of potential bond buyers is another consideration supporting the use of direct subsidy taxable bonds. Since many buyers of fixed income securities do not possess any federal tax liability, such as international buyers and US state and local government pension funds, tax exemption is of no value to these types of investors. However, these investors may be willing to purchase these securities as an alternative to other similar yielding taxable securities due to the relative safety of municipal bonds and as a way to diversify their bond portfolios. By selling bonds on a taxable basis that would be attractive to these investors, state and local governments may be able to increase the demand for their securities. The increase in investor demand should theoretically result in higher prices on the government's securities. Such increases in price will result in lower interest costs as the price of a bond is inversely related to its interest rate. The direct subsidy by the federal government would further reduce the interest costs for subnational government.

From the state and local governments' perspective, the potential downside of the direct subsidy approach is the potential reduction in its fiscal autonomy (Luby, 2012). Unlike the tax exemption where the federal subsidy effectively represents a transaction between the investor and the federal government with the subnational government benefiting from a reduction in its market interest rate, the direct subsidy approach establishes a direct relationship between the federal government and the state and local government through the provision of regular subsidy payments on the bonds. This is potentially problematic for state and local governments if they are in arrears with the federal government in other fiscal matters as the direct subsidy can 'offset' federal taxes or other amounts owed by the subnational government to the federal government. In addition, since the direct subsidy is a direct payment made by the federal government rather than a tax expenditure made through the tax code, the state or local government is hostage to the federal budget and appropriations process in its pursuit of receiving their subsidy.

From the federal government's perspective, the direct subsidy approach provides: (1) more influence in subnational financial policy; (2) greater transparency as to the cost of the subsidy; and (3) more flexibility in changing state and local government subsidy levels (Luby, 2012). First, the federal government can offer different direct subsidy levels to reflect the federal government's preference for various types of state and local government capital projects. Second, the direct subsidy approach, either in the form of a tax credit or direct subsidy, will reflect a line item in the federal budget, as opposed to an amount in the tax expenditure budget, offering more transparency on the federal budgetary cost of subsidizing state and local government capital activities. Finally, the federal government can more nimbly change the level of its generosity in providing its subsidy given different policy preferences as the subsidy would go through the annual federal budget process. In contrast, making changes to federal tax law as is required in changing the tax exemption subsidy has proven difficult in all federal policy areas, not just municipal finance. The recent federal policy experiment with BABs provides a prime example of the trade-off between federal policy effectiveness and subnational financial autonomy using taxable bonds.

7.   BUILD AMERICA BONDS (BABs)

Due to the lack of liquidity and credit availability as a result of the global financial crisis, Congress authorized the Build America Bond (BAB) program in the American Recovery and Reinvestment Act of 2009 (ARRA). BABs are taxable bonds issued by state and local governments whereby the federal government provides a direct subsidy of 35 percent of the interest costs of the bonds.[8] The BAB program aimed to unfreeze the credit market for state and local governments by expanding the universe of potential municipal bond buyers to include international investors and pension funds. The 35 percent subsidy also had the intended effect of providing a more generous federal subsidy for subnational capital-raising compared to the tax exemption. Previous research showed that tax-exempt bonds carried interest rates between 10 percent and 35 percent lower than comparable taxable securities (US Department of the Treasury, 2010a; Atwood, 2003; Poterba and Verdugo, 2008; Ang et al., 2010a; Longstaff, 2011).

Based on its usage by state and local governments, the BAB program was an overall success. As shown in Table 2.1, between 2009 and 2010 state and local governments sold over \$181 billion in BABs. Taxable BABs made up over 27 percent of the municipal bond market in 2010, far eclipsing the historical composition of taxable municipal bonds of roughly 6 percent of the market. Table 2.2 details BAB usage by state, showing that all 50 states employed the BAB program in varying degrees of usage. The BAB program and its generous subsidy was also effective in lowering borrowing cost for state and local governments vis-à-vis tax exemption. Several empirical studies illustrated this borrowing cost advantage. The US Department of the Treasury (2010a) performed a study that showed that BABs provide interest cost savings between 31 and 112 basis points depending on the bond maturity date, with a greater benefit on longer

Table 2.1 Monthly long-term municipal bond issuance, 2009 and 2010 ($ in billions)

	Build America Bonds	Total US Municipal Bond Issuance	% of BABs to Total Municipal Bond Issuance		Build America Bonds	Total US Municipal Bond Issuance	% of BABs to Total Municipal Bond Issuance
Jan 2009		23.2	N/A	Jan 2010	7.0	32.7	21.55%
Feb 2009		23.4	N/A	Feb 2010	7.1	27.2	26.25%
Mar 2009		38.9	N/A	Mar 2010	12.6	44.4	28.41%
Apr 2009	7.9	36.8	21.34%	Apr 2010	6.5	27.4	23.82%
May 2009	2.7	30.4	8.89%	May 2010	9.3	38.3	24.22%
Jun 2009	5.0	43.8	11.47%	Jun 2010	9.4	34.7	26.98%
Jul 2009	3.6	26.1	13.69%	Jul 2010	6.4	29.1	22.15%
Aug 2009	9.6	36.4	26.51%	Aug 2010	5.4	29.2	18.41%
Sep 2009	6.7	30.0	22.43%	Sep 2010	9.4	35.5	26.52%
Oct 2009	12.9	46.4	27.86%	Oct 2010	12.6	45.6	27.65%
Nov 2009	7.6	38.3	19.88%	Nov 2010	16.1	45.2	35.60%
Dec 2009	8.1	36.1	22.34%	Dec 2010	15.4	40.9	37.65%
2009 Total	**64.1**	**409.7**	**15.65%**	**2010 Total**	**117.3**	**430.1**	**27.27%**

Source: US Treasury.

Table 2.2 Build America Bond issuance by state and select US territories, 2009 and 2010 ($ in billions)

State	2009	2010	2009–10 Total	State	2009	2010	2009–10 Total
Alabama	0.22	0.41	0.63	North Carolina	0.70	0.95	1.65
Alaska	0.16	0.20	0.36	North Dakota	0.02	0.05	0.07
Arizona	0.62	1.40	2.02	Nebraska	0.33	0.67	1.01
Arkansas		0.03	0.03	New Hampshire	0.23	0.15	0.38
California	15.63	22.82	38.45	New Jersey	2.25	5.12	7.37
Colorado	1.56	2.48	4.04	New Mexico	0.06	0.22	0.28
Connecticut	0.84	1.07	1.91	Nevada	1.21	1.35	2.56
Delaware	0.18	0.34	0.52	New York	5.78	14.57	20.35
District of Columbia	0.96	0.99	1.95	Ohio	1.84	6.32	8.16
Florida	2.18	3.37	5.55	Oklahoma	0.30	0.52	0.82
Georgia	0.62	3.11	3.73	Oregon	0.02	0.93	0.95
Hawaii	0.09	1.18	1.27	Pennsylvania	1.33	3.69	5.02
Idaho		0.14	0.14	Puerto Rico		1.01	1.01
Illinois	3.68	7.77	11.46	South Carolina	0.47	0.73	1.19
Indiana	0.56	1.43	1.99	South Dakota	0.14	0.20	0.34
Iowa	0.49	0.28	0.77	Tennessee	0.31	1.53	1.84
Kansas	0.81	0.82	1.63	Texas	6.99	9.68	16.68
Kentucky	1.36	1.61	2.97	Utah	1.29	1.59	2.87
Louisiana	0.53	0.42	0.95	Virginia	1.34	2.50	3.84
Maine		0.09	0.09	Virgin Islands		0.04	0.04
Maryland	1.31	2.12	3.43	Vermont		0.13	0.13
Massachusetts	1.96	2.71	4.67	Washington	1.84	4.28	6.12
Michigan	1.17	1.45	2.62	West Virginia		0.09	0.09
Minnesota	0.44	1.06	1.50	Wisconsin	0.78	1.40	2.18
Mississippi	0.16	0.60	0.76	Wyoming	0.01	0.13	0.14
Missouri	1.38	1.58	2.95	Total	**64.1**	**117.3**	**181.4**

Source: US Treasury.

maturity bonds. Ang et al. (2010b) found that BAB issuers save 54 basis points, on average, over tax-exempt municipal bonds. Liu and Denison (2010) demonstrated a 70 basis point advantage for BAB issues compared to tax-exempt bonds. Luby (2012) looked at two representative transactions and found that BABs saved the State of Ohio between 36 to 90 basis points depending on bond maturity. The BAB program ended at the end of 2010. There have been several Congressional proposals to renew the program at different subsidy levels, but none have passed Congress.

While popular with many state and local government issuers, as a federal policy instrument, the BAB program has not been immune from criticism. As described in the previous section, many market participants worried about the 'reach' of the BAB program and its potential to undermine state and local government financial autonomy. For example, some members of Congress proposed altering the program to allow Congress to provide different subsidy amounts based on the funding purpose of the bonds. Senator Ron Wyden (D-OR) advocated for creating different types of BABs based on the project's job creation potential (Seymour, 2010). This would allow the federal government to encourage certain types of infrastructure projects over others. For example, one could speculate that transportation projects could receive a more generous direct subsidy, say 35 percent of the interest costs of the bond issue, compared to a government building project, which may receive only a 28 percent subsidy, due to the increased job creation benefits of a transportation project compared to the government building project. Compared to the tax exemption where the federal government generally does not provide different subsidy levels by project type, such varying subsidy amounts would represent significant encroachment by the federal government into the financial affairs of state and local governments.

While the above concern is speculative in the sense that varying subsidy levels were not included in the BAB program, the fear related to exposure to the federal budget process has been realized. Specifically, the across-the-board federal budget sequestration implemented in 2013 reduced all BAB subsidy amounts by 8.7 percent, or approximately $171 million in 2013 (DePaul, 2013). In addition, the federal government shutdown in October 2013 delayed subsidy payments from the federal government to state and local governments. Thus, state and local governments have had to find other permanent funds to pay BAB debt service to fill in the gap caused by the budget sequestration and procure financing for funds delayed due to the federal government shutdown. This has caused fiscal stress for many governments, especially small government entities that had limited slack in their budgets. In fact, as a result of the reduction in the BAB subsidy, several governments have refinanced their taxable BABs with tax-exempt bonds to eliminate their exposure to the federal budget. For example, the City of Columbus refunded $368 million in BABs with tax-exempt general obligation debt to eliminate its exposure to the federal sequestration (DePaul, 2013).

In addition, several governments have witnessed reductions in their BAB subsidy payments to reimburse the federal government for outstanding liabilities owed to it. As of March 2010, 2 percent of all BAB payments were 'haircut' to offset owed payments to the federal government (US Department of the Treasury, 2010b). While this is not a significant amount as a percentage of all direct subsidies, it does illustrate the increased power and reach of the federal government into the financial affairs of subnational governments under a direct subsidy approach.

8. SUMMARY

Tax status is a major distinguishing feature of municipal securities. The federal tax exemption of municipal debt is fundamentally important to the USA's fiscal federalist framework. The federal policy of tax credits to provide an indirect subsidy to subnational governments, and their taxpayers, is fraught with administrative difficulties and its expansion may undermine the fiscal sovereignty of subnational governments. While it may be fruitful for issuers to expand demand beyond the loyal, yet narrow demand provided by traditional municipal investors, the BAB program highlights the perils of over-reliance on the intergovernmental transfer system.

NOTES

1. In 2008 slightly over 5 percent of all securities sold in the municipal market were taxable. By 2010, this number had increased to 30 percent with the advent of the federal Build America Bonds (BABs) program started in 2009. The BAB program was allowed to expire at the end of 2010, so taxable bond issuance approximately returned to its 1986–2008 average of 6 percent.
2. In 46 states interest income on bonds issued in-state is also tax-free to in-state taxpayers.
3. Specifically, section 103(a) provides that federal gross income does not include interest on any state or local bond except as provided under section 103(b) (which refers to non-qualified private activity bonds).
4. The South Carolina v. Baker (1988) case was filed by South Carolina with the support of several states in response to the federal registration requirement. South Carolina believed, erroneously, that the Act usurped state rights and that the federal government did not have the constitutional authority to tax non-registered municipal bonds.
5. Specifically, private activity bonds are defined by section 141(a)–(c) of the IRS Code to be any debt instrument that meets jointly the private business use test and the private security test, or the private loan financing test. The private business and security (payment) tests are sometimes referred to as the two-part 10 percent rule, where if more

than 10 percent of the proceeds are used by a business, or 10 percent of the debt service is secured or paid by a business, then it is private activity debt. A debt issue meets the private financing loan threshold if the lower of 5 percent or $5 million of the debt issue is used to finance loans to individuals or businesses (see Congressional Budget Office//Joint Committee on Taxation, 2009).

6. Qualified private activity is either exempt facility or qualified 501(c) (3) debt. Governments may sell tax exempt debt 'on behalf' of 'qualified' non-governmental entities. Such qualified entities must be tax exempt 501 (c) (3) organizations and the proceeds must be used in fulfillment of their social welfare mission. Exempt facility debt is where at least 95 percent of issuer proceeds must be used to finance infrastructure listed in section 142 of the IRS code, which includes transportation, water and sewer, solid and hazardous waste and electricity, among other facilities. Qualified private activity debt may face one additional hurdle for tax exempt status. Several types of qualified private activity bonds are subject to state-level annual caps on the aggregate amount of private activity debt that can be issued on a tax exempt basis. Some private activity debt is not subject to the unified volume cap, such as educational and health care activities financed by tax-exempt 501 (c) (3) organizations. Qualified private activity debt subject to the cap is constrained, and activities must compete at the state level for their cap allocation (see Congressional Budget Office/Joint Committee on Taxation, 2009).

7. See US Government Accountability Office tax policy, 'Tax-Exempt Status of Certain Bonds Merits Reconsideration, and Apparent Noncompliance with Issuance Cost Limitations Should Be Addressed' (2008).

8. BABs can also be issued as a tax credit bond where the investor gets a tax credit worth 35 percent of the coupon rate of the BAB. However, all BABs were issued under the direct subsidy approach rather than the tax credit version.

3. States as fiscal 'sovereigns': implications for ability and willingness to pay in full and on time

In this chapter we discuss how state governments have used fiscal sovereignty to devise fiscal rules and institutions that provide a strong foundation underlying the debt issued by subnational governments. It is one of the more recent areas to be investigated by municipal market researchers, and contradicts claims that the market is fundamentally weak and prone to systematic upheaval.

State governments in the United States of America are not fiscal 'creatures' of the national government. Each state has its own power to raise revenue, spend money, borrow and take on debt, and have been doing so prior to the founding of the United States of America. Johnson and Rubin (1998) describe municipal debt prior to the founding of the United States of America, and they write that:

> states were issuing debt as far back as 1690 when the Commonwealth of Massachusetts issued bills of credit to pay soldiers who had participated in an unsuccessful raid on the City of Quebec – the bounty from the raid was supposed to have paid their wages. Throughout the next 100 years, Massachusetts and the other twelve colonies borrowed money for various purposes, mainly military, including the financing of the Revolutionary War. In 1790, the newly created federal government assumed the debts of all the original thirteen states in exchange for which they were forbidden to create money.

At this point, state borrowing was halted until the 1820s when 'states resumed borrowing to finance internal capital improvements rather than military endeavors' (Johnson and Rubin, 1998).

The federalist fiscal system created in the late 1700s remains intact today. Fiscal federalism separates revenue raising and spending functions across levels of government. The federal–state divide is enshrined in the Bill of Rights to the United States constitution. The Tenth Amendment states:

> The powers not delegated to the United States by the Constitution, nor prohibited by it to the states, are reserved to the states respectively, or to the people. (Amendment 10, ratified 15 December 1791).

The Tenth Amendment has been interpreted as giving the states autonomy over most of their fiscal affairs. Because of their fiscal autonomy and despite the fact that they are unable to print their own currency, states are viewed as fiscal sovereigns, and therefore each state's legal ability to borrow is constrained only by the federal constitution, its state constitution and its ability to obtain funds from investors. While the doctrine of reciprocal intergovernmental immunity originated in protecting the federal government and state governments from taxing one another, the basic notion of the federal and state governments keeping their hands off each other's fiscal affairs was carried over into the borrowing arena.

Because states have the right to levy taxes and raise funds from their own revenue sources, the pledge they provide to pay debt service in full and on time is a very strong repayment pledge. Most state revenue comes from compulsory income and sales taxes, which provide strong sources of repayment. Though local government revenue sources are subject to state authorization and oversight, local governments have been provided substantial autonomy over the property tax and have been allowed to augment their revenue from other sources as well.

Subnational governments have expanded their recurring sources of revenue by authorizing user charges and fees. The user charges and fees often finance services provided directly by general governments or by public benefit organizations established by governments such as special districts and public authorities. Such public benefit organizations are usually given legal authority to levy charges, fees or taxes to cover the cost of their services. Importantly, once debt is incurred and revenue pledged to finance the project, the ability to revoke pledged levies, fees and charges is often insulated from political pressure and beyond the legal reach of even the general government that established the special district or authority in the first place, providing a very strong, secure and legally enforceable repayment structure.

1. DO FISCAL RULES AND INSTITUTIONS STRENGTHEN THE MUNICIPAL MARKET?

The foundation underlying the modern repayment security of subnational government debt has been in existence since 1842, when subnational governments had to issue debt under some form of fiscal rule or institutional constraint (Johnson and Kriz, 2005; Heins, 1963). Subnational debt limitations started in the 1840s when several states were unable or unwilling to repay their debts during the 1839–43 economic depression, particularly debt sold on behalf of banks and canal and railroad debt (Wallis, 2005).

Historically, debt limitations and restrictions have taken the form of a limit on outstanding debt and procedural constraints on debt issuance such as requiring electorate approval prior to issuing new debt.

Largely in response to problems servicing debt in the 1840s, 11 states adopted new constitutions creating new procedural requirements for issuing debt (Johnson and Kioko, 2009). Government officials showed that they were capable of acting against the best interests of taxpayers, and therefore, taxpayers enacted constitutional procedures to constrain the behavior of their fiscal agents. Reforms to state constitutions were intended to give taxpayers the power to approve or disapprove debt issues by public referendum, taking the ultimate decision out of their representative agents' hands. Reforms also required government officials to get permission from voters to raise the level of taxes necessary to service the debt prior to any new debt being issued. The reforms intentionally reduced information asymmetries between fiscal agents and taxpayers throughout the debt issuance process including the permissible uses of proceeds and foreseeable debt-related tax burden.

Johnson and Kioko (2009) emphasize that taxpayers in the nineteenth century still recognized the need for subnational debt financing. Several states restricted issuing full faith and credit debt to times of extraordinary crisis (i.e. quelling an insurrection), but most states did not place hard ceilings on the total amount of debt a state could issue.[1] Taxpayers wanted more a priori control and influence over critical debt issuance decisions such as: the sources and uses of funds; how much full faith and credit debt should be issued; how much revenue would be required to repay the debt; and the revenue sources for debt service payments. By institutionalizing the monitoring function, the new *ex ante* procedural requirements increased direct debt issuance costs, but were expected to reduce the costs of monitoring fiscal administrators on a daily basis. The new procedural hurdles would help prevent the expropriation of future taxpayer wealth from unexpected increases in taxes from the financing of risky capital projects.

The new debt issuance procedural requirements also provided a self-selection benefit, according to Johnson and Kioko (2009). By requiring fiscal agents to bring a debt issue before the voters for approval, and asking them to raise the taxes necessary to repay the debt, officials were more (less) likely to propose projects that voters would perceive as in (against) their best interests and likely to approve (reject). Thus, the *ex ante* procedural requirement puts into 'motion a self-selection process that selects-in more worthy projects for taxpayer review and selects-out less worthy projects without direct monitoring' (Johnson and Kioko, 2009). This creates a system that reduces the number of 'bad' projects taxpayers have to scrutinize. Capital project financings that provide more benefits to fiscal agents than principals (taxpayers) are less likely to be brought forward for public scrutiny and approval because they are more likely to be voted down by taxpayers.

Subnational government fiscal systems that institutionalize monitoring of debt financing transactions may substantially reduce monitoring costs to taxpayers by reducing the moral hazard problem in debt finance. The moral hazard problem in debt finance is especially troublesome because the transactions are usually very large, expensive and long-term. Long after ribbon-cutting ceremonies are over, taxpayers are paying principal and interest. Moral hazard provides incentives for inefficient debt financing decisions, at least from the perspective of taxpayers' long-term interests. Procedural restrictions and limitations on full faith and credit debt are intended to better align the shorter-term interests of fiscal agents with the longer-term interests of taxpayers (Johnson and Kioko, 2009).

While the terms 'debt limits' and 'debt restrictions' are often used interchangeably, they differ in both substance and application (Kioko, 2010). Debt restrictions are procedural restrictions on debt issuance, and may cover several areas: requirements that debt is approved for issuance by legislative supermajority vote and/or voter approval; stipulations on the permitted use of proceeds; requirements dictating issuance processes (competitive vs. negotiated offerings); prescriptions on the allowable cost of issuance payable to contractors (Denison et al., 2006; Luby, 2009).

Debt limitations, on the other hand, are measures of affordability. Debt limits require states to determine and limit the maximum level of annual debt service (as a percentage of the general fund expenditures, for example) or the amount of outstanding debt (as a percentage of taxable property or personal income, for example). Historically, there has not been a direct link between debt limits and actual debt capacity, as such; debt limits were typically rules of thumb established to help manage the debt burden (Denison et al., 2006).

While debt restrictions and limitations provide a direct means for taxpayers to constrain and circumscribe the actions of officials issuing debt in their name, other fiscal rules and institutions are also important. Taxpayers can monitor and indirectly regulate debt issuance through revenue, expenditure and balanced budget requirements, commonly lumped together under the umbrella of fiscal rules and institutions (Poterba and von Hagen, 1999; Johnson and Kriz, 2005; Kioko, 2010). Balanced budget requirements and revenue and expenditure limits, often referred to as tax and expenditure limitations (TELs), are part of the fiscal regulatory framework that subnational governments must operate within in the United States. Fiscal institutions are intended to constrain officials from engaging in financial behaviors that do not represent the best interests of taxpayers and indeed, may impose current and future financial harm. In the spirit of prudent fiscal federalism, these rules and institutions, it should be noted, are imposed on state and local governments by state and local governments, not the federal government.

Beginning in the 1970s taxpayers in several states began clipping the power of government officials over subnational fiscal affairs by passing revenue and expenditure limitations.[2] In theory, such fiscal limits should make the repayment of debt issued by such governments more secure. But while fiscal limitations are intended to constrain profligate behavior by government officials, they are not insurmountable. Research has shown that fiscal limitations are not always binding constraints (Kioko, 2011); government officials can and do circumvent the limitations to produce fiscal outcomes that were clearly not intended by the authors of the limitations. For example, limitations on issuing full faith and credit tax-supported debt does not stop officials from issuing debt, it just changes the nature of the debt structure to include a variety of forms of non-guaranteed debt and often shifts state-level debt down to the local level (Kiewiet and Szakaly, 1996; Johnson and Kioko, 2009; Kioko, 2009, 2011). TELs also influence the structure of municipal debt indirectly by limiting the amount of general tax dollars available to repay tax-supported debt.

General obligation debt issued by state and local governments carries a full faith and credit pledge committing the government to levy whatever taxes are necessary to repay the debt. The extent of the seller's commitment to service general obligation debt was conveyed by official Census Bureau terminology. General obligation debt was referred to as 'guaranteed' debt by the Census Bureau because GO debt comes with a 'guarantee' by the government to come up with the money to meet debt service payments.[3] While there is no absolute guarantee that general obligation debt will be repaid in full and on time, taxpayers pledge that they will come up with the money from all of their available resources. If sufficient funds are not available at the end of the day after selling all of the government's assets and raising taxes to the infinite degree, then the money is simply not there to repay the debt. While not technically completely accurate, the term 'guarantee' does highlight the extraordinary nature of the pledge that taxpayers make when government officials issue general obligation debt in their name: in the future their taxes can be raised, their assets sold, their net incomes and net wealth reduced, by whatever amount is necessary to repay the debt. Thus, from a fiscal perspective, it is inaccurate to characterize GO debt as 'unsecured' debt. The 'security', however, is in the unconditional pledge.

In order for taxpayers to protect themselves from the potential risks of such open-ended pledges, they must monitor government officials. It is much easier and more efficient for taxpayers to limit their potential exposure by simply placing direct and indirect institutional constraints on the actions of government officials than engage in costly, daily monitoring. TEL institutions are an indirect way of regulating public debt and, according to Kioko (2011), they fall into two basic categories: '(a) general fund limits[4] on revenues, expenditures, or appropriations, or (b) procedural limits that restrict the taxing authority of a government'.

Procedural limits are technically different from general fund limits. Procedural limits impose a direct constraint on the taxing authority of the subnational government because they require voter approval or a legislative supermajority vote to levy new or higher taxes. Voter approval requirements mandate that the legislature request voter approval in a referendum for all tax increases and new taxes. A legislative supermajority requirement requires three-fifths, two-thirds, or three-quarters legislative vote before higher or new taxes can be levied. These limits are not part of the annual budgeting process and are only applicable if the government seeks to levy higher or new taxes.

A general fund limit constrains a government's current level of expenditures, but often debt service payments are explicitly exempted from the limit. Governments with debt service exemptions have an incentive to substitute current expenditures subject to the budget constraint with the proceeds of long-term debt that is not subject to the budgetary constraint. Long-term debt can be used as an alternative mechanism to expand the resources available for spending in a fiscal year (Denison et al., 2006). Such actions may allow the government to increase spending beyond the intentions of the limits' authors. Indeed, Johnson and Kioko (2009) find that 'states with limits on general fund spending have circumvented the spending requirements and substituted current spending with long-term debt'.

While issuing debt can often expand the resources available for spending beyond general fund limits, governments may face a real revenue constraint through their procedural limits. Since these limits require a supermajority vote of the legislature or direct voter approval prior to raising new revenues, government officials may not be able to levy higher or new taxes to meet new debt service obligations, especially for non-emergency or non-essential purposes. Therefore, states with procedural limits may be less likely to borrow routinely beyond their current fiscal capacity. Empirically, state procedural restrictions are effective at limiting GO debt, but not revenue debt or total debt (Johnson and Kioko, 2009; Hur, 2007; Clingermayer and Wood, 1995).

As indicated above, fiscal institutions may not always operate as intended.[5] Elected officials facing an ever-increasing demand for services, and confronting limitations on their taxing and spending powers will cause them to innovate and find ways to spend outside the confines of the official budget and voter imposed restrictions. So, fiscal institutions should not be viewed as absolute, inviolable, hard constraints. They do, however, provide a strong fiscal institutional foundation undergirding most municipal debt coming to market. Even when getting around certain limits, such as limits on general obligation debt, other vehicles may be created, like revenue debt issued by public authorities, which over many years and bond sales, develop their own solid legal foundation and repayment history. It usually does, however, come at increased cost to the government, at least initially. But for new debt products that can stand the tests of time and become market standards, significant excess costs typically fade away.

Fiscal rules and institutions affect the decision to issue debt, and credit ratings and borrowing costs, so they are felt throughout the market throughout the life of the debt issue. Research studies[6] have found that TELS affect borrowing costs and credit ratings. Studies show that revenue limits increase the cost of borrowing and lower credit ratings. Revenue limits are viewed by the market as constraints on the flexibility of the issuer to levy higher or new taxes in order to meet debt service obligations. On the other hand, limits on appropriations improve the rating of the issuer and reduce borrowing costs. They signal fiscal responsibility to the financial market and the likelihood that the government is spending within its resource constraints. Recent studies have not found evidence that debt limits reduce borrowing costs.[7] In fact states with debt limits have lower credit ratings (and indirectly, higher borrowing costs).

Generally, it is not fiscally prudent for subnational governments to borrow to balance their budgets and a number of states have placed limits on how much debt can be issued for deficit reduction. Poterba and Rueben (2001), Lowry and Alt (2001), Johnson and Kriz (2005) and Wagner (2004) found that balanced budget restrictions[8] may directly or indirectly (through a credit quality increase) reduce borrowing costs. However, like the general fund limit, a strict balanced budget requirement may provide an incentive to use long-term debt, especially if debt service payments are outside the general fund.[9]

Revenue to pay debt service on municipal revenue debt is often paid from funds outside the general fund. Towards the end of the 1960s governments started to issue more revenue bonds as the infrastructure demands on governments increased and the role of government expanded to include the financing of public debt for private purposes. Many governments created public authorities to finance non-general government activities such as hospitals, electrical power plants, mortgages and economic development projects, and most public authority financings were designed to be repaid from the enterprise or project being financed, not from general fund revenue from the general government.

Revenue debt represents a limited liability repayment pledge that is commonly based on the revenues from a project, such as an economic development project, or an enterprise, such as a transportation facility. Some revenue bonds are conduit bonds where the government gives a private firm access to the municipal securities market and the bonds are expected to be repaid by the private firm, often in the form of lease rental payments to the issuing (sponsoring) government. Revenue debt isolates and shifts the risk of non-payment away from general taxpayers to the users or beneficiaries of the project. Revenue debt financings more closely follow the benefit/burden principle: if you benefit you pay; and if you don't benefit, you don't pay.

In Bureau of Census publications revenue bonds were captured by the term 'non-guaranteed' bonds,[10] but some non-guaranteed bonds were also backed by a limited tax. More commonly, revenue debt is backed by the user charges imposed by a government or public benefit monopoly established to provide an essential service, such as water and sewer services. The service provider can be a government, non-profit or private firm operator that is often given a monopoly over providing the service (e.g. a bridge) in the area. The provider is also given authority to charge a user charge or toll for their service, and given the right to deny service for non-payment. Because of these legal arrangements and other safeguards that have been incorporated over decades into the fabric of revenue bonds, most revenue debt sold in the municipal securities market is very secure, the exception being mainly specific high-risk projects. Revenue debt, however, has traditionally been viewed as less secure than general obligation debt, and therefore more expensive to sell. Revenue bonds provide a limited, non-general (albeit specific and secured) pledge of future revenues, so investors have demanded a premium above the interest rate on general obligation bonds. Such an interest cost premium increases the cost of revenue debt compared to general obligation debt.[11]

2. THE 'LOCAL' IN SUBNATIONAL GOVERNMENT DEBT

The other subnational level of government in the United States that is neither part of, nor established by, the federal government is the local level of government – counties, cities, townships, special districts and so on. Local governments are established by and must operate within the legal framework established by their state government. The last section of this chapter covers three aspects of the local governments' debt financing system. First, we cover the constraints on borrowing placed on local governments by their state government, which are very much intertwined with those placed on all subnational government borrowers by the capital markets, and those self-imposed on state governments. Second, we discuss some mechanisms states have developed to facilitate or enable local government debt financing for the public benefit of the citizens of the state. Finally, we turn to the issues of local government default and bankruptcy.

2.1   State Constraints on Local Borrowing

While states have fiscal autonomy from the federal government, local governments are 'creatures' of the state and their borrowing is controlled by state constitutional provisions and legislative actions. Debt constraints imposed by state governments affect the subnational debt structure by affecting the portfolio of local government debt. States directly and indirectly influence local government borrowing. Indirectly, state-level fiscal rules and institutions that constrain state borrowing also influence borrowing at the local level. Indeed, local government debt grew dramatically after constraints were placed on state government borrowing in the 1840s (Wallis and Weingast, 2006). Moreover, higher levels of local government borrowing have been found in states whose state government is prohibited from issuing GO debt (Kiewiet and Szakaly, 1996; Wallis and Weingast, 2006). Kioko (2011) notes that 'when states imposed limits on their general obligation borrowing authority it fostered growth in local government debt. . .'

Direct state controls over local borrowing often cover outstanding debt, voter approval requirements, allowable debt purposes and uses of debt proceeds. The most widely used state constraint on local borrowing has been the imposition of a debt ceiling, generally relating the amount of local debt outstanding to property tax revenues or to property values. Debt limits imposed by states may apply universally to all local governments or may vary by type, level or size of government.

A line of research has estimated the impact of fiscal institutions on local debt. Studies have consistently found that total debt – both GO and revenue – is lower in local governments subject to debt limits imposed by the state (Heins, 1963; Bunch, 1991; Nice, 1991; Kiewiet and Szakaly, 1996; Hur, 2007; Johnson and Kioko, 2009; Kioko, 2009). Kioko (2009; 2011) finds that voter approval requirements result in less debt issued – both GO and revenue debt.[12] Finally, other fiscal institutional constraints also affect local debt. Property tax limits[13] constrain local government borrowing and fiscal (revenue and expenditure) constraints affect the mix of GO/revenue debt.

2.2   State Enabling Local Borrowing

State governments enable local government borrowing directly by granting local governments the power to borrow, and indirectly, enabling local governments to raise revenue. Historically, of the Big '3' tax revenue sources state governments have generally shared the income tax base with the federal government, had exclusive domain over the general sales tax base, and given local governments substantial, when not exclusive, autonomy over the property tax base to raise local own-source revenue. More recently, state governments have enabled local general governments to augment their property tax revenue with either sales or income, often in the form of a local option tax. Local governments are also allowed to generate revenue from non-tax revenue sources, such as user charges, licenses and fees.

State governments can facilitate local government borrowing by serving as financial intermediaries. States establish financial intermediaries as financing conduits to help local governments raise more capital for particular purposes at lower cost. Bond banks and state revolving funds are some of the most frequently established state financial intermediaries. State bond banks commonly issue their own bonds and use the funds to purchase local obligations, or pool several smaller local obligations into one large issue to sell. Bond banks should be able to provide the local government with lower borrowing costs for several reasons.

First, the bond bank is established by the state government, which usually has a higher credit rating than most, if not all, of the local governments in the pool. Moreover, the issuer may be able to structure the state intermediary's debt so that its rating is higher than the state's general government, GO rating. Second, the bond bank should have substantial expertise in creating highly marketable debt for sale, and much more experience than the average participating local government. Third, local governments should benefit from the economies of scale the bond bank offers in selling a debt issue that is larger and backed by a more diversified repayment structure. The bond bank is going to market with a much larger issue than an individual local government. The credit risk is lower because the debt service is being paid from a diversified pool of local loans, rather than a single local government, and it is usually structured with substantial debt service coverage. All of the above benefits should produce lower effective borrowing costs for local governments. Hildreth and Zorn note (2005) that:

> most observers agree that bond banks have achieved their stated goals. They provide smaller governmental units affordable access to regional and national capital markets. They overcome constraints on access faced by these units of

government, such as relatively high legal and administrative costs per dollar of debt, lack of information about small issuers among underwriters and investors, and the lack of a bond rating.[14]

State governments have also developed a form of financing called the state revolving fund (SRF).[15] SRFs are similar to bond banks, but they have been established in conjunction with the federal government to help local communities raise money to satisfy water and wastewater infrastructure capital improvements mandated by federal laws. Revolving funds were initially established to help localities meet the Water Quality Act of 1987. According to the United States Environmental Protection Agency, 'total funds available to the program since its inception exceed $77 billion'.[16]

The revolving fund structure is designed to provide local utilities with funding, but also to retain and expand the equity capital base of the state. The revolving funds were initially capitalized with federal grant funds, and a required 20 percent state matching contribution. The capitalization funds (the corpus) are then used as leverage to float large amounts of debt to finance the capital improvements. Most bonds are sold by a state financial intermediary, on behalf of the pool of local entities. The local entities receive loans from the SRF, at a subsidized rate, that must be repaid to the SRF. The loan repayments are then recycled, and used to provide more loans to local entities. The revolving cash flow structure is designed to provide a continuous stream of funds.

In addition, state governments have also provided enabling legislation to facilitate particular types of local government borrowing. One of the most pervasive local debt financing programs is tax increment financing (TIF).[17] Typical TIF financing programs enable local governments to lever their property tax base to finance targeted economic development projects. Property tax TIF programs have at one time or another existed in all 50 states,[18] and are currently in 48 states and the District of Columbia.[19]

TIF was originally created by state governments as a local government tool for self-financing the redevelopment of blighted communities. TIF has been successful in fulfilling its original intent, but it became increasingly controversial as it expanded into other areas and began capturing a greater share of local property tax revenues.[20] Most TIF development funds are generated through the sale of TIF debt. TIF debt service payments are usually secured by the incremental property tax revenue generated from the expected increase in property values generated from the new development in the project area.

2.3 Local Government Bankruptcy and State Remedies

States are fiscal sovereigns and vary in how they choose to manage local jurisdictions within their boundaries. Among a number of fundamental fiscal management concerns, states are responsible for maintaining the borrowing credibility of their local governments in capital markets. In other words, they guard access to municipal markets by instituting fiscal rules and institutions that attempt to bring fiscal discipline to municipalities. Occasionally, states also must deal with managing fiscal emergencies that may result due to business cycles or due to ineffective or absent fiscal institutions. The states, however, vary in their approaches to fiscal management of local governments during times of fiscal distress from being very involved ever-watching sovereigns to neutral and impartial observers.

This variation in management approaches, particularly vis-à-vis fiscally distressed local governments, came to the fore with renewed significance during and after the Great Recession. A number of local general-purpose governments across the United States defaulted on their liabilities, with some of these governments filing for bankruptcy protection. During this process, it has become apparent that states deal with fiscally distressed municipalities differently, based on the particular set of rules each state has governing municipal bankruptcies. Moreover, while the federal bankruptcy code applies to local bankruptcy cases, Chapter 9 of the code provides very limited powers to the courts but extended powers to fiscal sovereigns, that is state governments (Laughlin, 2005; Spiotto, 2012; Gillette, 2012). Unlike in Chapter 11, bankruptcy courts in local government cases cannot rule that assets be liquidated, expenditures for core services be stopped, or revenues be increased. Thus, in local government bankruptcies the bankruptcy courts are arbiters of last resort, albeit resigned to neutral observance of the debt restructuring process. States themselves, as fiscal sovereigns, cannot file for Chapter 9 bankruptcy protection (Lewis, 1994; Spiotto, 2012).

Extant literature distinguishes between local government defaults and bankruptcies. While certainly related, not all defaults may result, or even can result, in bankruptcy (Moody's, 2012; Spiotto, 2012; De Angelis and Tian, 2013). In fact, 23 states prohibit or do not specifically authorize Chapter 9 filings for their local governments. For example, local governments in Georgia are prohibited from filing for bankruptcy, while local governments in Indiana may not file for bankruptcy because the state has not specifically granted them the authority to do so. There are 15 states that authorize Chapter 9 filings to their local governments, albeit under a set of conditions and limitations. These conditions and limitations are diverse, and local governments may need to satisfy additional state-specific rules beyond those that are identified in the US bankruptcy code.

Local governments in California may need to use 'neutral evaluators' to assess the level of fiscal emergency, with the California Debt and Investment Advisory Commission (CDIAC) playing an important role. Local governments in Michigan may need to work under an emergency financial manager placed on behalf of the state who would deal with fiscal distress as well as with any subsequent bankruptcy filing procedures. Finally, 12 states specifically authorize bankruptcy filings for their governments. Under severe fiscal distress, governments in Arkansas and Nebraska have the required authority to file for Chapter 9 bankruptcy in order to restructure their liabilities under bankruptcy court protection. This is usually done when all other mechanisms of debt restructuring that are implemented in good faith fail.

There are eligibility rules for governments to file for Chapter 9 protection that are specifically reflected in the US bankruptcy code. Under these rules, municipalities must satisfy five major conditions (see for details Laughlin, 2005; Spiotto, 2012; De Angelis and Tian, 2013). First, an entity that files for Chapter 9 protection must be a municipality, where 'the term "municipality" means political subdivision or public agency or instrumentality of a State' (US GPO, 2013, p. 10). States may sometimes limit this definition to a narrower set of jurisdictions (by excluding counties or special districts from eligibility, for example). Second, states must give authorization to file for bankruptcy protection. As already discussed, not all states in the US do so. Third, the petitioning municipality must be insolvent. Insolvency is measured based on whether the petitioner is paying its debts or may not be able to pay its debts when they become due. Fourth, the municipality must show a 'desire to affect a plan', which involves a genuine desire to restructure one's debt and not simply eliminate it due to non-financial reasons. Finally, the municipality must show that it has negotiated with its creditors in good faith or otherwise explain why it cannot do so. Ideally, most creditors are on board with the bankruptcy restructuring process. If not, there can be a cram down decision, even in the presence of a sizable number of dissenting creditors, if the municipality has negotiated in good faith. When there are too many creditors or the creditors are forcing their position, and thus not demonstrating good faith themselves at negotiations, the bankruptcy courts may waive the fifth requirement.

On 19 December 2010, CBS aired on its *60 Minutes* TV program the opinion of Meredith Whitney, a Wall Street Analyst, that there would be a 'spate' of municipal defaults, worth hundreds of billions of dollars.[21] Certainly, very large defaults of Harrisburg, PA; Jefferson County, AL; Stockton, CA; or Detroit, MI since the Great Recession may give an impression that the municipal market 'meltdown' is underway. However, a tsunami of municipal defaults and/or bankruptcies is unlikely. Moody's (2012), Spiotto (2012), and Bergstresser and Cohen (2011) do not find that the number of municipal bankruptcies has increased dramatically. Indeed, among Moody's rated municipalities, there were 71 defaults during 1970–2011. A great number of these were in the 1980s and 1990s, predominantly for debt issued for housing and hospital purposes (Moody's, 2012). Spiotto (2012) tallies that there were 31 bankruptcy filings in the US in 2009 to 2012, which is not anywhere more dramatic than the frequency of bankruptcy filing in the 1980s and 1990s. Therefore, in terms of the frequency as well as aggregate dollar volume of municipal defaults and/ or bankruptcies as percentages of the total municipal market, a spate of defaults is rather unlikely. However rare municipal defaults and/or bankruptcies may be, fiscal distress is viewed negatively by the capital markets. The approach and mechanisms states use to steer their municipalities back to proper fiscal health are critically important and fundamental to their role as fiscal sovereigns.

Most states have significant leeway in actively managing their municipalities in times of fiscal crisis. States may set up early warning mechanisms to prevent fiscal crises. North Carolina has one of the more involved local government fiscal management and debt monitoring mechanisms, and is often cited for its required continued disclosures of municipalities' fiscal data. Generally, having one's fiscal house in order is recognized favorably by the markets, while poor fiscal choices and rules are disciplined by the markets (Bayoumi et al., 1995). When crises do occur, some states may take over the distressed city and walk the municipality though its bankruptcy, as was the case for Central Falls, RI, or try to prevent Chapter 9 filing altogether, as was the case for Harrisburg, PA. The major difference between state governments versus bankruptcy courts is that states can push through the sale of assets or recommend tax increases while bankruptcy courts are merely impartial observers in the bankruptcy process. The state role is very important in finding fiscal solutions for municipalities during times of distress because they have the powers of fiscal sovereigns. Bankruptcy filing should be a tool of last resort when all else has been tried.

A recent study by Moldogaziev et al. (2013) finds that municipal markets recognize variations in bankruptcy rules in the US states. Using a large sample of US municipal government debt issues sold from 2005–10, they discover that municipalities in the states that authorize bankruptcy filings pay a bankruptcy premium (i.e. higher yields) on their general obligation debt. Moreover, the premium appears to increase as the authority to file for bankruptcy becomes relatively less stringent. Similarly, a study by Moessinger et al. (2013) examines the effects of bailout rules for distressed municipalities in Swiss cantons on cantonal bond yield spreads. They find that a credible no-bailout rule of municipal debt by cantons lowers cantonal debt yield spreads. Therefore, there is empirical evidence that default and/or bankruptcy laws are recognized and priced in the subnational government bond markets on both sides of the Atlantic.

Several states have statutory liens protecting select kinds of debt during the bankruptcy restructuring process. These liens determine the priority order of debtors in the recovery line for certain protected or pledged revenues. In Michigan, revenue pledges for revenue debt cannot be claimed by 'full faith and credit' general obligation debtholders until the claims of revenue debtholders are satisfied and operating expenditures are paid out, which is playing out in the case of Detroit in its 2013 bankruptcy process (Chappatta, 2013). Rhode Island went further by passing legislation that bonded general obligation debt be honored first before general-purpose liabilities such as pension liabilities are considered (Spiotto, 2012). In effect this legislation has subordinated pension liabilities to general obligation debt service. Moldogaziev et al. (2013) argue that markets recognize statutory liens. For example, municipalities in the states that allow statutory liens appear to be paying a subordination premium on their general obligation bonds. In other words, investors penalize municipal general obligation bond issuers in states where full faith and credit bonds become subordinated to revenue or limited obligation bonds in bankruptcy workouts. Municipal revenue or limited obligation bond investors may, on the other hand, prefer extra protections on their pledged sources should municipal bankruptcies occur. Similarly, investors in Central Falls' general obligation debt in Rhode Island must have been somewhat relieved in 2011 to see that their debt service comes first at the expense of general-purpose liabilities, of which pension liabilities were the most prominent item.

3. SUMMARY

In the beginning of this chapter we asked the question: 'do fiscal rules and institutions strengthen the municipal market?' We have argued that they do, at both the state and local levels of government. Fiscal sovereigns and the citizens they represent have availed themselves of the US federalist system to strengthen the debt issued in the municipal securities market.

The tax pledge supporting general obligation debt and user charges from monopoly providers creates a very secure repayment stream for most municipal debt. Repayment security is strengthened further by fiscal rules and institutions – debt limits and restrictions, balanced budget rules, tax and expenditure limits – that state and local governments must operate within. While these are not always hard, binding constraints, they have created additional layers of repayment security, along with additional hurdles to issuing debt.

Local governments are creatures of the state. Local governments operate within the fiscal and legal framework provided by their state government. Therefore, in a local government default or bankruptcy the onus is shared by the local government and the enabling state government – as is the solution. Local governments should not default on their debts, nor should states let them. After all, the state government has the authority to grant or not grant local governments the power to petition for bankruptcy in the first place, and ultimately, it is responsible for the local government restructuring process.

NOTES

1. Eleven states imposed outstanding debt dollar volume caps on debt issuance or strictly limited the sale of debt: Arizona, Colorado, Iowa, Idaho, Indiana, Kansas, Kentucky, North Dakota, Nebraska, South Dakota and Wyoming (Johnson and Kioko, 2009).
2. The increase in municipal revenue debt precedes the proliferation of revenue and expenditure limits in the 1970s.
3. After survey year 2005 the Census Bureau no longer distinguished between guaranteed and non-guaranteed debt. The distinction the Bureau made after 2005 and still continues is: 'public debt for private purposes', and 'public debt, unspecified public purposes'.
4. According to Kioko (2011), 31 states have general fund limits.
5. Johnson and Kioko (2009) find that balanced budget rules have been found to be effective at limiting GO debt, revenue debt and total outstanding debt; they state: 'balanced budget rules are more effective than any debt restriction and limitation (at limiting debt) other than direct prohibition'.
6. See, for example, Poterba and Rueben (2001), Johnson and Kriz (2005) and Wagner (2004).
7. According to a survey of state debt restrictions and debt limits provided by Johnson and Kioko (2009), six states have no GO debt restriction; 11 states strictly (or effectively by statutory requirements) prohibit GO debt; 21 states have a voter approval requirement; 13 states have a legislative supermajority requirement; and 18 states have a debt limit.
8. Balanced budget requirements are found in most states. According to the Fiscal Survey of the States (National Governors Association/NASBO, 2012), the governor must submit a balanced budget in 44 states; the legislature must pass a balanced budget in 41 states; and the governor must sign a balanced budget in 37 states.
9. Von Hagen (1991) found that states with strict BBRs held significantly less FFC debt, but their NG debt holdings were not significantly different from states with lax BBRs. Ellis and Schansberg (1999) find weak evidence that a state's BBR may reduce its total debt while Nice (1991) and Kiewiet and Szakaly (1996) found BBRs to have no significant impact on state government debt holdings.
10. Revenue debt is included in both 'public debt for private purposes', and 'public debt, unspecified public purposes' Bureau of Census debt categories. Conduit debt should be categorized as 'public debt for private purposes'.
11. The Bond Buyer Revenue Bond Index has always been higher than the 20-Bond GO index and the 11-Bond GO index.
12. Earlier studies indicated that voter approval requirements for GO debt issues resulted

in less GO debt, but more revenue debt. This result is most pronounced for localities without a procedure for exceeding the debt limit (Farnham, 1985).

13. These include limits on property tax assessments, rates and levies.
14. See also studies on bond banks by Robbins and Kim (2003) and Yusuf and Liu (2008).
15. See studies by Holcombe (1992), Johnson (1995), Travis et al. (2004) for more on the financial economics of the SRF program.
16. Downloaded from http://water.epa.gov/grants_funding/cwsrf/basics.cfm, on 30 December 2013.
17. For a thorough discussion of tax increment financing (TIF) see Johnson and Man (2001).
18. Some states have authorized sales tax increment financing programs (STIFs). STIFs have been authorized in only a few states, have not been used frequently, nor have they been very successful where employed.
19. California was the first state to pass a TIF law (referred to as 'tax allocation'), but it eliminated redevelopment agencies in 2011, prohibiting them 'from engaging in new business and (providing) for their windup and dissolution' (California Supreme Court (S194861), California Redevelopment Association et al., v. Ana Matosantos, December 29, 2011). Arizona repealed its TIF law in 2006 (Kerth and Baxandall, 2011).
20. According to Johnson and Robinson & Cole LLP (2002), TIF bond proceeds commonly finance projects in non-blighted, as well as blighted areas, and for a variety of purposes associated with redevelopment, development, or related physical infrastructure improvements, such as elementary and secondary educational facilities, roads, bridges, parking facilities, recreational facilities, water and wastewater facilities, and electrical power plants.
21. The full program is available at: http://www.cbsnews.com/video/watch/?id=7166293n. Last accessed on 30 October 2013.

4. The federalist framework: fiscal sovereignty, federal regulation and disclosure

In this chapter we review how the fiscal federalist structure has affected the way the municipal securities market regulatory framework has developed. The US federalist system provides a legal framework resulting in a complex, disjointed regulatory web across multiple levels of government. The regulatory structure amplifies the diversity and complexity of the marketplace. The federal government exercises overall responsibility for US financial markets, and over the twentieth and into the twenty-first century has expanded its direct regulatory control over most financial markets, except for the direct control of municipal issuers. Traditionally the federal government's involvement was mostly intended to limit their exposure to tax expenditures resulting from the tax exemption of municipal securities, but now the federal government does have extensive involvement in the municipal market. We cover this growing involvement with our discussion of Dodd–Frank, and continuing disclosure and post-issuance requirements.

The fiscal federalist structure provides the basis and the scope of the regulatory framework for municipal debt. Before the 1960s the municipal securities market was mostly free from federal regulation (Temel, 2001). As previously mentioned, right after the Sixteenth Amendment to the US Constitution was passed in 1913, Congress passed the Revenue Act of 1913 which explicitly exempted the taxation of interest on state and local debt. State and local governments were also explicitly exempted from specific federal regulatory requirements, including securities registration and disclosure obligations imposed on corporations by the Securities Act of 1933 (Public Law 73-22 15 U.S.C. sec. 77a) and the Securities Exchange Act of 1934 (Public Law 73-291, 15 U.S.C. sec. 78a). Municipal issuers were not subject to mandatory reporting requirements nor were they legally required to follow uniform standards for accounting and financial reporting. Even though issuers were subject to the general anti-fraud provisions of federal securities laws, the municipal securities market functioned for decades largely free of federal regulatory interference.

This all changed in the late 1960s, which marks the birth of the modern federal framework for regulating municipal securities. The regulatory framework consists of direct and indirect rules governing different aspects of the municipal securities market, but still leaves state and local governments largely free to manage their own borrowing affairs. Beginning in 1968 a series of federal laws were passed limiting the federal tax expenditure on interest income from tax-exempt bonds. The laws placed limits on the types of bonds allowed to be federally tax-exempt, basically defining bonds as either 'good' bonds, meaning they are issued to finance a public purpose, and therefore should remain federally tax-exempt, or 'bad' bonds, meaning that in the eyes of federal government officials they are not financing a public purpose, and therefore limits should be placed on their federal tax exemption.

The other strategy was to create the Municipal Securities Rulemaking Board (MSRB) in 1975 (Securities Act Amendments of 1975; Public Law 94-29) to regulate the activities of financial service providers involved in municipal securities transactions, focusing initially on municipal securities brokers and dealers. Indeed, while the most important document involved in selling municipal debt to investors – the debt prospectus – was subject to the general anti-fraud provisions of the 1933 Securities Act, it was not subject to direct federal regulation until Securities and Exchange Commission (SEC) Rule 15c2-12 (17 CFR Parts 240-241) effective 1 January 1990. The prospectus, or official statement, provides the market with credit quality information, it is the issuer's disclosure statement to bidders and investors, and it reduces the costs to underwriters and investors of acquiring credit information. The official statement is designed to provide potential investors with all the necessary information they need to make an informed investment decision regarding the bond issue (Johnson and Rubin, 1998). In the official statement issuers are expected to provide timely, full and accurate disclosure of all significant events that could influence a rational investor's decision to purchase its bonds.

Prior to the rule the industry had voluntary followed the Government Finance Officers Association's (GFOA) 'Disclosure Guidelines for State and Local Government Securities', published in 1976. SEC Rule 15c2-12 was intended to improve disclosure practices for new issues, and marks federal incursion, beyond enforcing anti-fraud laws, into setting municipal disclosure requirements. The rule requires that before bidding on the purchase of a new debt issue, the underwriter must obtain and review an official statement that the issuer deems 'near final' at the time of its offering. This 'near final' official statement must provide complete disclosure about the issuer, the issue, and the structure of the financing. As a result, the underwriter and issuer cannot plead ignorance of material commissions or omissions made in the offering statement used to market the debt to investors. Once the bonds are awarded, the official statement is disseminated in 'final' form, with updated information on sources and uses of proceeds, pricing and other important information for bondholders.

The SEC further demonstrated its commitment to improving information flows in the market over the life of the security by establishing in 1994 a continuing disclosure system with amendments to Rule 15c2-12. The first amendment prohibits bond dealers from purchasing or selling bonds in a primary offering if the issuer does not pledge in writing to provide a nationally recognized municipal securities information repository (NRMSIR) with annual financial information and timely notices of material events for as long as the bonds remain outstanding. The second amendment prohibits dealers in the secondary market from recommending the purchase of a bond to investors if the dealer does not have a system in place that informs the dealer of significant events regarding the security.[1]

The amendments continue the SEC's strategy of indirectly regulating municipal issuers by directly regulating the behavior of brokers and dealers. The MSRB regulates the municipal securities through broker-dealers and banks that underwrite and trade securities by setting rules pertaining to issuing and trading municipal securities. The rules are enforced by the SEC and other regulatory organizations, but the SEC has no direct authority over issuers, except regarding matters of fraud. Municipal securities are not registered with the SEC, nor are municipalities subject to uniform accounting and financial reporting standards.

State and local government accounting standards are developed in the US by the Governmental Accounting Standards Board (GASB). GASB is recognized in the accounting profession and by investors in the bond market as the official source of generally accepted accounting principles (GAAP) for state and local governments. While not federally required to implement GASB accounting and financial reporting standards, most municipal government accounting and reporting follows GASB standards. Indeed, municipal debt issuers that do not perform well on these GASB standards are punished in the market by paying higher yields on their debt issues (Kioko et al., 2012).

1. DODD–FRANK

In response to the Financial Crisis, Congress passed H.R. 4173 (Public Law 111-203), otherwise known as 'Dodd–Frank'. Subtitle H of Title IX in Dodd–Frank broadly expands the role of the federal government in regulating the municipal securities market by: enhancing the role and responsibilities of the MSRB (Sec. 975 (b)); creating an Office of Municipal Securities in the SEC (Sec. 979); and providing additional funding and an annual budget for the GASB (Sec. 978).

Dodd–Frank also contains provisions which expand the federal regulation of subnational government finance service providers, to include substantive authority over credit rating agencies and independent municipal financial advisors. Federal regulators are now the official gatekeeper for the independent (non-broker-dealer) municipal financial advisory industry and they have significantly expanded their monitoring and control role over firms in the credit rating industry.

Subtitle H of Title IX of H.R. 4173 provides the first federal regulation of independent, municipal financial advisors. Political momentum for Subtitle H comes from the Financial Crisis, but as Johnson states, 'aspects of the nascent industry that might lend itself to regulatory oversight had been long known, but it took time and the right circumstances for the knowledge to be codified in law' (Johnson, 2013). Indeed, the path to Subtitle H is a case of law following professional practice, theoretical development and empirical research. Municipal financial advisors now have an explicit, legal fiduciary duty as the issuer's agent, and are now required to register with the federal government. Subtitle H states that: 'It shall be unlawful for a municipal advisor to provide advice to or on behalf of a municipal entity . . ., unless the municipal advisor is registered in accordance with this subsection.' (H.R. 4173, Subtitle H-Municipal Securities, Sec. 975 (a) (1) (B)).

According to Subtitle H, a 'municipal advisor' is a 'person who provides advice to or on behalf of a municipal entity. . .with respect to financial products or the issuance of municipal securities, including advice with respect to the structure, timing, terms, and other similar matters concerning such financial products or issue. . .' (H.R. 4173, Subtitle H-Municipal Securities, Sec. 975 (e) (4) (A) (i)).

Regarding the codification of the municipal financial advisor's official fiduciary duty, Subtitle H states:

> A municipal advisor . . . shall be deemed to have a fiduciary duty to any municipal entity for whom such advisor acts as a municipal advisor, and no municipal advisor may engage in any act, practice, or course of business which is not consistent with a municipal advisor's fiduciary duty or that is in contravention of any rule of the Board. (H.R. 4173, Subtitle H-Municipal Securities (c) (2)).

Since passage, Dodd–Frank's provisions related to municipal advisors have proven to be quite controversial to some municipal market participants. The initial challenge under the law was in determining who constitutes a municipal advisor. Can it be a board member who provides advice to the government entity he/she oversees? How about elected officials?

What about accountants and engineers? The second concern relates to the flow of information from broker-dealers to state and local governments. Prior to Dodd–Frank, for better or worse, many state and local government financial managers relied on broker-dealers for informal advice on capital market strategies. There is a concern that Dodd–Frank's strong demarcation of who a municipal advisor is will shut off this flow of information from the broker-dealer community to the detriment of government debt issuers. Finally, the increased regulation, including certification requirements and continuing education standards, may drive out of the industry some small firms that provide local, tailored advice to small, infrequent issuers. While time will tell how these concerns ultimately manifest themselves, Dodd–Frank's municipal advisor requirements clearly represent federal encroachment into the municipal securities market.

Prior to Dodd–Frank the internal procedures of credit rating agencies or the performance of the ratings themselves were not regulated by the SEC. But it was not the first time the rating agencies found themselves in the 'cross-hairs' of federal regulators. The first major set of federal regulations directly aimed at the credit rating industry was the 'Credit Rating Agency Reform Act of 2006', which gave the SEC authority to regulate the credit rating industry. The 2006 Act created the official legal designation 'Nationally Recognized Statistical Rating Organization (NRSRO)', and advised rating agencies to apply to the SEC for registration as an NRSRO (Johnson, 2013). Now, rather than just being rating agencies, they were asked to become NRSROs. The penalty of not being designated an NRSRO was that buyers would be likely to place less value on a rating provided by a non-NRSRO credit rating agency. In order to remain in the business of selling credit ratings, rating agencies had to conform to the new rules (Johnson, 2013). Prior to the Act no governmental regulatory body had oversight authority over the credit rating industry. The two main rating agencies – Moody's Investors Service and Standard and Poor's – had set their own rules.

While Dodd–Frank attempts to plug holes in the federal regulatory structure regarding protections for issuers and investors from the actions of independent municipal financial advisors and credit rating agencies, bond insurers are conspicuously omitted from the massive legislation and are still not regulated by the federal government. Bond insurers provide credit support for state and local government securities by guaranteeing the full and timely repayment of debt service to investors. Bond insurers are regulated by the state in which they are domiciled and licensed. The state of New York, however, has become the monoline industry's 'de facto' regulator and standard setter. The industry became codified in law when New York State passed Article 69 of Chapter 68 of the Consolidated Laws of New York in 1989, restricting firms underwriting financial guarantee insurance policies to only financial guarantee insurance. These firms were 'monoline' insurers because they were legally limited to only providing financial guarantees and prohibited from writing other types of policies. Since most insurers at the time were domiciled and licensed to write insurance in New York State, and because New York's Appleton Rule requires that 'a foreign multiline insurance company may not issue in any state a product which comes within the New York definition of financial guaranty insurance' – at least if it wishes to become or remain licensed in New York, the New York rules effectively became standard industry regulation, with most other states adopting the same monoline standard (Moldogaziev, 2013). We continue the analysis of the bond insurance industry before and after the Financial Crisis in Chapter 12.

2. CONTINUING DISCLOSURE AND POST-ISSUANCE ACTIVITIES

The debt management activities for state and local governments do not end on the date bonds are issued. There is a litany of post-issuance activities that a subnational government must carry out to ensure the prudent management of its outstanding debt portfolio. These post-issuance activities can be broken down into three types: (1) disclosure; (2) bond proceeds investment; and (3) debt service monitoring and payment. Securities and Exchange Commission Rule 15c2-12 requires that state and local governments disclose certain information to investors while their bonds are outstanding. This post-issuance disclosure consists of two main types: (1) government financial and operating condition; and (2) event notices. State and local governments are required to disclose annual financial and operating information. This information release is usually satisfied by disclosure of a government's annual financial statements. Event notices refer to events that happen to an issuer after bond issuance that impact its ability to pay in full and/or in a timely fashion the principal and interest on the bond, or to changes that can impact the value of the bond in the secondary market. Some typical event notices that must be disclosed include bond defaults, delayed principal and interest payments, rating changes, adverse tax opinions, unscheduled draws on reserve funds or credit facilities, and adverse tax opinions, to name some of the primary event notice types.

Once the state or local government closes on the bonds, it must make a decision on how to invest the bond proceeds pending expenditure for the project. The investment of bond proceeds attempts to maximize earnings while maintaining adequate liquidity to fund the project on a timely basis. As such, state and local governments generally invest bond proceeds in short-term, highly rated securities. These government entities often use treasury bills, treasury notes, agency securities, commercial paper, certificates of deposit and money market funds as investment devices for their bond proceeds. The specific types of bond proceeds investments are usually governed by the bond trust indenture and/or state law. While most debt managers take a very conservative approach in their investment of bond proceeds, there have been instances in the past when government entities have not been risk-averse in their investment decisions. Such risky investment strategies have often backfired, most notably in the 1995 Orange County California bankruptcy, which was the result of a failed pooled investment strategy that was funded in part by bond proceeds. Although rare, such prominent investment failures provide grist for supporters of a more centralized fiscal federalism approach to financial management.

Subnational governments also interact with the federal government in bond proceeds investment as it relates to arbitrage rebate. Specifically, the federal government generally prohibits subnational governments from earning a rate of return on its bond proceeds greater than the borrowing cost of the bonds. The federal government put this arbitrage requirement in place to prevent governments from issuing municipal bonds for the sole purpose of 'arbitraging' the difference between its tax-exempt borrowing rate and the taxable investment rate it could receive on its bond proceeds. In the event that the state or local government does have bond proceeds earning in excess of the earning amount that would have been realized if the proceeds were invested at the interest rate on the bonds, the government must 'rebate' those excess earnings back to the federal government. Failure to make rebate payments can result in the Internal Revenue Service declaring the state or local government's bonds in question taxable. The calculation of arbitrage rebate is very technical and demands a mastery of the tax law that governs municipal bonds. As such, most governments contract with auditors or tax lawyers to provide these calculations. State and local governments must prepare calculations and remit arbitrage rebate payments, if incurred, to the Treasury Department every five years and at the final maturity date of the bonds.

Debt service monitoring and payment is an ongoing process throughout the term of the bonds. Working with the bond trustee, issuers remit periodic debt service payments that are ultimately paid to investors. For fixed rate debt, such periodic payments are known as of the closing date of the bonds. For variable rate bonds, these amounts change at each interest rate reset period. Such calculations need to be verified by the issuer to ensure it is not under- or overpaying its investors. To the extent that the bonds include interest rate swaps, the issuer has to confirm that those payments are accurate and made on time. In the case of direct subsidy taxable bonds like Build America Bonds, the subnational government has the added responsibility to file a request with the Internal Revenue Service for the direct subsidy payment in advance of the taxable bond interest payment date. For Build America Bonds, such filing occurs between 30 and 90 days before the bond interest payment date so the government can receive the subsidy in time to make the debt service payment. Filing for the direct subsidy injects state and local governments into the fiscal affairs of the federal government which at times can be problematic for these governments. For example, the sequestration of 2013 resulted in all Build America Bonds subsidies being reduced by 8.7 percent. Subnational governments must plan for such federal subsidy changes in its post-issuance activities and be able to replace the lost revenues payable for debt service associated with such a federal sequester. In the course of managing its debt service payments, issuers also regularly monitor their outstanding bonds for refinancing opportunities. The opportunity to refinance outstanding debt at lower interest rates can provide significant operating budget savings for government entities. The ongoing monitoring of its debt portfolio allows for issuers to capitalize on market opportunities that may produce such interest cost savings. Chapter 10 details bond refinancing transactions in much greater depth.

3. SUMMARY

The last several decades have witnessed greater federal encroachment and oversight of the capital markets relied on by state and local governments. Such encroachment has manifested itself through several seminal court rulings and a few pieces of major tax and regulatory legislation. The most recent federal legislation, Dodd–Frank, sought greater regulatory oversight of the various 'players' that provide financial services to subnational governments in the United States. All of this legislative activity has placed a greater administrative burden on state and local governments before, during and after issuance of their securities. While 'paternalism' may have influenced such intervention by the federal government in the hope of facilitating a more efficient and transparent securities market, such actions have also compromised the fiscal autonomy of subnational governments and tilted the balance of power more towards the federal government in this sphere of the fiscal federalist structure.

NOTE

1. The 1994 continuing disclosure requirements were intended to produce a secondary market disclosure system roughly parallel to the corporate disclosure requirements under section 15 (c) of the 1934 Securities Act.

PART II

Creating debt instruments for the municipal market

The discretionary space that subnational governments occupy over their own debt issuance affairs continues to shrink from greater federal involvement. Subnational government issuers, however, are still largely responsible for their own debt issuance policies and practices. Moreover, the debt policies and practices that state and local governments develop and implement has taken on even greater importance, because of the difficult fiscal times governments have endured through the Great Recession. Difficult economic times throughout the US have served to highlight the importance of sound financial decision making at all levels of government. While the federal government's involvement in the market has grown, state and local governments are still responsible for their basic debt issuance and management decisions.

This part of the book examines how subnational government financial instruments are created. It starts by offering first principles along with a policy framework that can prudently guide financial decision making in the municipal finance sphere. Next is an illustration of the actual primary market process of bringing a municipal securities issuance to market followed by a discussion on the details of a basic debt issue. Finally, this part concludes by detailing the secondary municipal securities market, which provides critical liquidity for investors in municipal securities after the primary market sale by the government.

5. Subnational government debt financial management I: financing principles and policies

In the life of a community, debt issuance decisions can be of remarkable importance. This chapter covers the principles and policies that should guide such decisions. The financing–investment decision is appropriately represented by the sale of long-term debt to finance a major capital infrastructure investment. Such a financing and investment decision represents the essence of the debt decision, which is to contractually trade expected future revenues for a large increase in current funds. Debt financing has an inevitable budgetary impact – the debt must be serviced over the life of the issue, and principal and interest payments may crowd out future spending. The sale of debt creates a future liability that must be repaid as debt service expenditures until the debt matures. The more that is paid in future debt service expenditures, the fewer funds available to finance the rest of the budget.

Indeed, 'because of the large, binding and long-term nature of debt obligations, debt issuance and management practices should be guided by a formal debt policy'[1] which is based on fundamental debt financing principles. Debt policies should be grounded in basic financial economic and democratic principles that help create a sustainable capital financing program. Issuing and managing debt is a public trust. Debt policies should specifically detail what that public trust entails and administrative practices emanating from those policies should strengthen the trust between government officials and the citizens they represent.

The right of subnational governments to engage in debt financing free from national government interference is at the heart of fiscal federalism. Subnational governments have the right to debt finance, but in order to maintain that right in a free marketplace, they must exercise it responsibly. Prudent debt policies can help steer officials from engaging in practices that could put their debt financing franchise in jeopardy. In fact, some may argue that recent federal legislative activity (e.g. Dodd–Frank) directed at the municipal securities market could be interpreted as an attempt to federally legislate more prudent behavior by state and local government issuers and their financial service vendors. Indeed, better and more diligent use of debt policies across subnational governments may have forestalled recent federal interventions.

Each debt issuer should have a debt policy statement that is written in language that is easy to understand, publicly adopted, comprehensive, integrated into the capital budget and improvement plan, and that clearly communicates the role of debt financing in helping to realize public policy goals (Simonsen et al., 2001; Larkin and Joseph, 1991). Unfortunately, as rational as this seems, this has not always been the practice of many subnational governments. Specifically, previous research has suggested that most state governments did not have a comprehensive, detailed set of formal debt policies, but rather relied on their own standard practices or mere rules of thumb (Robbins and Dungan, 2001).

Debt policies must be inclusive enough to cover multiple stakeholders, elected officials and appointed debt managers, taxpayers and ratepayers, investors and vendors. Since government officials contract with private firms for much of the financial services involved in debt issuance and management, including municipal advisors, attorneys, auditors, bond insurers, credit rating agencies and underwriters, debt policies should guide appropriate vendor relationships and help officials make sound financial contracting decisions.

Debt policies should be comprehensive enough to provide debt managers with clear guidance as they engage in the process of raising capital, without constraining them from responding to changes in financial markets and generally making good contemporary financial decisions. The policies should be clear and transparent to the general citizen as well as providing guidance for the professional expert. Perhaps most importantly, debt policies should help public administrators make decisions that strengthen the trust citizens have placed in them to use their money wisely. In the remainder of this chapter we cover the foundational principles that debt policies should be rooted in: accountability and transparency, equity, efficiency, effectiveness, management flexibility, certainty and measurability. These principles have been established in the debt management literature (Petersen and McLoughlin, 1991; Johnson and Rubin, 1998; Luby, 2009; Bifulco et al., 2012), and we conclude the chapter by discussing the three strands of prior research.

1. PUBLIC ACCOUNTABILITY AND TRANSPARENCY

Public accountability refers to the ideal in a democratic society that 'elected officials are answerable to their constituents' (Lee and Johnson, 1998). In debt management, public accountability is part of the basic premise that whoever is responsible for repaying the debt obligation (taxpayer, ratepayer, etc.) should have a voice in the decision to incur the obligation (Johnson, 1996). There should be political and administrative channels for citizens to participate in debt issuance decisions, such that taxpayers can hold government officials accountable for long-term debt incurred in their name (Johnson, 1996).

Violating the accountability principle can result in disastrous consequences for taxpayers and debtholders. For example, without getting direct voter approval, local governments in Orange County, California, sold over $1.2 billion in short-term taxable notes solely to invest in the Orange County investment pool.[2] Many of these governments in past years had successfully executed this arbitrage strategy (selling tax-exempt securities and investing the proceeds at a higher, taxable interest rate) to generate substantial interest income for their operating budgets. This time the arbitrage strategy did not work, resulting in financial catastrophe for taxpayers and debtholders. The recent bankruptcy filing in Jefferson County, Alabama provides some of the latest evidence for the importance of public accountability. The bankruptcy is the result of the excessive use of financial derivatives along with nefarious corruption activities by the district's elected officials and financial managers related to its debt financings.

Debt financing is fundamentally riddled with principal–agent problems because of the incentive for administrators to leverage the resources of future taxpayers for their own pecuniary and non-pecuniary gains (money, votes, power, prestige, etc.) (Johnson and Kioko, 2009). The cost to taxpayers for monitoring and constraining the financing decisions of government officials can be expensive, but it begins with government officials being transparent about the full consequences of the initial decision to issue debt and its recurring costs and benefits. According to Bifulco et al. (2012) transparency 'refers to the extent to which an action is widely recognized as committing future resources and the extent to which those commitments are considered in public deliberations'. In order for taxpayers (and ratepayers) to make good debt financing decisions, they must be fully informed regarding their current and future obligations, along with the opportunity costs associated with their decisions.

2. EQUITY

Fairness or equity is an important guiding principle in developing a debt policy. In the context of long-term borrowing, equity has three related dimensions: net benefits (benefits minus costs), ability-to-pay and intergenerational equity. For debt sold to finance pure public goods, all of the beneficiaries from the facilities and services financed by the debt issue should be liable for repayment, which may be the entire jurisdiction (e.g. city, county, region or state). Such is the case when a jurisdiction sells full faith and credit general obligation debt to finance a public good.

For debt sold to finance non-pure public goods, the equity principle incorporates the idea that those not benefiting from the project should not have to pay for it (Petersen and McLoughlin, 1991). Only the direct beneficiaries should be required to pay for projects associated with goods that are not purely public: private goods, toll goods and common-pool resources. Officials may want to make an exception to this rule based on vertical equity. For example, a poor, rural area of a state may not have the money to pay for mandated infrastructure improvements, such as water and sewer infrastructure improvements in furtherance of clean and safe drinking water standards. Therefore, the state government might sell unlimited tax bonds backed by state revenues to finance the improvements. Or, the state and/or federal government might provide local communities with other forms of subsidy, like the capitalization grants and direct interest rate subsidies provided in SRFs.

Similarly, the government may want to expand the payers beyond direct beneficiaries when the debt proceeds may be used to extend positive spillovers and reduce negative spillovers. Financing a pollution control facility is intended to reduce the amount of pollution, a negative spillover; financing an elementary education facility is intended to expand the amount of education produced, a positive spillover. In such cases, however, the indirect beneficiaries responsible for repaying the debt should have a say in their level of financial participation. A debt service cross-subsidization policy could address the broad policy issues of when, why and how they could participate, and the extent of their financial obligation.

As it relates to debt finance, intergenerational equity refers to the incidence of a debt burden among different generations of taxpayers, both present and future (Johnson and Rubin, 1998). Usually, it deals with one generation placing an undue debt burden on another generation. Each generation should share equitably in the distribution of the costs and benefits from long-term investments financed with debt. One upside of debt financing is that it can smooth the payment for and consumption of capital facilities over a long period of time; the downside is that the current generation has an incentive to place a greater burden on future generations. Having the present generation pay for a long-term asset over a short period is inequitable because it places an undue burden on the current generation. Likewise, having future generations pay for current projects with short useful lives is also inequitable, because it can leave future generations paying for worthless assets. The debt policy statement should incorporate the perspective that while using debt to finance capital investments can generate a smoother revenue and expenditure profile across generations and lead to greater consumption for each generation, the incentive in debt finance to enjoy the benefits today and move the costs into the future must be guarded against.

One recent example of a financing strategy violating intergenerational equity principles is the use of school district capital appreciation bonds (CABs) sold in California. From 2000–12 California school districts sold roughly $20 billion of CABs, 6.2 percent of which had 39- or 40-year maturities.[3] Moreover, there was a pattern of CABs being issued with no debt service payments for more than a decade, and no call option. The Santa Ana Unified School District sold a $35 million CAB issue in 2009, with no debt service payable until 2026.[4] The case that is credited with influencing a change of state debt policy is the Poway Unified School District non-callable $105 million CAB issue, which has a 40-year maturity date and debt service costs totaling 'nearly $1 billion'. Moreover, reportedly the bond issue was passed because it was inequitable. According to Lovett (2013), since 'payments on the bond do not start for 20 years, current school board members faced little risk of resistance from property owners'. In an attempt to reduce the intergenerational inequities in local school district CAB debt financing, on 2 October 2013 the Governor of the State of California signed Assembly Bill No. 182[5] into law. Among other debt policy reforms, the law prohibits the ratio of total debt service to principal from exceeding four to one, requires that after 10 years the CABs must be callable, and requires more frequent and detailed public disclosure of the terms and the financial impact of the CAB issue.[6]

In a debt refinancing, as an example, the benefit to one (current) generation of taxpayers should be proportional to another (future) generation. The refinancing should not place an increased debt burden on one generation while reducing the debt burden on another. This would be the case if the debt refinancing provided interest cost savings in the near term but increased debt service costs in later years even if the present value savings were positive in aggregate. Also, it is inequitable to extend the repayment period beyond that of the original debt issue without increasing the useful life of the asset. Such a refinancing transaction is actually a debt restructuring and should not be done without buying new, useful assets or without full disclosure of such practice to current and future stakeholders. Without buying new, valuable assets with the new, longer-term debt, the practice extracts from the future generation the accumulated patrimonial value they should have inherited, leaving them with debt on assets likely in need of costly maintenance and repair. Therefore, the duration of principal and interest payments should approximate the useful life of the capital asset being financed (Johnson, 1996).

3.   ECONOMIC EFFICIENCY, EFFECTIVENESS AND MANAGEMENT FLEXIBILITY

Efficient debt policies should provide guidance for officials to minimize borrowing costs. According to Johnson (1996), 'debt policies should promote low-cost, high-quality contracting for services from financial professionals and should include general guidance on characteristics of bond issues' that can help lower borrowing costs. The policy should strike a balance between motivating managers to avoid risky behavior without unnecessarily constraining their ability to manage their debt financing affairs and unintentionally increasing borrowing costs (Johnson, 1996).

An effective debt policy helps officials obtain all the capital needed, when it is needed. The policy should help officials maintain timely access to the market and the capacity to raise additional debt at reasonable cost. Effective policies also provide management with future decision-making flexibility. It involves not making decisions now that constrain unnecessarily or unwisely future decision making. For example, converting 'soft' liabilities, where officials may be able to control the timing of payments, to 'hard' liabilities, such as contractual payments to bondholders, may limit management flexibility. The sale of pension obligation bonds (POBs) to provide funding for unfunded liabilities is an example of this type of flexibility constraining action. Moreover, the negative consequences of creating such hard, fixed debt service obligations can also bleed over into other areas of the budget and cause financial problems.

This is precisely what occurred when the city of Stockton, California sold $125 million POBs in 2007 to finance their unfunded pension liability. The purpose of the Stockton POBs, like POBs in general, was an arbitrage play that backfired. The city invested the POB proceeds in investments intended to produce a higher rate of return than the cost of borrowed funds. Unfortunately, investments bought with POB proceeds declined in value rapidly during the Financial Crisis, resulting in estimated losses of 50–65 percent of principal value in less than three years.[7] The loss in POB proceeds, coupled with the stark decline in housing prices, among other systematic problems facing local governments in California, resulted in the city of Stockton filing for bankruptcy in June 2012.

4. CERTAINTY AND MEASURABILITY

The principles of certainty and measurability were initially developed by Bifulco et al. (2012), and expanded by Luby (2014). We view them as related concepts. In debt financing, ideally the costs and benefits should be measured with certainty. While this is not always possible, the precise use of proceeds is almost always prescribed prior to debt issuance. On fixed rate debt, the future costs (i.e. principal and interest payments) are published in a debt service schedule in the official statement. However, debt issues often have much more complicated structures than fixed rate debt. Indeed, officials should not enter into debt contracts where the potential liabilities are highly uncertain and largely immeasurable. Such has been the case with certain variable-rate debt instruments and interest rate swap contracts. Also, in the case of debt refinancing the interest cost savings of a refinancing should be measured (measurability) and are 'locked-in' (certainty) at the transaction's execution.

In upcoming book chapters we further develop the theme of developing debt policies and implementing financial management practices that reduce uncertainty and potential liabilities associated with sophisticated financial instruments. In Chapter 9 we analyze the uncertainty associated with interest rate swaps, particularly estimating termination value. In Chapter 10 we evaluate debt refunding transactions against basic debt financing principles, and in Chapter 11 we analyze the revealed interest rate reset uncertainty associated with MARS.

5. PREVIOUS RESEARCH ON DEBT POLICIES

The aforementioned principles should guide the development of a debt policy and, thus, the debt finance decisions made by subnational governments. The normative importance of debt policies has been identified by public finance researchers. In fact, there is a robust empirical literature on state and local government debt policies governing the management of traditional municipal bond activities including the sale, structure and monitoring of their debt portfolios. This research can be split into three strands: (1) studies that attempt to offer a normative framework for the development of debt policies; (2) studies that describe and evaluate subnational debt management policies actually in place; and (3) studies that empirically assess the impact of debt management policies on debt management decision-making and financial outcome variables.

The first category includes studies by Petersen and McLoughlin (1991), Larkin and Joseph (1991), Zino (1994), and Johnson and Rubin (1998), which provide a framework that has informed debt management policies best practices. The second category involves describing and evaluating current policies in work by Hackbart and Leigland (1990), Miranda et al. (1997), Simonsen and Kittredge (1998), Robbins and Dungan (2001) and Luby (2009). In general, these studies found that state and local government debt policies are not nearly universally adopted, are usually very technical in nature, and often exclude broad policy issues and sometimes may lead to unintended consequences.

Finally, the third strand of previous research, which includes Simonsen et al. (2001) and Levine (2011), explores the impact of state debt management policies on debt management decision-making and financial outcome variables. These studies found that inclusion of certain debt policy elements was perceived as having greater importance by financial managers (Simonsen et al., 2001) and that debt policies had a very limited impact on bond borrowing costs with only policy elements related to improving transparency being associated with lower borrowing costs (Levine, 2011).

6.   SUMMARY

While there is general support for the theoretical import of debt policies, the way state and local governments have written and used these policies has mitigated their effectiveness to the point where there is a certain degree of skepticism about their efficacy. Recognizing such skepticism and in the absence of better standardized policies, this book relies on the previously described debt management principles to serve as guideposts in our discussion of specific debt management activities and decisions considered by subnational governments. In addition, our approach is congruent with the recent policy stance at the federal government level through the Dodd–Frank legislation that has generally required a more systematic and formalized approach to subnational debt management.

NOTES

1. See Johnson (1996).
2. See Johnson and Mikesell (1996).
3. Jensen (2012).
4. Lovett (2013).
5. California Assembly Bill No. 182. Chapter 477 (Legislative Counsel's Digest, 2013).
6. See Sophia Kwong Kim (2013), California Senate Analysis of AB 182, 29 August.
7. Baumgartner et al. (2013), unpublished manuscript.

6. Subnational government debt financial management II: bringing an issue to market: networks and practices

Financial autonomy for state and local governments in a decentralized system is predicated on these governments' ability to effectively and efficiently raise resources through the capital finance markets. If subnational governments lack this skill and expertise, justification for autonomous subnational financial decision making weakens. However, bringing a bond issue to market is not a quick or simple task. It is an extended process that does not begin and end on the bond pricing date. Rather, it starts with the capital budgeting process and often ends decades later when the government entity makes its final debt service payment on the bonds. In addition, capital financing is not a closed system but rather relies on the skills and counsel of many types of financial intermediaries and consultants who reside both inside and outside of government.

This chapter details the management network that state and local governments rely on to bring a municipal securities issue to market. It places the debt management network in principal–agent theory identifying the potential conflicts of interest that reside in the network. Also detailed are the various specific decisions debt managers need to make that can have considerable economic implications for their securities transactions both in the short and long run. The chapter concludes with a discussion of the academic research that addresses many of these debt management decisions as a means of providing some empirical justification behind industry best practices.

1.   THE DEBT MANAGEMENT NETWORK

Once a state or local government decides to issue debt, it contracts with several types of financial intermediaries and consultants to help the government raise capital in the municipal bond market. These financial intermediaries reside in a debt management network where each member's tasks are clearly delineated but where they work together in the network in the pursuit of a successful capital-raising outcome for the government. Miller and Justice (2012) describe three basic types of debt management network members: (1) those who interpret the bond market for the government; (2) those who interpret the law for the government or underwriter; and (3) those who interpret the government for the underwriter and investor. Municipal advisors interpret the bond market for the government. Bond counsel and underwriter's counsel interpret the law for the government and underwriter, respectively. Accountants, engineers, credit rating agencies and credit enhancement providers interpret the government for the underwriter and investor. The following paragraphs describe each of these debt management network members.

Municipal advisors (MAs) are financial consultants to state and local governments that advise on various municipal securities, instruments, financial products and capital market strategies. As defined by the Dodd–Frank Wall Street Reform and Consumer Protection Act of 2010 (the 'Dodd–Frank Act' or 'Dodd–Frank'), MAs include financial advisors with respect to the issuance of securities and investment of bond proceeds, swap advisors, and third-party solicitors to state and local governments. The importance of these MAs in the financial activities of state and local governments is indisputable. As measured by municipal bond sale activity, municipal advisors advised on approximately 70 percent of the total volume (by par amount) of state and local government debt in 2008 (Municipal Securities Rulemaking Board, 2009). However, solely looking at MA usage on primary bond market sales underestimates the influence of these actors as it is commonly understood that they provide financial counsel on a number of other financial policy areas not captured in the bond sales data (Petersen and Watt, 1986; Joseph, 1994; Wood, 2008). Since Dodd–Frank, municipal advisors now have a fiduciary responsibility to the state or local government it is serving. This fiduciary responsibility is aimed to mitigate principal–agent problems inherent to the debt management network as will be described in more detail later in this chapter.

State and local governments retain bond counsel in order to provide legal opinions as to the legal status of the municipal securities. The legal opinion of bond counsel seeks to assure investors that the securities are legal, valid and binding obligations of the government. These opinions also speak to the taxability of the securities, that is, whether the bonds are tax-exempt from federal, state and/or local income taxes. Bond counsel represents the government entity and serves as its counsel on matters related to the sale of the bonds. On the other side of the transaction, underwriter counsel serves as counsel to the underwriter drafting the purchase agreement of the bonds from the government to the underwriter. Underwriter's counsel advises the underwriter on federal and state securities issues and also ensures that the offering documents do not omit any information or include any misleading information as it relates to disclosure.

The underwriter purchases the bonds from the government entity and resells these bonds to investors. Depending on the type of bond sale, negotiated versus competitive, the underwriter has different roles and responsibilities. In a negotiated bond offering, the underwriter works with the MA and government entity to design the plan of finance and pre-market the bonds. The underwriter advises the government on market timing, assists in drafting bond documents, and 'runs numbers' as it relates to the proposed financing. In a negotiated underwriting, the underwriter actually consists of several investment banks that combine forces to act as an underwriting syndicate for the bonds. The lead or book-running senior manager manages this syndicate distributing the bonds to the syndicate members based on predetermined criteria. In a competitive offering, the underwriter submits a bid to the government entity to purchase the bonds, with the government selecting the underwriter that offers the highest dollar amount/lowest interest rate for the bonds. Regardless of the type of bond sale, underwriters should maintain an arm's-length relationship with the state or local government in bringing the issue to market, which, it should be noted, is a different relationship from the one a government has with its MA or bond counsel. Acting in a fiduciary role for the bondholder with whom the underwriter ultimately places the bonds is the trustee. The trustee serves to enforce the terms of the bond indenture including the timely payment of principal and interest on the bonds. The trustee also often invests the proceeds of the bonds for the issuer in accordance with legal restrictions on such investment.

There are several other consultants that interpret the government entity and its debt offering for investors. A government's comprehensive annual financial report (CAFR) includes financial statements that provide a glimpse of the government's financial condition. A government contracts with accountants to audit its financial statements to ensure they are being assembled according to Government Accounting Standards Board (GASB) requirements. Investors and other stakeholders such as credit rating agencies and credit enhancers rely on such financial statements in making purchase and credit rating decisions regarding the government's bonds. In a revenue bond offering, state and local governments often rely on engineers or feasibility consultants to project the future revenues and expenses associated with a revenue-producing asset. These projections are critical in helping credit rating agencies assess the default risk of the revenue bond financing and investors, once again, in making a bond purchase decision.

The credit rating agencies (Standard and Poor's, Moody's and Fitch) use publicly available information and their own internal analyses to assess the credit quality of the bonds. Investors heavily rely on credit ratings in making their bond purchase decisions. Credit enhancers such as bond insurance companies and bank letter of credit providers support a government's credit in exchange for an up-front or ongoing fee. Thus, if the government entity cannot pay its debt service on the bonds in a timely fashion, the credit enhancer steps in and makes the payment to investors on behalf of the government. Bond insurance is generally used on fixed rate municipal securities while letters of credit and liquidity facilities provide credit support on variable rate securities.

2. PRINCIPAL–AGENT THEORY AND THE MUNICIPAL BOND PROCESS

A helpful framework for state and local governments to use in understanding their relationship with the various intermediaries and each player's interests is principal–agent theory (Simonsen and Hill, 1998; Luby, 2010). The municipal bond issuance process is a web of principal and agent relationships whereby some groups are both principals and agents while other groups may only be an agent or a principal. Figure 6.1, which is adapted from Simonsen and Hill (1998), details this web of principal–agent

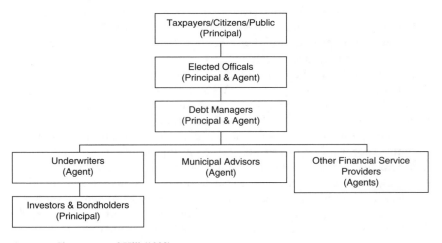

Source:	Simonsen and Hill (1998).

*Figure 6.1	Principal–agent framework: general municipal bond issuance*

relationships. Figure 6.2, which is adapted from Luby (2012) focuses on the principal–agent relationships most germane to the government entity directly and the goals and interests of these participants in this process (i.e. the public, elected official, and government financial manager).

From an agency theory perspective, in the case of issuing municipal bonds, the public is the principal and only a principal. The working assumption is that the public favors prudent, long-term public financial management decisions made on its behalf by elected official and financial managers. The public values the principles of efficiency, equity and accountability. In general, they do not favor public finance decisions that undermine inter-generational equity or, more specifically, decisions that produce short-term benefits at long-term costs. Such short-term and reckless decisions made by the current generation only serve to burden the current taxpayers or future taxpayers. Thus, the public's goal is the long-term cost efficient and equitable management of government debt (Luby, 2010).

Complicating this goal, however, is the fact that the municipal bond process and its substantive decision-making part is very technical, complicated and often not transparent. That is, public financial management decisions made by elected officials working through their debt managers are often not transparent or well understood by the citizenry. This results in a decision-making context where there can be strong information asymmetry between the principal (the public) and its agents (elected officials and financial managers) related to the specific aspects of the substance and process of bond financing decision making. This information asymmetry can lead to principal–agent problems whereby the agents act in their own interest rather than in the interest of the principal.

At the other extreme of the web are investors who are also only principals. Underwriters are agents to principals. The underwriter's loyalty is ultimately to the investor in delivering securities at the most favorable price. That is, the underwriter strives to provide investors with securities at the lowest price at which the government entity is willing to sell. However, the underwriter also has an agency relationship with the government entity in helping to structure and market the debt to investors. In fact, in the bond pricing process, the underwriter may represent to the government entity that it is trying to find investors who are willing to pay the highest price for the government's securities. Clearly, this evidences a potential conflict of interest for underwriters. However, government entities must understand that the underwriter's first loyalty is to investors whom they often serve daily in finding and placing securities with these investors.

The principal–agent relationship between the public and the elected official working through her government financial managers is complicated. The elected official (usually the chief executive of the government

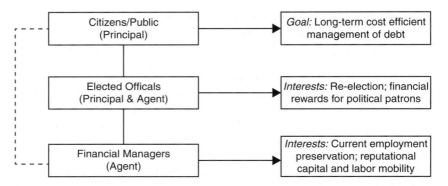

*Figure 6.2   Principal–agent relationships in state and local government
debt issuance choices, goals and interests*

entity) is ultimately responsible for the government's debt management activities. She thus acts as an agent to the public. The elected official is also the principal to the government's financial managers (usually the budget director or debt manager) as these financial managers are hired by the elected official and must be responsive to her policy preferences. The interests of the elected official are assumed to be short-term with an emphasis of securing re-election at the ballot box. The re-election goal is achieved by keeping taxes low (or reducing taxes) and maintaining or increasing public provision of goods or services. Debt finance activities can facilitate these re-election goals through the use of debt in financing capital projects or reducing operating budget costs in the case of debt refinancing. Re-election is further achieved by maximizing campaign contributions which can be partially achieved directly or indirectly by providing bond financing contracts to certain financial market participants (e.g. financial advisors, investment banks, bond counsel) either in the form of bond underwriting, financial advisory arrangements or legal contracts.

The elected official's interests are operationalized through the debt financing decisions of her agent, the financial manager. Since the financial manager is motivated by self-preservation and/or professional promotion (at least in the short-term), she is inclined to make debt finance decisions that strive to achieve the elected official's primary goal of re-election. However, these debt finance decisions may be short-sighted from the perspective of the public and not reflect their interests. The empirical literature has cited many different ways that governments have employed budget gimmicks through the use of debt to satisfy balanced budget requirements at the expense of the long-term fiscal health of the government (Briffault, 1996; Petersen, 2003; Bifulco et al., 2012; Luby, 2012).

Thus, one can see a diversion between the goals of the public and the interests of elected officials (working through their debt managers making financial decisions) in an arcane area of public financial management which offers the potential for acute agency problems to exist. However, the financial manager is also motivated to maintain her long-term value in the labor market, and participating in reckless or imprudent financial management practices threatens this value. Thus, financial managers' interests may be in conflict somewhat and it is an empirical question as to which interest is more influential in their decision making (i.e. loyalty to the public official, professional norms, and/or future professional employment opportunities). In the event that agency problems do not exist in public financial management, one could hypothesize that the longer-term professional interests of financial managers may serve to mitigate this potential agency problem between the public and elected officials (Luby, 2010).

3. CONTRACTING FOR SERVICES REQUIRES MAKING KEY DECISIONS

Intertwined with the use of the aforementioned financial intermediaries and consultants are several key policy decisions that a state or local government makes as it relates to its proposed debt issuance. Often, the first decision a state or local government makes as it begins the process of bringing its debt issue to market is whether to sell the bonds via a competitive or negotiated method of sale. On a conceptual basis, the academic literature has documented the pros and cons of both underwriting methods of sale over the last 30 years (Leonard, 1994). Nevertheless, the debate over which sale method is preferable has not been settled. The primary advantages cited in the literature for competitive bond sales are threefold. First, the 'all or nothing' dynamic inherent in competitive bidding provides a clear-cut incentive for underwriters to offer their lowest bid. Second, gross underwriter spreads have historically been lower on competitive sales than negotiated ones. Finally, competitive sales provide a political buffer to government finance officials in that they avoid the appearance of unfairness.

The general disadvantages cited in the literature for competitive bond sales are also threefold. First, pre-sale marketing may be minimal since underwriters are not assured of the awarding of bonds. This may result in a higher interest rate than if the underwriters knew in advance that they were selling the bonds. Second, competitive sales restrict an issuer's flexibility in changing the timing or structure of the bond sale. In addition the issuer does not receive the underwriter's expertise in tailoring the bond issue (e.g. adjusting coupons, structuring term bonds) to meet current investor demands under a competitive sale. Finally, an issuer does not control the distribution of bonds to specific types of syndicate members in a competitive sale. This may undermine other worthy government policy goals such as the encouragement of greater participation in the underwriting syndicate by local, minority, woman-owned or other disadvantaged and emerging firms.

Negotiated bond sales enjoy four general advantages over competitive sales. First, a negotiated underwriting may reduce the need for a municipal advisor or more knowledgeable issuer staff since the investment bank can perform most origination services. Second, negotiated sales allow underwriters to perform a more exhaustive pre-sale marketing effort with potential investors, which may result in lower overall borrowing cost on the bond issue. Third, negotiated sales offer issuers greater flexibility to time the bond market and structure the issue to meet changing investor demands both prior to and during the actual bond pricing. Finally, an issuer can control the distribution of bonds and the composition of the underwriting syndicate in a negotiated offering.

The general disadvantages of negotiated bond sales are threefold. First, the pre-selection of a managing underwriter(s) may deflate competition in the bond sale, thus resulting in a higher true interest cost to the issuer. Second, it may be difficult for an issuer to discern whether they are receiving fair value for each component of the underwriter spread since the investment bank performs several services in a negotiated offering. Finally, some outside observers may view negotiated sales as less transparent or fair especially in light of the fact that most issuers have the ability to sell bonds competitively.

Some public policy implications about bond method of sale can be drawn based on the above cited advantages and disadvantages. First, government finance officials should not restrict themselves to only one bond sale method. Retaining flexibility may be the optimal course of action in ensuring that a particular government entity receives the highest price for its securities. Second, state and local elected officials should resist any temptation to statutorily mandate a minimum amount of competitive or negotiated bond sales over any given time period given the benefits of one method or the other in certain market and bond credit conditions. Finally, state and local government finance officials should not be hesitant in selling their bonds on a negotiated basis. While the openness of competitive bidding may be highly valued in the government finance sector, the premium for such government decision-making transparency may be costly to the taxpayers should negotiation allow for a substantial reduction in an issuer's borrowing costs.

State and local governments also must decide on whether to use a

municipal advisor in their bond financing. This decision is somewhat connected to the decision to sell bonds on a competitive or negotiated basis. In
a competitive sale, many state and local governments need the services of
a municipal advisor for the bond origination services that an underwriter
would perform in a negotiated sale. In addition, the municipal advisor
coordinates the competitive bid process for the issuer, ensuring that the
government selects the underwriter who submits the lowest bid based on
the true interest cost of the issuer. The municipal advisor also counsels the
issuer on the most advantageous bond structure and market timing given
investor demands and bond market conditions.

Given these tasks for the municipal advisor in a competitive sale, one
might be tempted to claim that an MA's services would not be needed in a
negotiated offering since the underwriter could perform these same tasks.
While it is true that the underwriter could perform many of the origination
services, the role of an MA is somewhat different in a negotiated sale and
potentially even more valuable. That is, the MA serves as an independent
advisor to the government whose fiduciary responsibility is solely to the
government (now as required under Dodd–Frank). Contrast this with the
underwriter who technically has an arm's-length relationship with the government entity. Thus, in a negotiated sale, the municipal advisor provides
an independent voice as to the proper bond structure and market timing
for the bond issuance, taking into account the sole interests of the state or
local government. Should a state or local government rely on the recommendations of its underwriter, there is no assurance that such direction
would serve the best interest of the government given the underwriter's
position as an agent to the government's investors.

In addition to the decisions to use different financial intermediaries and
methods of sale, the state or local government also faces important decisions related to the actual structure of its bond offering. A key decision
relates to whether the state or local government wants to have its interest
rates 'fixed' through the term of the bonds or whether they are comfortable
with a variable interest rate structure. The benefit of fixed rate debt is that
the government entity knows exactly what its interest costs will be over the
term of the issue. There is no uncertainty related to borrowing costs that
need to be taken into account in future budgets. The benefit of variable
rate debt relates to the term structure of interest rates. Specifically, variable rate bonds have short-term interest rate resets and thus can provide
benefits to the state or local government due to the historical interest cost
advantage of short-term rates compared to long-term rates assuming an
upward sloping yield curve. That is, short-term interest rates are generally
lower than long-term interest rates, resulting in borrowing cost efficiency
for a state or local government. However, the interest rate on variable rate

bonds resets at periodic times and there is no assurance that such interest rate resets will be less than the fixed interest rate available at the original pricing date of the bonds.

In addition, variable rate bonds require credit and liquidity support from banks or insurance companies whereby the future availability and cost efficiency of these credit enhancement devices is uncertain. The Government Finance Officers Association recommends that state and local governments exercise caution with the use of variable rate debt, carefully evaluate how such financial instruments meet financial management objectives, and ensure that the government entity has a plan for managing the various risks associated with variable rate debt (GFOA, 2010).

Related to the use of variable rate debt, another decision that state and local governments face is whether to use financial derivatives such as interest rate swaps to mitigate the risks associated with floating rate securities. Chapter 9 provides a fuller explanation of financial derivatives. Related to this section on bringing the bond issue to market, state and local governments often consider using an interest rate swap that attempts to effectively convert the variable rate debt to fixed rate debt. This conversion can result in a lower fixed interest rate than would be available to the state or local government if it just sold fixed rate debt without the interest rate swap. However, interest rate swaps, like all financial derivatives, carry many financial risks. These risks materialized during the recent global Financial Crisis whereby many state and local governments ended up paying much higher interest rates than expected under the interest rate swap given the tremendous volatility in the bond markets during that time period. As in the general case of variable rate debt, the GFOA recommends that state and local governments exercise significant caution before using financial derivatives and evaluate the various potential risks related to these financial instruments (GFOA, 2010).

Other bond structural decisions involve the bond size, bond refunding and bond amortization schedule. Generally, the size of the bond issue emanates from the capital budgeting process. The decision on the timing and amount of bond proceeds should be based on the capital budget and the specific requirements of the projects(s) being financed. However, state and local capital projects often entail years of time in their construction so debt managers must make a decision of when to sell the debt. That is, they need to decide on the optimal timing of selling the debt as it relates to when the proceeds are needed, and how much the government can earn on bond proceeds pending expenditure, taking into account expectations for future interest rates. State and local governments also often decide to increase the size of the bond issue if there are opportunities to refinance its existing bonds at a lower interest rate. In this event, the state and local government will try to take advantage of advantageous bond market conditions by selling additional bonds and using the bond proceeds to pay off the higher interest rate existing bonds. However, the decision to refinance bonds is a complicated one whereby issuers must assess whether to wait and refinance the bonds later if they expect interest rates to decline further. Chapter 10 discusses such bond refinancing decisions in greater depth.

Finally, the state or local government must decide on how quickly or slowly it wants to pay off the bonds. This decision refers to the amortization structure of the bonds. Generally, the state or local governments decide between an accelerated, level or deferred amortization structure. The debt is paid off fastest and usually at a lower overall interest cost under an accelerated structure and is paid off slowest and at the highest interest cost under a deferred interest cost structure. However, the amortization structure decision often takes into account other non-interest payment factors such as future financial flexibility, yield curve efficiency and revenue bond capacity. Chapter 7 details the amortization structure decision.

4. EMPIRICAL RESEARCH ON INTERMEDIARIES AND DEBT ISSUANCE

Keeping up with municipal bond market best practices and the empirical literature in public finance is one way for governments to ensure that their decisions lead to the most effective and efficient use of the capital markets. Many of the decisions that debt managers make relating to bringing a debt issue to market have been studied by researchers, often for decades. This section will review the empirical literature on the debt management decisions most studied by researchers. These decisions include bond method of sale, use of underwriters, use of municipal advisors, number of credit ratings, and use of debt management policies.

4.1   Bond Method of Sale

Government finance researchers have studied bond method of sale for decades. Unfortunately, there is still a split in the researcher community on the most effective method of sale as it relates to reducing borrowing costs. In the first phase of this research, Leonard (1994) reviewed 32 studies on the cost efficiency of negotiated versus competitive bond sales, presenting three notable findings. First, most studies found that a higher level of competition, measured by number of bidders and the intensity of bids, reduced underwriter spreads and reoffering yields. Second, several studies found that competitive versus negotiated cost differentials depended on the level of bidding competition and the degree of uncertainty about investor demand. Finally, Leonard concluded that the lower cost method of sale depended on the characteristics of a particular issue and issuer as well as the bond market conditions at the time of sale. From a public policy perspective, Leonard argued that these studies' empirical results demand that issuers maintain a flexible policy in selecting competitive bidding or negotiated sales at least until the results of new research is available.

Since Leonard's (1994) literature review on underwriting method of sale, the academic community has produced several more empirical studies on this topic as it relates to the municipal bond market. Simonsen and Robbins (1996) explored the cost efficiency of negotiated offerings in light of the many changes that occurred in the municipal bond market in the 1980s and 1990s. Simonsen and Robbins (1996) utilized a multivariate regression model to determine the impact of method of sale on the true interest cost of local government general obligation bonds issued in the State of Oregon in 1992 and 1993. The researchers found that, on average, competitive sales resulted in lower interest costs to issuers compared to negotiated sales and that this difference increased with the number of bids received. Robbins (2002) analyzed sales data for revenue bonds sold by the State of New Jersey Treasury Department and other state authorities before and after the 1993 enactment of an executive order encouraging competitive bid bond sales. This legislation allowed for a natural social scientific research experiment whereby the author could evaluate whether statutory restrictions lead to higher borrowing costs. Robbins found that there were significant cost savings for those issues sold through competition both before and after the enactment of the aforementioned executive order. Using a very large sample of California bonds issued in 2000–07, Guzman and Moldogaziev (2012) found that competitive sales performed as well as negotiated bids in terms of true interest costs for the riskiest debt issue purposes. However, they argue that the bond issues for lower risk debt obligations are almost always better off if sold using competitive bids.

Leonard (1996) further explored the topic of negotiated versus competitive bond sales by attempting to answer two questions: (1) whether issuers select method of sale rationally; and (2) whether yield differences between negotiated and competitive bond sales are attributable solely to the method of sale utilized. In this study, Leonard analyzed a sample of all municipal bonds issued between August 1992 and December 1992 utilizing regression analysis to explain method of sale decisions and cost efficiencies. With respect to Leonard's first research question, the author finds that issuers tend to act rationally in making a bond method of sale selection. Leonard finds that the probability of negotiation increased when: (1) market conditions were more unsettled; (2) issue size increased, (3) for low-rated issues and (4) for issues with complex structures. Regarding his second question, Leonard did not find any statistical support for competitive bid yields being lower than negotiated sale yields.

In their 2003 study, Jun Peng and Peter Brucato analyzed the underwriting method of sale debate from the theoretical perspective of financial certification. The authors claimed that sale method can be viewed as a certification mechanism as issuers self-select themselves into either competitive or negotiated groups based on their belief of how well the issue will be accepted by investors. In general, the authors concluded that for issuers with little or no information asymmetry, neither sale method has a significant cost advantage over the other. In contrast to almost all previous research on this topic, Peng and Brucato's results show that even large, well-established and higher-rated issuers may be able to benefit from negotiated offerings vis-à-vis competitive bidding. Kenneth Kriz's 2003 research on financial certification theory offers more evidence for the potential efficacy of negotiated offerings. After correcting for self-selection bias through his two-stage model, the author finds that for a nationwide sample of state general obligation bonds sold between 1990 and 1997, negotiated offerings have at worst no higher and perhaps lower true interest costs than competitively bid bonds. In fact, Kriz estimates that negotiated bond sales were associated with a 24 basis point reduction in true interest costs relative to competitive sales for those issuers that actually use a negotiated offering.

4.2   Use of Underwriters

The empirical research on use of underwriters has focused on several characteristics related to type of underwriters and their impact on bond borrowing costs. Clarke (1997) tested whether financial advisors who participate in the bidding process impact the interest cost of debt. Clarke assessed nearly 1000 competitively sold municipal debt issues in the state of Texas from 1991 to 1995, analyzing the impact of financial advisors turned underwriters on the net interest cost of bonds. For general obligation debt and state backed school bonds, there were no interest cost implications for allowing an advisor to bid on bonds. However, for unrated issues, advisors are much more likely to win the bid, indicating that cities should be concerned about the guidance of their advisor when that advice is to take unrated issues to market (Clarke, 1997).

More recent studies have focused on extending the research on municipal underwriting fees to even more specific variables of interest including underwriter prestige, the use of 'local' underwriters and the financial advisor–underwriter relationship. Daniels and Vijayakumar (2007) analyzed a sample of municipal bonds issued between 1990 and 1999 and found that issues underwritten by more reputable investment banks were associated with lower underwriting spreads. Butler (2008) analyzed a sample of taxable municipal bonds issued from 1997 to 2001, exploring whether underwriter 'location' mattered. Butler found that 'distance' mattered in that investment banks with an ongoing presence in the state were associated with lower underwriting fees. Butler's research also confirmed Daniels and Vijayakumar's (2007) finding on underwriter reputation with higher reputation investment banks associated with lower underwriting spreads (Butler, 2008).

Luby and Moldogaziev (2013) analyzed the empirical determinants of underwriter fees with more recent data, more sophisticated econometric modeling and different variables of interest. The authors found empirical support for much of the previous literature on the previous discussed variables associated with underwriter fees. However, Luby and Moldogaziev also found some interesting results relating to the underwriter–financial advisor relationship that had not been explored previously in the literature. Specifically, they found that financial advisors and underwriters who work together frequently are associated with higher underwriting fees. Luby and Moldogaziev suggest that this finding implies that issuers need to be very mindful of the level of interdependence in crafting their debt management networks so as to reduce their borrowing costs as much as possible.

4.3   Use of Municipal Advisors

There have been a number of academic studies on MAs. The initial wave of research was mostly normative in tone, offering prescriptive advice for state and local governments (Petersen and Watt, 1986; Joseph, 1994; Johnson, 1994a; Moyer, 2003). In the last couple of decades, researchers have tried to empirically assess the efficacy of MAs. Forbes et al. (1992) tested the impact of MAs on various bond borrowing cost components. The authors used their analysis to test two hypotheses: (1) the underwriter monopsony power hypothesis; and (2) the certification hypothesis. The underwriter monopsony power hypothesis claims that underwriters overcharge for their services due to their access to private information on the investor demand for a state or local government's municipal securities as well the level of effort they will need to distribute the securities. By extension, the hypothesis claims that using entities, such as municipal advisors, to monitor the bond sale should result in lower underwriter fees to the government. However, the authors' results provided evidence that the use of municipal advisors only modestly lower underwriter fees to state and local governments compared to not using an MA on a transaction. The certification hypothesis asserts that MAs mitigate information asymmetries between issuers and investors by certifying the true price of a municipal security offering. However, Forbes et al. (1992) found no statistically significant evidence supporting the certification hypothesis related to bond offering yields.

In subsequent research, Johnson (1994b) found some support for the certification hypothesis as it relates to municipal advisors. Johnson found that issuers of 'riskier' government entities (i.e. smaller, lower rated or infrequent issuers) were more likely to use a municipal advisor. From this finding, Johnson claimed that use of an MA is a result of the demand from investors for additional issue price certification (Johnson, 1994b). Vijayakumar and Daniels (2006) also evaluated the efficacy of municipal advisors with more recent bond sales after the MA market had evolved for a couple of decades. These researchers found that municipal advisors are associated with lower borrowing costs, reoffering yields and underwriter gross spreads. These results show strong support for the use of MAs as it relates to both the underwriter monopsony and certification hypotheses (Vijayakumar and Daniels, 2006). However, this study found no statistical effect as it relates to MA prestige, another variable of interest to state and local governments as they contemplate what firms should advise them. Allen and Dudney (2010) also studied the MA prestige issue and found that the use of reputable financial advisors (as measured by market share) is associated with lower bond yields, with this effect being even more pronounced for 'riskier' securities.

Robbins and Simonsen (2003) studied the relationship between the use of 'independent' municipal advisors and bond method of sale choice and found that 'independent' MAs were associated with a higher likelihood that a government entity would choose a competitive bond sale. Conversely, the authors found that government entities that used MAs that were closely associated with one underwriter (or were an underwriter themselves) were more likely to choose a negotiated sale (Robbins and Simonsen, 2003). These results led Robbins and Simonsen to conclude that there is a relationship between bond method of sale and municipal advisor 'independence'. This finding lends indirect credence to the underwriter monopsony power hypothesis, assuming one supports the supremacy of competitive sales compared to negotiated sales in lowering borrowing costs.

4.4 Number of Credit Ratings

Credit rating agencies serve as certification agents in capital markets by screening and sorting debt issues for investors (Wakeman, 1981; Johnson, 1999; Johnson and Kriz, 2002). Rating agencies provide a certification of a debt issues default risk – the likelihood that the debt issuer will pay debt service in full and on time. After a rating agency gathers and processes information to assess the credit quality of the debt issue, they assign higher (lower) credit ratings to issues that reflect lower (higher) default risk. *Ceteris paribus*, credit ratings directly affect the cost of borrowing. Debt issues with a higher (lower) credit rating exhibit lower (higher) borrowing costs. In addition, Johnson and Kriz (2002) find that the number of ratings can impact borrowing costs. Issuers that purchase a third credit rating receive a net cost benefit, once a 'two AAA rating threshold (is) reached'. They conclude that this 'indicates that obtaining "double" certification of prime quality status is valued by the market'.[1]

5. SUMMARY

Bringing a municipal securities issue to market is a complicated process that relies on extensive capital market expertise within and outside the subnational government. The process is plagued by principal–agent problems related to conflicts of interest and information asymmetries. Much of the federal government's recent regulatory and legislative activity in the municipal securities market is aimed at minimizing these information asymmetries and to ensure that subnational governments are receiving financial advice from capable intermediaries. Within this process, governments make several key decisions related to the process and actual structure of their bond financings. These decisions have real economic implications related to the ultimate borrowing cost of the transaction as well as to which taxpayers, current and future, must bear the cost of the transactions. Fortunately for state and local governments, there is a rich empirical academic literature on many of these key decisions that can provide empirical support for making a decision one way or the other given current financial and market conditions.

NOTE

1. The authors found no empirical evidence of a net benefit in 'the A and AA' categories (Johnson and Kriz, 2002).

7. The serial debt issue structure

The previous chapter discussed the process in which state and local governments sell municipal securities to finance their capital and operating activities. This chapter provides greater detail into the specifics and structure of those securities. Municipalities sell debt issues by combining individual bonds along the term structure into a debt issue, called a serial debt issue. Serial debt issues attract a range of investors that have varying maturity preferences.[1] A municipal bond issue with a principal amount of $10 million consists of 2000 bonds with a principal value of $5000 each.[2] On serial issues, a portion of the total principal of the debt issue is scheduled to mature at regular intervals over the life or term of the issue. The schedule (dates and amounts) of the principal maturities of the issue is referred to as the principal maturity schedule. Table 7.1 shows a typical maturity schedule for a serial debt issue. On a $10 million bond issue, $2 million matures annually over a five-year period, so the entire bond issue is retired five years after the date of issuance. All 2000 individual bonds, therefore, do not have the same final maturity date; they mature annually over the five-year period at roughly equal intervals (e.g. 400 bonds mature each year). The principal amount of $2 million is retired (repaid) each year for the next five years.[3]

Most bond issues have an increasing coupon interest rate and yield structure which corresponds with an upwardly sloping market yield curve. The typically upward sloping schedule of interest rates (3.00–5.00 percent) and yields (2.30–3.50 percent) reflects the need to compensate investors for additional risks on longer-term bonds. Interest is generally paid semi-annually and decreases over the life of the debt issue, despite being paid on

Table 7.1 Principal maturity schedule, issue size: $10 000 000

Maturity (1 January)	Principal amount ($)	Interest rate (%)	Initial yield (%)
2011	2 000 000	3.00	2.30
2012	2 000 000	3.00	2.50
2013	2 000 000	3.50	3.00
2014	2 000 000	4.00	3.20
2015	2 000 000	5.00	3.50

higher coupon rate bonds. In our example in Table 7.2a, it decreases from $462.50 in period 1 to $125 in period 10 for a notional $5000 bond (assuming semi-annual coupons) using the maturity schedules from Table 7.1. Interest on a bond is paid until the bond matures, but not after the final maturity date, so as bonds mature, interest payments decrease since interest is only paid on the remaining maturities.

We can calculate the total coupon payments an issuer will pay for the first period using the numbers in Table 7.2a. As shown in Table 7.2b, since there are 400 bonds in the first serial issue maturing in 2011 ($2 000 000/$5000), in the first period an issuer should expect to pay $30 000 (400 × $75) in coupon payments for all bonds in this serial issue. Similar estimations are done for other serial bonds with later maturities. For serial bonds maturing in years 2012, 2013, 2014 and 2015, the total coupon payments in period 1 are expected to be $30 000, $35 000, $40 000 and $50 000 respectively. Therefore, the aggregate coupon payments across all serial bonds are what the issuer owes in coupon interest in period 1, which in our case equals $185 000. In period 10, however, the aggregate coupon payment falls to only $50 000, because serial bonds with earlier maturities (2011 to 2014) are already retired by then.

Notice that the coupon payments within each serial bond are fixed. Also, notice that at the end of the first year (period 2) the serial bond maturing in 2011 will be retired. Therefore, at the end of the first year the issuer must pay $185 000 in coupon interest payments and the principal amount of $2 000 000 for the first serial bond. In the beginning of the second year (period 3) only four serial maturities will be outstanding, and so on until the final maturity of the entire debt issue.

Several types of individual bonds are used to construct an individual serial bond issue. It is not uncommon to see a serial bond issue that contains one or more of the following types of bonds: serial, term, variable, and capital appreciation (zero). Term bonds are usually subject to a mandatory sinking fund because the entire bond principal matures on a single date.[4] Like a typical bond, term bonds pay interest semi-annually, but their principal payments are paid (or sunk) through annual installments to a sinking fund. For example, a $25 000, five-year term bond pays semi-annual interest to bondholders, but also may pay $5000 ($25 000/5) per year to the sinking fund.[5] The sinking fund then pays such principal amounts out to the bondholders per the mandatory redemption schedule. The sinking fund is effectively an escrow fund and once the sinking fund payment goes into the escrow fund the issuer no longer has a legal right to the money.

Variable rate securities are municipal securities whose interest rate

Table 7.2a   *Coupon payments per serial bond for maturity schedule in Table 7.1 (for a notional $5000 bond and serial totals, assuming semi-annual coupons)*

Coupon periods	Bond maturity 2011	Bond maturity 2012	Bond maturity 2013	Bond maturity 2014	Bond maturity 2015	Total
Period 1	($5000 × 0.03) /2 = $75	($5000 × 0.03) /2 = $75	($5000 × 0.035) /2 = $87.5	($5000 × 0.04) /2 = $100	($5000 × 0.05) /2 = $125	$462.50
Period 2	$75	$75	$87.50	$100	$125	$462.50
Period 3		$75	$87.50	$100	$125	$387.50
Period 4		$75	$87.50	$100	$125	$387.50
Period 5			$87.50	$100	$125	$312.50
Period 6			$87.50	$100	$125	$312.50
Period 7				$100	$125	$225
Period 8				$100	$125	$225
Period 9					$125	$125
Period 10					$125	$125

Table 7.2b   *Coupon payments per serial issue for maturity schedules in Table 7.1 (assuming semi-annual coupons)*

Coupon periods	Bond maturity 2011	Bond maturity 2012	Bond maturity 2013	Bond maturity 2014	Bond maturity 2015	Total
Period 1	400 × $75 = $30000	400 × $75 = $30000	400 × $87.5 = $35000	400 × $100 = $40000	400 × $125 = $50000	$185000
Period 2	$30000	$30000	$35000	$40000	$50000	$185000
Period 3		$30000	$35000	$40000	$50000	$155000
Period 4		$30000	$35000	$40000	$50000	$155000
Period 5			$35000	$40000	$50000	$125000
Period 6			$35000	$40000	$50000	$125000
Period 7				$40000	$50000	$90000
Period 8				$40000	$50000	$90000
Period 9					$50000	$50000
Period 10					$50000	$50000

fluctuates over time. These securities can be long-term bonds or short-term notes. The distinguishing feature is that the interest rate changes at set specified dates and such reset is subject to bond market and issuer credit conditions. The benefit of variable rate securities is the historical interest rate advantage related to the term structure of interest rates, with these securities typically bearing short-term interest rate resets with long-term maturities. The disadvantage of variable rate securities is the uncertainty related to the future interest rates on these bonds and notes. Capital appreciation bonds (CABs) or zero coupon bonds are securities sold at a deep discount from par, with the principal value of the bond growing or appreciating in value to the par amount at maturity. These bonds do not pay coupon interest. Rather, investors in capital appreciation bonds receive a principal payment at the maturity date of the bonds.[6] The benefit of CABs or zero coupon bonds is that state and local governments can avoid any debt service payments on these bonds until maturity, providing greater budgetary flexibility. The downside of CABs is that these securities tend to be very expensive as measured by bond yield as investors demand a premium for bonds since they receive no payments until final maturity.

1.   UNDERSTANDING DEBT SERVICE

Debt service is principal plus interest. In our example, total debt service is $11 210 000 ($10 million principal payments plus coupon payments of $1.21 million). According to Table 7.3, the issuer faces only coupon payments in the first period – an amount of $185 000 – because no serial bond is maturing. In the end of the second period (the end of the first year) the debt service has two parts, principal of $2 000 000 and aggregate coupons

Table 7.3   Debt service schedule for $10 000 000 bond issue from Table 7.1 (assuming semi-annual coupons)

Periods	Principal payments	Interest payments	Total debt service
Period 1		$185 000	$185 000
Period 2	$2 000 000	$185 000	$2 185 000
Period 3		$155 000	$155 000
Period 4	$2 000 000	$155 000	$2 155 000
Period 5		$125 000	$125 000
Period 6	$2 000 000	$125 000	$2 125 000
Period 7		$90 000	$90 000
Period 8	$2 000 000	$90 000	$2 090 000
Period 9		$50 000	$50 000
Period 10	$2 000 000	$50 000	$2 050 000
Total	$10 000 000	$1 210 000	$11 210 000

of \$185000. In period 10 (end of year 5), debt service involves \$2000000, which is the principal payment on the very last maturing serial bond, and \$50000 in coupon interest for the last period. Debt service represents the amount of money the issuer has to legally come up with to service the debt, and therefore represents the direct budgetary burden the issuer agrees to when issuing debt.

Debt service structures can be either flat (level), ascending or descending. The example in Table 7.3 shows a descending debt service structure with recurring principal retired every year. It is not always the case that all the serial issues in a single bond issue have the same size, which in this case was \$2 million for each of the five serial maturities. If desired, the issuers could choose to 'back-load' the principal by structuring four serial issues of \$1 million each and a fifth serial issue of \$6 million. In that case, the debt service structure would become less descending. Debt service may also be back-loaded, where debt service payments increase over time. Governments often have prescriptions against back-loading debt service, and it can be a very inequitable way to finance capital improvements.

Similarly, maturity and coupon structures can be adjusted to shape one's debt service structure. An issuer could choose to sell four zero coupon serials (zerials), and have only the last serial maturity with a coupon that pays current interest. That coupon structure would effectively create a flat debt service structure. In a flat debt service structure annual debt service payments are roughly equal over the life of the debt issue.[7] In front-loaded debt service structures total annual debt service declines at a faster rate over time. The more rapid the debt service declines, the greater the front-loading.[8] If desired, the issuers could choose to front-load the principals in serial issues in Table 7.1 by structuring the first three issues of \$3 million each and have the remaining two series to have issue sizes of \$0.5 million each.

According to Johnson et al. (2010), each debt service schedule has pros and cons and can be understood in terms of trade-offs. Front-loaded schedules have rapid principal repayment which 'takes advantage of the normally upwardly sloping yield curve to produce lower coupon interest rates attached to earlier principal maturities'. A front-loaded schedule may also strengthen intergenerational equity, since current users (who enjoy greater benefits) will pay more than future users.

In a flat debt service structure less coupon interest is paid at the short-term end of the yield curve, because principal is amortized at a slower rate, placing relatively less pressure on upcoming annual budgets. Also, deferring debt service payments into the future could produce present value savings. While back-loaded structures may be the most efficient on a present value basis, they may violate the fundamental principle of matching the debt service structure to the useful life of the asset being financed. Moreover, Johnson et al. (2010) argue that:

> such a repayment scheme would be severely penalized by credit rating agencies with added pressure towards a lower rating, and by investors in the form of higher borrowing costs.[9] In general, investors prefer to get their money back sooner, rather than later, and rating agencies prefer more front-loaded than back-loaded debt service arrangements.

However, Johnson et al. (2010) find evidence that the standard debt service schedule rules, 25 percent/5-year and 50 percent/10-year,[10] encourage debt service schedules that are too front-loaded, especially when going into an economic slowdown. They find that state governments went into the 2007–08 recession with heavily front-loaded debt schedules, exacerbating the fiscal squeeze of the recession, and they argue in favor of level debt service schedules.[11]

2. TRUE INTEREST COST (TIC)

Debt issues are sold to investors through an origination and marketing process that involves a number of participants. Usually, issuers sell their debt by competitive (auction) bid or negotiated offering to an underwriting syndicate that in turn resells the debt issue to investors.[12] In an auction sale, the issuer awards the bonds to the underwriting syndicate submitting the lowest interest cost bid. The lowest cost bid should be determined on the basis of true interest cost (TIC).[13] The TIC is the rate that discounts the issue's debt service payable to its present value, or net proceeds. Issuers and financial advisors should also use a TIC-based measure to evaluate the cost of debt on negotiated offerings.

In order to estimate TIC for the serial debt issue in Table 7.1, we show in equation (7.1) a generic cash flow discounting equation. The goal is to find the yield that would equate the debt proceeds to all the debt service cash flows until final maturity.[14] From Table 7.1 we know that issue size is $10 million, with debt service cash flows spread out throughout the life of the bond issue. Equation 7.1 helps to find the true interest cost for this bond issue.

$$IssueSize = \frac{C_1}{\left(1 + \frac{TIC}{2}\right)^1} + \frac{C_2}{\left(1 + \frac{TIC}{2}\right)^2} + \ldots + \frac{C_n}{\left(1 + \frac{TIC}{2}\right)^n}$$

$$IssueSize = \sum_{i=1}^{N} \frac{C}{\left(1 + \dfrac{TIC}{2}\right)^n}$$ (7.1)

From the discussion of debt service in Table 7.3 we know the following:

$$\$10,000,000 = \frac{\$185,000}{\left(1 + \dfrac{TIC}{2}\right)^1} + \frac{\$2,185,000}{\left(1 + \dfrac{TIC}{2}\right)^2} + \ldots + \frac{\$2,050,000}{\left(1 + \dfrac{TIC}{2}\right)^{10}}$$

Table 7.4   Iterated TIC rates (semi-annual compounding)

	TIC /2	Issue size ($)
High TIC scenario	0.030000	9 469 957
Actual TIC	0.020078	10 000 000
Low TIC scenario	0.010000	10 582 828

It is apparent from the above equality that a closed form solution for TIC does not exist as we need to find a single number that satisfies the polynomial of tenth power. (In Appendix B, we provide a detailed introduction to pricing of fixed income securities. If necessary, we encourage the readers to refresh their skills in basic mathematics of bond valuation before proceeding further with TIC.) Instead, one must use an iterative method of solution to find the true interest cost that helps to balance the equality. Generally, a good place to start in the iterative selection of TIC is to select rates that are somewhat close to the expected coupon rates.

From Table 7.4 one can find that an assumption of 6 percent TIC, or to be precise TIC/2 = 3% due to semi-annual compounding, would result in $9 469 957. This would be less than the issue size of $10 million. Thus, this assumed TIC is too high and one needs to select a lower level of TIC. Further, from the same table one can find that an assumption of a 2 percent TIC, or TIC/2 = 1% due to semi-annual compounding, would result in $10 582 828. This is now greater than the issue size of $10 million. Therefore, a greater level of TIC must be selected. After these two initial steps, one can infer that the true interest cost must be between 2 percent and 6 percent for the bond issue in Table 7.1. In other words, we locked in on the range where TIC is located. After a bit of tinkering with potential TICs back and forth (selected iteratively), we discover that the true interest cost in this bond issue consisting of five serial components is 4.0156 percent (or 2.0078% × 2 due to semi-annual compounding). This rate balances the left- and right-hand sides in equation (7.1), and is, therefore, the true interest cost for the total bond issue.[15]

3.   PRICING DEBT ISSUES

The previous section detailed the mechanics of the true interest cost of a municipal securities issue. The inputs (coupon rates, yields, principal amounts) of the true interest cost are determined at the pricing date of the bonds. Bond pricing is one of the most important and technical financial management activities for state and local governments. Bond pricing refers to the setting of the maturity date, principal amount, coupon rate, bond yield and call provisions on each maturity in a bond issue. It is the bond pricing that determines: (1) the timing and amount of principal and interest payments a government must make on its bonds; (2) the early call provisions of the bonds that determine future refinancing opportunities; and (3) the amount of bond proceeds received from the debt sale. More technically, bond pricing determines whether the bonds are sold at par, at a discount or at a premium. In a competitive sale, underwriters submit bids with coupon rates and bond yields for the bonds at each maturity, with the underwriter submitting the lowest bid as measured by the true interest cost winning the bond issue. In a negotiated sale, the government entity, often aided by a municipal advisor, negotiates the 'price' and other details of the bond issue with an underwriter. In a competitive sale, the 'price' is determined by an underwriter using the debt structuring criteria we discussed in the sections above. This section, therefore, will focus on negotiated sales as it relates to bond pricing due to the generally higher prevalence of negotiated sales and the greater skill needed by state and local governments in negotiating a bond pricing.

The bond pricing process begins well before the pricing date of the bonds. Once a state or local government decides that they are going to sell their bonds via negotiation, they select a senior managing underwriter that will lead the bond sale. At this point, the underwriter will task its sales team to begin pre-marketing the bonds to investors. These bond salesmen attempt to get a sense for the general appetite and view of the government's proposed securities from potential investors. Based on this information and given their financing needs, the state and local government works with the senior managing underwriter to structure the bond issue to 'optimize' the financing as it relates to bond pricing. This optimization may entail reaching out to investors to inform them of the details behind their bond indenture and structuring the bonds to satisfy investor demands. A few days before the pricing date, the senior managing underwriter develops a pre-pricing 'scale' that details the level for the coupon rate and bond yield in each maturity given current market conditions and perceived investor demand. The government entity and senior managing underwriter review this pre-pricing scale and make changes to it based on strategies aimed to minimize the borrowing cost on the issue.

On the morning of pricing, the senior managing underwriter and government entity meet again and collectively determine the initial coupon rates and bond yields that the underwriter is going with to the market to solicit investor demand. After the initial canvassing of investors, the underwriter and government entity meet again (usually a couple of hours later) to see what the current level of demand is for each bond maturity in the issue at the initial prices. At this point, they make a decision to adjust the coupon rates and bond yields up or down (or keep them the same) based on the level of investor demand determined by the senior managing underwriter. After another canvassing of investors, the senior managing underwriter meets again with the government entity to detail the results of their revised bond pricing efforts. To the extent that government officials want to make further changes to the coupon rates and bond yields, this process can continue back and forth. At some point, the senior managing underwriter makes an offer to purchase the bonds at specific coupon rates and bond yields. If the government entity accepts the offer, the bonds are sold to the underwriter at the coupon rates and bond yields as specified in the offer.

In aggregate, the price of the bond issue that investors pay for and the government issuer receives is a function of the issue date, bond's face value, maturity date, call provisions, coupon interest rate, and stated yield on each bond maturity in the issue. Thus, in determining how much a state and local government will receive in proceeds from a bond sale, we can calculate the price of the issue taking into account all those factors for all the bonds in the issue. In a negotiated bond sale, the negotiation between the government entity and underwriter mainly revolves around adjustments up or down on the individual bond maturity yields. Given the issue size of many state and local government bond issues that can range from hundreds of thousands to multi-billion dollar issues, relatively small changes in bond yields can lead to big differences in the amount of bond proceeds received from a sale.

Table 7.5 details a \$315 million State of Illinois general obligation bond issue sold in April 2005. It compares the actual maturity-by-maturity bond prices and aggregate bond issue price to a hypothetical bond issue that had

Table 7.5 *State of Illinois general obligation bonds, series of April 2005: actual bond sale proceeds vs. hypothetical bond sale with yields adjusted 21, 12 and 7 basis points*

Maturity date	Principal amount ($)	Actual bond pricing			Hypothetical bond pricing		
		Interest rate (%)	Price ($)	Bond sale proceeds	Interest rate (%)	Price ($)	Bond sale proceeds ($)
2006	12 600 000	2.60	100.626	12 678 876	2.39	100.830	12 704 580
2007	10 800 000	2.86	104.097	11 242 476	2.65	104.510	11 287 080
2007	1 800 000	2.86	100.267	1 804 806	2.65	100.671	1 812 078
2008	10 320 000	3.06	105.490	10 886 568	2.85	106.106	10 950 139
2008	2 280 000	3.06	100.537	2 292 243	2.85	101.135	2 305 878
2009	12 600 000	3.25	106.488	13 417 488	3.04	107.300	13 519 800
2010	12 600 000	3.42	107.182	13 504 932	3.21	108.182	13 630 932
2011	12 600 000	3.60	107.475	13 541 850	3.39	108.652	13 690 152
2012	12 600 000	3.75	107.616	13 559 616	3.54	108.962	13 729 212
2013	12 600 000	3.88	107.625	13 560 750	3.76	108.482	13 668 732
2014	12 600 000	3.98	107.640	13 562 640	3.86	108.584	13 681 584
2015	12 600 000	4.05	107.736	13 574 736	3.93	108.764	13 704 264
2016	12 600 000	4.13	107.058	13 489 308	4.01	108.078	13 617 828
2017	12 600 000	4.20	106.468	13 414 968	4.08	107.481	13 542 606
2018	12 600 000	4.25	106.049	13 362 174	4.13	107.058	13 489 308
2019	12 600 000	4.30	105.632	13 309 632	4.18	106.636	13 436 136
2020	12 600 000	4.34	105.300	13 267 800	4.22	106.300	13 393 800
2021	12 600 000	4.38	104.969	13 226 094	4.31	105.549	13 299 174
2022	12 600 000	4.42	104.640	13 184 640	4.35	105.217	13 257 342
2023	12 600 000	4.47	104.229	13 132 854	4.40	104.804	13 205 304
2024	12 600 000	4.50	103.984	13 101 984	4.43	104.557	13 174 182
2025	12 600 000	4.55	103.577	13 050 702	4.48	104.148	13 122 648
2026	12 600 000	4.57	103.415	13 030 290	4.50	103.984	13 101 984
2027	12 600 000	4.60	103.172	12 999 672	4.53	103.740	13 071 240
2028	12 600 000	4.63	102.930	12 969 180	4.56	103.496	13 040 496
2029	12 600 000	4.64	102.849	12 958 974	4.57	103.415	13 030 290
2030	12 600 000	4.65	102.769	12 948 894	4.58	103.334	13 020 084
Total	315 000 000			331 074 147			333 486 853
Difference				2 412 706			

Source: Governor's Office of Management and Budget http://www.state.il.us/budget/officialstatements.asp.

bond yields slightly lower by 21, 12 and 7 basis points in years 5, 10 and 20 respectively. Bond price and yield are inversely related so that when yield goes down, price goes up. Also note that bond yield changes are generally quoted in basis points. A basis point is one hundredth of a percentage point. For example, a 10 basis point increase in bond yield of 4.67 percent would result in a 4.77 percent bond yield. As shown in the table, this modest decrease in bond yields would generate over $2.4 million in additional bond proceeds for the State of Illinois. This is not an insignificant amount of money for any state or local government to spend on capital projects.

Bond pricing is also critically important for refinancing transactions. In the event of a refinancing, changes in bond yield have a direct impact on the present value savings of the transaction. In fact, changes in bond yield could generate interest saving levels whereby the state or local government may decide to execute or not execute all or a portion of the proposed refinancing. For example, a sudden increase in bond yields on the day of pricing may result in a situation where it does not make economic sense to refinance some or all of the bonds in the contemplated transaction since the interest costs savings from refinancing the bonds have decreased. Conversely, a sudden decline in bond yields may expand the universe of bonds that the state or local government may want to refinance as the savings levels have increased. Chapter 10 discusses bond refinancing in much more detail.

Bond pricing is also important for the other parameters that are set in the pricing process. More specifically, the coupon rate (assuming a fixed rate issuance) will determine the annual amount of interest the government will pay as long as the bonds are outstanding. Thus, bond pricing locks the government entity into a stream of fixed costs that covers the entire term of the bonds, which can be as long as two or three decades. The optional call provisions will determine the timing and price at which the issuer will be able to call the bonds early in the event that a refinancing makes economic sense or if the issuer needs to redeem the bonds early due to other legal considerations. The specifics of the call provisions will determine how expensive it will be for the state or local government to refinance the bonds for these aforementioned purposes. In sum, bond pricing has both short-term and long-term impacts that necessitate skillful and thoughtful handling by public financial managers at the subnational government level. To the extent that such expertise is not available 'in-house', state and local governments often rely on the expertise of municipal advisors who specialize in capital market bond pricing.

4.   REVENUE BOND CAPACITY AND BOND SIZING

The amount (i.e. 'size') of a bond issue is a function of constitutional, statutory and/or bond market constraints. In financing its capital program, subnational governments will often be restricted as to the amount of debt they can issue. Thus, the size of a particular bond issue or series of bond issues will be a function of such legal restrictions and the amount of bond proceeds needed by the government. This is often the case with general obligation bonds where states must abide by legal constraints in the amount of GO debt they can issue.

On the other hand, the maximum size of a revenue bond issue is often only constrained by market factors. Specifically, bond investors usually demand a certain level of debt service coverage, where the expected revenues pledged for the repayment of a revenue bond issue must equal or exceed the expected debt service by some factor. A government cannot issue revenue debt that lowers debt service coverage below a certain level. For example, a state or local government may be constrained in structuring their revenue bonds so that the total amount of expected revenues can never be below two-times the expected revenue bond debt service. This is known as a debt service coverage factor (DSCF). From the investor perspective, the two-times debt service coverage factor provides the investor with some cushion in the event the actual revenues or revenue bond debt service varies from their expected levels. From the government's perspective, the debt service coverage factor effectively serves as a constraint in the amount of debt service it can pay on the revenue bond issue(s). Thus, it eliminates the government's ability to leverage all its future revenues for debt service since at least half the expected revenues (under a two-times debt service coverage factor) will be available for other capital purposes after paying revenue bond debt service.

From a bond mathematical perspective, the maximum revenue bond size is just the present value of the expected debt service payments. That is, the amount of bond proceeds a government can raise is the present value of the annual principal and interest payments using a discount rate of the bond borrowing cost. In effect, public financial managers determine the maximum debt they can issue for a revenue bond sale by present valuing the pledged revenues available for debt service over the expected life of the bond issue. As such, to determine maximum bond size (also known as 'bonding capacity'), one needs four types of data points: (1) expected annual revenues; (2) debt service coverage factor; (3) expected interest rate; and (4) bond maturity structure including amortization type (equal principal, level debt service, deferred principal or accelerated principal) and final maturity date. Using these data points, one can estimate the maximum revenue bond size that the state or local government can issue.

An example in Table 7.6 illustrates this type of analysis. Assume that a subnational government is considering building a new toll road expected to generate $100 million in net toll revenues each year for the next 20 years with 2 percent annual growth expected in toll revenues. The government plans to structure the proposed revenue bonds with a two-times debt service coverage factor and estimates its interest rate to be 5 percent. The debt is structured so that total debt service at a 5 percent interest rate is

Table 7.6 *Revenue bond size capacity analysis (2× debt service coverage factor (DSCF), 20-year final maturity, 5% interest rate)*

	2014	2015	2016	2017	2018	2019	2020	2021	2022	2023
Net toll revenues	100000	102000	104040	106121	108243	110408	112616	114869	117166	119509
DSCF	2.00	2.00	2.00	2.00	2.00	2.00	2.00	2.00	2.00	2.00
Debt service	50000	51000	52020	53060	54122	55204	56308	57434	58583	59755
Pay-as-you-go	50000	51000	52020	53060	54122	55204	56308	57434	58583	59755
	2024	2025	2026	2027	2028	2029	2030	2031	2032	2033
Total revenues	121899	124337	126824	129361	131948	134587	137279	140024	142825	145681
DSCF	2.00	2.00	2.00	2.00	2.00	2.00	2.00	2.00	2.00	2.00
Max debt service	60950	62169	63412	64680	65974	67293	68639	70012	71412	72841
Pay-as-you-go	60950	62169	63412	64680	65974	67293	68639	70012	71412	72841

Maximum Bond Size (Present Value of Debt Service) = $733.270 million
Available Pay-As-You-Go (Present Value Basis) = $733.270 million

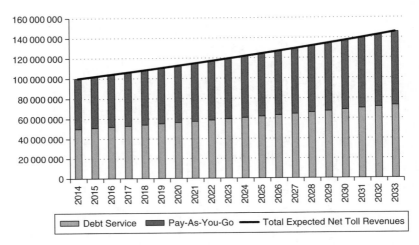

Figure 7.1   Revenue bond size capacity analysis (2× debt service coverage factor (DSCF), 20-year final maturity, 5% interest rate)

equal to available revenues each year (taking into account the debt service coverage factor) with a final maturity of 20 years. The cash flows and debt service for such a capital project look as shown in Table 7.6.

The subnational government can issue bonds in the maximum amount of $733.270 million based on expected revenues, interest rate, debt structure and debt service coverage factor in Table 7.6. Since the debt service coverage factor is two-times, the government also has access to $733.270 million on a present value basis in residual revenues after paying debt service. These residual revenues can be used to pay for a portion of the cost of the project on a pay-as-you-go basis and can be used to pay for operation and maintenance of the toll road on an ongoing basis over the next 20 years. Figure 7.1 shows visually the allocation of net toll revenues for debt service and available for pay-as-you-go spending.

In analyzing their revenue bond capacity, state and local governments often perform various sensitivity analyses since the various parameters in the analysis can change and are often not 'set in stone'. For example, in structuring their capital program using revenue bonds, the subnational government often wants to know the maximum bond size under different interest rate environments. Market conditions can change from the formulation of the capital program to the time when the government goes to the market with a bond sale. Also, when initially structuring a revenue bond, the governmental entity may not know what the investor threshold will be regarding the revenue bond DSCF. Given these uncertainties, the state

Table 7.7   *Revenue bond size capacity analysis (20-year final maturity amortization, in millions)*

Interest rate	Debt service coverage factors		
	1.5	2.0	2.5
4%	$1 072.776	$804.582	$643.666
5%	$977.693	$733.270	$586.616
6%	$894.457	$670.843	$536.674

Table 7.8   *Revenue bond size capacity analysis (2× debt service coverage factor (DSCF), in millions)*

Interest rate	Final maturity		
	20	25	30
4%	$804.582	$961.452	$1 103.808
5%	$733.270	$859.207	$968.152
6%	$670.843	$772.176	$855.779

or local government can perform sensitivity analyses varying these two parameters. Tables 7.7 and 7.8 show that for a 20-year bond amortization, the government can raise between $536 million and $1.072 billion with interest rates ranging from 4 to 6 percent and debt service coverage factors ranging from 1.5-times and 2.5-times.

Alternatively, the government entity may have more uncertainty regarding the market interest rate and the maturity length of the revenue bonds. In this scenario, the government could run a sensitivity analysis assuming a two-times debt service coverage factor and various bond maturity lengths and market interest rates. Tables 7.7 and 7.8 show that assuming a two-times debt service coverage factor, the state or local government can raise between $670 million and $1.103 billion with interest rates ranging from 4 to 6 percent and bond final maturity varying from 20 to 30 years. Both of these sensitivity analyses illustrate the sizeable variability in revenue bond capacity given relatively modest changes in the bonding capacity parameters. They also show the importance of carefully designing the debt finance portion of a government's capital program anticipating the impact of exogenous changes usually related to changing bond market conditions and investor preferences.

5. SUMMARY

The structure of municipal securities and the pricing process are very technical in nature and require strong knowledge of fixed income mathematics. State and local government financial managers have many choices in structuring these securities and these choices have real economic policy implications. Moreover, these policy implications are not just short-term in nature but may have material impacts on the government entity for decades. That is, the financial structure policy choices made by financial managers often require basic trade-offs between time periods that can impact multiple generations of taxpayers. As such, these financial technicalities and policy choices demand strong finance and public policy acumen on the part of government financial managers.

NOTES

1. In addition to maturity structure, often bonds with longer maturities will be imbedded with various options and a credit enhancement mechanism, which reflects the greater risk exposures for securities with larger durations.
2. Very large bond issues may be sold in larger principal denominations, $25 000 or $50 000.
3. It is not necessary that serial bonds are retired at equal intervals or every year in this example. It is also not necessary that equal proportions from total debt are retired with every serial bond maturity or $2 million in the example.
4. In the early years of the municipal bond market most bond issues were structured as term bonds.
5. Technically, the annual sinking fund payment is set so that the annual payment plus investment earnings will reach $25 000 at the maturity date. So, the actual annual payment would be less than $5000.
6. The appreciated value is sometimes viewed or accounted for as interest income, but it is not. The accreted value is a function of yield, not coupon interest.
7. Special escrow funds may be set up to flatten or smoothen expected debt service liabilities. In our case, instead of facing a principal of $2 000 000 every other year (in addition to coupon payments), an issuer may choose to send a portion of that amount annually or semi-annually to an escrow account or fund.
8. Front-loaded debt service is often referred to by its principal maturity structure which is level or equal principal.
9. Debt service structures that are back-loaded structures may be justified for other reasons, such as to account for expected inflation in hyper-inflationary environments. However, any particular benefits from back-loading must be explicitly weighed against its potential intergenerational inequity.
10. The 25%/5-year and 50%/10-year guidelines are described in Standard & Poor's Public Finance Criteria (2007, p. 63) handbook, where Standard & Poor's writes:
   'An average maturity schedule for capital projects is one in which 25% of the debt rolls off in five years and 50% is retired in 10 years.'
11. Johnson et al. (2010) also develop new debt service structure measures for understanding, measuring and managing debt service structures.
12. Issuers only rarely sell their debt directly to the ultimate buyers of their debt in a private placement.

13. Before the advent of microcomputers, net interest cost (NIC) was commonly used as the basis of award. NIC is an average interest cost rate. NIC is an inferior measure and should no longer be used; it ignores the timing of interest payments. It is calculated on the basis of simple interest and does not account for the time value of money.

14. The left-hand side of the TIC equation should be the net proceeds from the bond issue. The net proceeds equals the gross proceeds minus the fees and costs of financial intermediation, such as fees for legal counseling, financial advisors, credit enhancement, credit ratings, underwriters and so on.

15. True interest cost can also be found using representative bonds from each of the serial bonds in Table 7.1, which totals $25 000 ($5000 × 5). Debt service on these individual bonds from the five series can be obtained from Table 7.2. The equality set-up for finding TIC is below:

$$\$25\,000 = \frac{\$462.5}{\left(1 + \dfrac{TIC}{2}\right)^1} + \frac{\$5\,462.5}{\left(1 + \dfrac{TIC}{2}\right)^2} + \ldots + \frac{\$5\,125}{\left(1 + \dfrac{TIC}{2}\right)^{10}}$$

The right-hand side of the equation balances to $25 000 when one assumes the true inte. rest cost of 4.0156% (or 2.0078% semi-annually). The iterations, therefore, produce the same true interest cost for individual bonds from each of the five series in a single debt issue. While the method of iteration may appear tedious, fortunately various calculators and spreadsheets allow for a quick estimation of true interest costs.

8.   Secondary market disclosure

Information disclosure is an important condition for smooth and efficient functioning of any capital market. Information disclosure improves market efficiency by increasing liquidity, matching investors to issuers by risk preferences, and leads to better price discovery. Secondary market continuing disclosure is an attempt by regulators to motivate state and local issuers to provide all the pertinent financial and operating condition information to municipal investors. Due to the segmented and loosely organized nature of the municipal over-the-counter (OTC) market, timely information discovery becomes a key concern for municipal secondary market participants. Certain important events regarding issuers' fiscal condition or material decisions (such as defaults, ratings changes, or bond calls to name a few) are required to be reported to the Electronic Municipal Market Access (EMMA) of the Municipal Securities Rulemaking Board (MSRB) in a timely manner. There is also a set of voluntary disclosures that are encouraged to be reported to EMMA. Issuers, or financial intermediaries acting on their behalf, may choose to exercise their discretion and disclose additional information as a self-certification or quality signaling tool. In this chapter we describe the US municipal secondary market and how it is different from other bond markets. We then discuss the role of municipal market indices, the link between information disclosure and pricing, and current mechanisms for municipal disclosure. Finally, we assess the link between the secondary and primary markets.

1.   OVER-THE-COUNTER (OTC) MARKET

The initial municipal bond issue transaction between the issuer and the underwriter occurs on the primary market. After the initial placement of municipal bonds, anyone that wishes to buy or sell (trade) the bonds they hold must do so on the municipal secondary market, which is an over-the-counter (OTC) market. This market is a continuous market as trades are executed continuously for bonds that arrive to the market. The municipal OTC market is a broker-dealer dominated market that, and according to most of the recent empirical studies, holds the poorest record in terms of transparency and resulting difficulties in price discovery and liquidity (Chakravarty and Sarkar, 2003; Harris and Piwowar, 2006; Green et al., 2007a, 2010; GAO, 2012a, 2012b). Unlike the corporate bond market, there is no centralized exchange where one could gauge the price quotes in the market for pre-trade purposes. Moreover, very little post-trade data was available on municipal secondary trades until the early 2000s before the MSRB began providing secondary post-trade data to the public through its EMMA website. Today one can find certain post-trade information on secondary trades (generally within 15 minutes of trade execution) from EMMA.[1] This new feature provides greater levels of post-trade transparency, which was largely not available a decade or so ago.

Secondary trades occur on a 'yield basis and spread' criterion (Lamb, 1992). Bid trades are quoted in yields less the spread or concession; that is, the final price is determined based on these two moving parts. Buyers can manipulate both – lower (raise) the yield and concession at the time to quote the highest (lowest) bid price. Ask trades may also consist of these two components, in which case the logic reverses. The role of broker-dealers in the secondary market is to provide liquidity and price discovery by bringing the buyers and sellers of municipal bonds together. Their profits are a function of the secondary market spread between the ask price and bid price or round-trip transaction spread, and any concessions in each transaction.

Table 8.1 is an example of secondary market trading activity for a serial bond.[2] Most municipal bonds are thinly traded and end up in buy-to-hold investor portfolios. As seen in Table 8.1 (top left corner), the principal amount at issuance for a serial bond is $325 000, coupon rate of 3 percent, and maturity of about 3.5 years. Initial offering price is 100.855 of par; therefore, it is a premium bond with a yield rate of 2.8 percent.

It also appears that the entirety of the bond issue was placed with two investors on a 'when-issued' basis at a reoffering price/yield. 'When-issued' bonds are sold off to investors conditional on bond issuance before the bonds are even sold in the primary trades (first two rows in the transaction register). Such pre-sale of municipal bonds lowers the placement risks of municipal underwriting firms (Moldogaziev et al., 2013). We can further observe in Table 8.1 that the secondary trades for these 3 percent bonds occurred sporadically. An investor sold $35 000 about five months after issuance at a price/yield of 102.371/2.401 percent. This amount was sold off the same day at a price/yield of 102.657/2.33 percent. These transactions are highlighted in the table. The broker-dealer in this transaction has captured a spread of 7.1 basis points.

Table 8.1   Illustration of secondary market post-trade transactions

| Dated date: 05/27/2009 |
| Maturity date: 01/01/2014 |
| Interest rate: 3% |
| Principal amount at issuance: $325 000 |
| Initial offering price/yield: 100.855 |

Trade date/time	Settlement date	Price	Yield (%)	Trade amount ($)	Trade submission type	Notes
05/13/2009: 12:20 PM	5/27/2009	100.855	2.800	250 000	Customer bought	When-issued
05/13/2009: 12:34 PM	5/27/2009	100.855	2.800	75 000	Customer bought	When-issued
10/20/2009: 12:12 PM	10/23/2009	102.657	2.330	35 000	Customer bought	
10/20/2009: 12:12 PM	10/23/2009	102.371	2.401	35 000	Customer sold	
09/09/2010: 12:01 PM	9/14/2010	104.894	1.473	40 000	Customer sold	
09/16/2010: 04:24 PM	9/16/2010	105.625	1.250	40 000	Customer bought	
02/13/2013: 04:52 PM	2/19/2013	102.102	0.565	250 000	Customer sold	
02/14/2013: 08:51 AM	2/20/2013	102.085	0.576	250 000	Inter-dealer Trade	
02/14/2013: 08:52 AM	2/20/2013	102.095	0.565	250 000	Customer bought	
02/14/2013: 11:54 AM	2/20/2013	102.095	0.565	250 000	Inter-dealer Trade	
07/17/2013: 02:38 PM	7/22/2013	100.900	0.952	35 000	Customer sold	
07/17/2013: 02:39 PM	7/22/2013	101.100	0.503	35 000	Customer bought	

2. WHAT MAKES THE 'MUNI-OTC' MARKET DIFFERENT?

The municipal OTC market provides liquidity to investors. The MSRB is the central entity in regulating the municipal secondary market in that it writes the rules of the game and provides informational support to the brokers, dealers, banks and financial advisors. All broker-dealers must register with the MSRB, and simultaneously with the Securities and Exchange Commission (SEC), before they are able to operate in the OTC market. The Financial Industry Regulatory Authority (FINRA) is a self-regulatory entity, which oversees every firm that has broker-dealer functions. A report by the Government Accountability Office (GAO, 2012a) states that the MSRB and the SEC have had insufficient capacity to review the quality of self-regulation by FINRA, or the timely direct assessment of registered broker-dealers. Therefore, any monitoring of broker-dealers is assumed to be patchy at best. However, even if the MSRB were to have sufficient capacity to monitor broker-dealers, it lacks any enforcement authority. Instead, FINRA is expected to discipline the members that violate its industry-wide standards.

Furthermore, the reporting requirements for broker-dealers are the most relaxed of all capital markets. There is no central location for any of the secondary pre-trade information on municipal securities; that is the 1700 or so registered broker-dealers maintain their own databases of bid and ask prices.[3] Some of the dealers may provide directly to their customers their own bid and ask quotes for the securities in their own inventories; however, no such information is available at the market level. Even the requirements on post-trade transparency are not very stringent. All that gets filed to the MSRB by broker-dealers is information on the size and time of transactions and whether any given transaction is a customer sale, customer purchase, or an inter-dealer transaction. Yet, this information is not enough to assess the round-trip transaction prices (and hence broker-dealer spreads) since no information on how the trades were matched is required for reporting.[4] Therefore, even this new effort to provide post-trade transparency may be insufficient to the smaller and less sophisticated market participants as the reported information is incomplete and may not allow these investors to learn from prices.

Consequently, the municipal OTC market is characterized by very low levels of pre-trade price transparency, lack of bid/ask quotes by all dealers, lack of centralized exchange or market (Green et al., 2007a, 2010; Harris and Piwowar, 2006), less transparent trading data (Downing and Zhang, 2004), high transaction costs (Harris and Piwowar, 2006), and an inferior position of uninformed smaller investors compared to informed institutional investors (Green et al., 2007b; GAO, 2012b). To summarize, smaller and uninformed investors suffer significantly due to the fundamental market information asymmetries.

However, recent studies suggest that the price behavior in the municipal secondary trades can be partially explained by high inter-dealer transaction costs (Schultz, 2012), broker-dealer network structures (Marlowe, 2013) and/or underwriter placement risks (Moldogaziev et al., 2013), and not always necessarily by fraudulent and adverse behavior by broker-dealers. At the same time, evidence from market building efforts for sovereign and corporate bond markets suggests that an introduction of a centralized bid/ask platform for dealer markets generally tends to significantly stabilize fixed income bond prices for issuers of securities with a stable investor demand base (World Bank/IMF, 2001; Freire and Petersen, 2004).

Further, the extant literature suggests that the municipal bond market is a segmented market rather than a unified and integrated single market. Therefore, individual borrowing costs and market yields, in both primary and secondary markets, are likely to be affected by market segmentation. Market segmentation may result from a number of factors. For example, the tax code reforms in the 1980s and 1990s have resulted in a shift of holders of municipal bonds from larger financial institutions to smaller household investors. Except for bank qualified bonds, banking institutions do not benefit from the income tax exemption that characterizes the municipal market (Marlin, 1994; Brown and Sirmans, 2013). Denison (2003) found that states compete by utilizing bond insurance, a competition that he argues results in market segmentation by credit quality. Chen et al. (2013) argue that regulatory rules that govern rating-based allocation of investment portfolios result in bond market segmentation by credit class category. Schultz (2012) and Pirinsky and Wang (2011) maintain that asymmetric tax exemption of municipal bonds in the states creates adverse conditions for interstate investment choices, which results in geographic market segmentation. All of these factors are found to be important in scholarly works and are expected by market participants to be relevant for price formation in both primary and secondary market pricing.

After the Great Recession, the US Congress passed provisions (as part of the Dodd–Frank 'Wall Street Reform and Consumer Protection Act') to reassess the structure of the municipal secondary market and to provide recommendations for its improvement. The Act has mandated that the GAO produce reports relevant to the OTC market – one report on the quality of municipal disclosures and another on the structure of the OTC market and prices. The MSRB and the SEC have been tasked to follow up on these reports and adopt appropriate regulatory measures. Moreover, the Act requires that the MSRB, the SEC and FINRA conduct biannual meetings and share their notes on broker-dealer regulatory responsibilities with each other (GAO, 2012b). It is too early to assess whether Dodd–Frank will result in major reforms for the municipal OTC secondary market and result in substantial federal government involvement. It is equally too early to predict whether a single centralized exchange platform or pre-trade bid–ask quotes on a market-wide basis will be required to inject more transparency in subnational government debt secondary trades.

3. MUNICIPAL MARKET INDICES

A useful way of gauging the developments in the municipal secondary market is to monitor market indices. There are a variety of indices that follow the trends in the secondary market, such as *The Bond Buyer 20* index (BBI20) or Moody's municipal market indices. *The Bond Buyer* is a daily newspaper that puts together indices for general obligation and revenue bonds. Similarly, *Moody's Investors Service* provides indices for municipal bonds of varying credit quality and maturity. These indices help market participants in their decisions regarding market timing as well as credit or options choices.

For illustration purposes, in Figure 8.1 we depict the trends for Moody's Aaa-rated and A-rated 20-year general obligation bonds. For comparison, we also plot the Bond Buyer 20-year general obligation bond index. In this figure, we also plot the differential between the Aaa-rated and A-rated bonds for Moody's indices. It is clear that during and after the Great Recession the gap between Aaa-rated and A-rated bonds widened dramatically, from about 15–30 basis points to about 60–100 basis points, reflecting the credit quality uncertainties during that period (see the shaded area at the bottom of Figure 8.1 in relation to the y-axis on the right). Indices are also useful to evaluate the market yield curve. In Figure 8.2 we provide the trends for Moody's Aaa-rated 20-year and Aaa-rated 10-year general obligations. The differential between these two indices reflects the market participants' interest rate expectations in the future, as the only difference between the two is bond maturity (hence, the term 'maturity risk premium').

It is also possible to compare the yields in the municipal bond market to the treasury- or corporate yields in order to assess cross-bond market yield differences. Such cross-market yield differential comparisons become useful during varying market conditions when flight-to-liquidity or flight-to-quality phenomena may drive out or pull in institutional and individual investors from/to the municipal secondary market. These cross-market movements of capital are expected to affect municipal secondary market

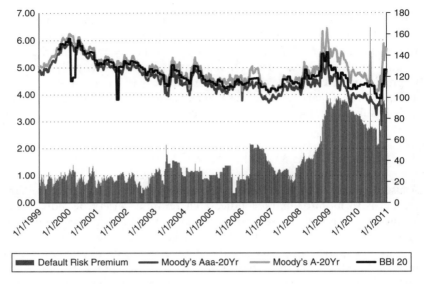

Source: *Bloomberg* and *The Bond Buyer*.

Figure 8.1 *Moody's Aaa, Moody's A 20-year indices, A–Aaa credit spread (shaded area, in basis points), and the Bond Buyer 20 Municipal Bond Index*

yields and liquidity provision in the OTC market. The recent meltdown of the mortgage-backed securities market had an enormous impact on all other corners of capital markets during and after the Great Recession, which had a significant impact on yields and liquidity in the corporate and municipal secondary markets.

4. INFORMATION DISCLOSURE AND SECONDARY MARKET PRICING

Pre- and post-trade information disclosure is important for efficient markets. Information-based trading is important for both 'on-the-run' and 'off-the-run' securities, terms that describe new (a period starting from up to 30 to 90 days since issuance) and older (a period beyond 90 days since issuance) municipal bonds. While pre-trade transparency helps with initial investment decisions and mitigates placement risks, post-trade transparency helps with secondary market liquidity and risk monitoring of individual securities.

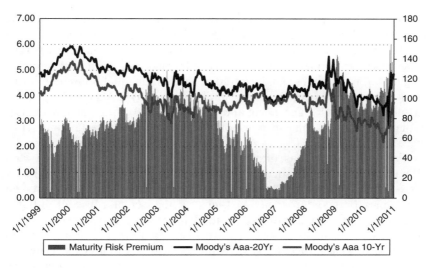

Source: Bloomberg.

*Figure 8.2   Moody's Aaa 20-year, Moody's Aaa 10-year indices, and the
Aaa 20-year vs. Aaa 10-year spread*

Pre-trade transparency is also important for market makers. Broker-dealers, in the absence of a centralized bid/ask quoting system, must rely on their own ability to price municipal securities. Such price discovery efforts may become very costly, which may ultimately result in large gross mark-ups or wide dealer spreads. Large dealer spreads are also likely to backfire, as costly sales or purchases by individual investors may prevent them from trading more frequently, thus creating environments that are unfriendly to liquidity provision. This could create conditions of limited retail capacity for broker-dealers, which in return would limit the desire and ability of underwriters to compete on primary transactions.

Currently, it is neither feasible for anybody, including the regulators, to efficiently assess municipal price structures in the municipal bond market nor possible to use price as a signal to attract attention from potential investors, except for narrow client-bases of a select few underwriting firms. Of course, there are very small issuers in the municipal market that are unlikely to have high levels of liquidity. In addition, municipal markets are highly segmented due to underwriter retail capacity, investor locations and preferences, and state tax asymmetries. However, any attempts to compare pre-trade prices for relatively similar small-scale municipal issuers within a state or across state boundaries are unlikely to be successful.

Post-trade transparency has improved during the last decade, enabling a growing number of empirical studies. Based on this new access to secondary trading data (now via EMMA), Green et al. (2007a, 2007b) argue that excessive market opacity created informed and uninformed pricing regimes in municipal secondary trades, where individual household investors appear to lose out the most. Similar studies by GAO (2012a, 2012b), Moldogaziev (2012) and Deng and McCann (2013) confirmed incidences of large mark-ups, some in excess of 500 basis points, for certain municipal secondary trades.

The latter study has drawn the ire of the Securities Industry and Financial Markets Association (SIFMA), the self-regulatory industry association, which cited large transaction costs and lack of clarity on guidelines or standards on mark-ups as the actual cause of inflated mark-ups rather than industry fraud. This position may not necessarily be faulty as recent studies discover that secondary market prices, among other factors, are affected by high broker-dealer search costs related to their market-making roles (Schultz, 2012), the size of underwriter placement risks (Moldogaziev et al., 2013), or the roles of firms in underwriting syndicates and networks (Marlowe, 2013). Nonetheless, it is evident that lack of sufficient market transparency is not producing the most efficient outcomes currently in the municipal secondary OTC market.

There are two major measures of secondary market trades that the federal regulators are interested in, in light of recent Dodd–Frank induced proposals for market reform. The first one is the measure of gross mark-ups while the second is the measure of midpoint/round-trip transaction price. Green et al. (2007a) provided the earliest evidence on municipal OTC gross mark-ups. Their measure of gross mark-up is the differential between the transaction price and the reoffering price.[5] Using a sample from the pre-EMMA post-trade information disclosure era (i.e. broker-dealer transactions prior to 31 January 2005), they find significant mark-ups in the municipal broker-dealer OTC market, some individual bonds experiencing mark-ups in excess of 500 basis points. These mark-ups also appear to grow with bond age as fewer investors are potentially informed about the bonds in the opaque markets with little pre-sale and post-trade transparency. This, the authors argue, happens because relatively smaller household investors may face very high search costs to become informed about bond prices in the absence of trading data and broker-dealers and institutional investors are uninterested in sharing information as market opacity brings excess profits to them at the expense of uninformed investors.

Schultz (2012) finds that with the introduction of post-trade transaction reporting requirements (that improved market transparency after 31 January 2005) mark-ups have shrunk substantially; however, transaction price dispersions still remained in the broker-dealer OTC markets. These remaining price dispersions, he argues, can be explained by higher transaction costs that the intermediaries incur in the relatively sparsely traded municipal market. Nevertheless, these larger transaction costs still appear to be passed on to relatively uninformed household investors in the post-2005 improved transparency era (Deng and McCann, 2013; Moldogaziev, 2012; GAO, 2012b). The federal government's desire to reign in gross mark-ups stems from the SEC's role in protecting capital market participants. Gross mark-up is important because it is the spread between the initial offering price and transaction price normalized by the initial offering price.[6] Arguably, large mark-ups signal significant underpricing in the initial distribution of municipal bonds in the market. In addition, incidence of large mark-ups for some unsophisticated investors compared to institutional investors could also be a sign of preferential treatment of certain investors by broker-dealers. By requiring more transparency in gross mark-ups the federal government may potentially solve the problems of underpricing and investor mistreatment, but it would also require a firmer grip on the state and local government bond market.

Federal regulators are also interested in the midpoint/round-trip transaction price in municipal secondary trades. This price is mainly related to the liquidity provision role of the OTC market. Municipal broker-dealers, in addition to their initial placement role, earn a spread by buying from investors and reselling to other investors. In other words, the dealer after-market spread is the difference between the transaction price at which a customer buys (CB) from the dealer and the price at which a customer sells (CS) to the dealer any given bond(s). Due to the general lack of sufficient broker-dealer transaction information, regulators and scholars have grappled with the task of estimating the prices for municipal securities from prices recorded for customer purchases, customer sales and inter-dealer trades. The price of interest to regulators is then the midpoint of the 'round-trip' CB–CS pair. The practical problem, however, is that the municipal OTC market does not provide information on how the CB–CS pairs match (even on the EMMA post-trade data). Moreover, it is not reported to the public how inter-dealer transactions interact with buyer–seller matches. Often the dealers aggregate purchases from several customers and sell to one buyer; they may also buy in large chunks and resell bonds to many customers by splitting these large purchases. In the meantime, individual dealers may balance their inventories by trading with one another.

In the corporate bond market, secondary market bond pricing studies became possible in the early 2000s with improved disclosure requirements in the corporate bond markets (Hong and Warga, 2004; Schultz,

State and local financial instruments

2001; Kalimipalli and Warga, 2002). Municipal secondary market pricing research, however, is not as robust as the corporate or treasury bond market secondary pricing scholarship. Chakravarty and Sarkar (2003), Hong and Warga (2004), and Downing and Zhang (2004) are the earliest research efforts in municipal secondary trade pricing.

The first two studies assess CB–CS pair spreads by matching similarly sized daily customer sells to customer buys sequentially. However, there is little evidence that this method matches actual bonds that transferred hands from the selling customer to the buying customer (with the help of a broker-dealer). Some of these bonds may indeed be the pairs of a single buy–sell 'round-trip' transaction; however, others may not be the actual pairs. This approach seems like a 50–50 method of matching – some guesses will be correct, yet others will be incorrect. Furthermore, transactions in the municipal bond market are rather thin, and even weekly aggregations may not find CB–CS pairs. Hence, in addition to serving as an exercise of 'educated guessing', the CB–CS matching approach ends up discarding most of the trading data.

Harris and Piwowar (2006) and Edwards et al. (2007) propose an econometric time-series approach to estimate effective spreads in municipal and corporate secondary transaction costs. This approach retains non-trading days in the sample; however, it requires some hefty assumptions and faces identification concerns. Two studies by Green et al. (2007b) use two different approaches to estimate secondary market prices (one of which is similar to Chakravarty and Sarkar (2003) and Hong and Warga (2004) CB–CS pair matching approaches).

A recent study by Green et al. (2010) recognizes the difficulties in estimating secondary trade prices and proposes a relatively straightforward approach. There is an average price, on any given day, in the market at which the dealers buy from customers (CS), sell to customers (CB), or transact with one another (IDT). This average price is a midpoint between the lowest price of customer buy (CB) and the highest price of customer sell (CS) transactions on a given day. However, quite often the secondary municipal markets trade inactively; hence, one does not observe buys and sells during the same day. When one or both of these buy and sell prices are missing, Green et al. (2010) propose using the average price on all inter-dealer transactions as the mean market price. If the distribution of trades is sparse (i.e. markets are illiquid), then instead of daily averages of customer buy and customer sell transactions in the secondary trades, it is possible to resort to weekly or even monthly averages. The wider the period between trades, however, the smaller the value of trading prices for price discovery may be. Indeed, with bond age, municipal secondary transactions appear to involve uninformed investors rather than informed ones

(Green et al., 2007a).[7] Therefore, the presence of multiple pricing regimes in municipal secondary prices is of interest to the SEC in their investor protection responsibilities. By regulating secondary price formation, the SEC would potentially give more power to the federal government over the state and local debt market in the US.

5. MECHANISMS FOR MUNICIPAL DISCLOSURE

With the approval of the SEC, the MSRB now requires continuing disclosure filings by responsible parties through its EMMA filing portal starting from 1 July 2009. Details for such continuing disclosure requirements are stipulated in the Securities and Exchange Commission Rule 15c2-12, hereinafter the disclosure rule. Continuing disclosure files must be submitted either by the issuers, obligated persons, or special designated agents, which are designated by issuers/obligated persons. Designated persons can be undesignated at any time on EMMA by issuers/obligated persons. The MSRB writes that:

> Under Rule 15c2-12(b)(5), an underwriter for a primary offering of municipal securities subject to the rule currently is prohibited from underwriting the offering unless the underwriter has determined that the issuer or an obligated person for whom financial information or operating data is presented in the final official statement has undertaken in writing to provide certain items of information to the marketplace. Rule 15c2-12(b)(5) provides that such items include: (A) annual financial information concerning obligated persons; (B) audited financial statements for obligated persons if available and if not included in the annual financial information; (C) notices of certain events, if material; and (D) notices of failures to provide annual financial information on or before the date specified in the written undertaking. (MSRB, 2009, p. 1).

Therefore, municipal regulators have been attempting since 2009 to improve information disclosure to the secondary market both prior to issuance and for periods when bonds are outstanding. However, it is not clear as to what happens to the issuers, obligated parties or designated agents, should they fail to provide continuing disclosures to EMMA at prescribed intervals. The MSRB has no authority to punish non-filers that fail to provide required financial materials.

Required continuing disclosure data are related to annual financial information of issuers or borrowing entities, other financial statements that are not in the annual statements, notices of certain material events, or notices of failure to deliver the required files by the designated deadlines. Kioko et al. (2012) find a lengthy delay of annual financial disclosures even by the most sophisticated state issuers, sometimes delays in excess of 6 to 12 months. Hence, notices of failure to deliver files on time would be quite frequently filed. Timely arrival of financial information could improve price discovery in secondary trades, yet very old news is likely to have diminished value for municipal secondary market participants. Issuers can improve price discovery for their securities by filing important financial information in the municipal market in a timely manner.

EMMA also has a list of information items that issuers can submit voluntarily. Issuers can provide financial information on a more frequent basis, quarterly or semi-annually, as well as files on budget, investment and operating reports on a rolling basis. This tool can be used for self-certification purposes or signaling of extra qualities by municipal borrowers. Therefore, there is an opportunity for issuers (and their underwriters) to actively engage in additional delivery of issuers' financial information to relevant market participants to improve liquidity for their securities, both for soon-to-be-sold debt obligations and for seasoned bonds outstanding in the market. Prudent continuing disclosure practices will help in solving information asymmetry problems in primary and secondary transactions and result in lower price uncertainties for all of the involved market participants. Ultimately, improved information dissemination decreases investment uncertainties and may result in lower borrowing costs for municipal issuers and their taxpayers.

Furthermore, individual states may establish more stringent rules for municipal disclosure above and beyond the MSRB requirements. California and Texas are two states that have very active state regulatory bodies. Fortunately, these two states are also a home for many top issuers of municipal debt securities in the United States. California, through its Department of Treasury webpage, and Texas, though the Bond Review Board Online, provide a great deal of relevant issuer and primary market financial information to the public. Other states are less forthcoming and transparent about issuers of municipal debt securities within their jurisdictions.

6. WHAT CAN ISSUERS LEARN FROM THE SECONDARY MARKET?

There are a number of important factors that municipal issuers can learn from trading in the secondary market. These factors can be important both for market timing of new issues and issuer borrowing costs. In the more established corporate bond market, the existing literature suggests that cross-market effects are economically significant (Chordia et al.,

2001; Harris and Piwowar, 2006; Beber et al., 2009). Corporate issuers and underwriters canvass the secondary market for price discovery that in turn shapes their price structures for new securities. Even if corporate issuers are not frequent issuers of bonds or are involved in an IPO, they still need to monitor the secondary market to gauge investor demand.

In municipal secondary trades, the same reasons apply. More frequent issuers can learn from demand for their bonds during initial placements and subsequent trading in order to demand better prices in the underwriting process for new deals. Underwriters would also benefit from knowing the pulse of the secondary market as these are potentially relevant for their bids in competitive and negotiated underwritings as well as for their mitigation of placement risks. In other words, more liquid transactions for existing debt must be a positive factor for any given municipality's borrowing costs and an overall liquid market must be a positive factor for lowering transaction costs for broker-dealers in the secondary OTC market. Due to market segmentation, issuers may face differing pricing regimes for their debt issues, however. Therefore, both issuers and financial intermediaries will benefit from staying informed about differing dynamics in various sectors of the municipal bond market, be it segmentation due to regional, statutory, or credit class preferences.

The daily periodical of the municipal bond market, *The Bond Buyer*, occasionally reports individual stories that underwriters indeed canvass the secondary market for liquidity and pricing information before making decisions on their primary market commitments. For example, a piece in this newspaper reported that in Illinois the state capital markets director, financial advisors and underwriters apparently consulted the broker-dealers concerning the spreads and yields in the secondary trades for Illinois general obligation bonds before deciding whether to issue new bonds (Shields, 2013). In fact, the plan to hold a competitive sale had to be postponed for about three months because the state was worried that the adverse conditions at the time for outstanding Illinois debt in the secondary market would significantly increase true interest costs for new bonds. When the conditions were right and the bond sale was finally held, the newspaper further claimed that the spreads for true interest costs on the 10-year maturity bonds received from 10 competitive bids were all tightly aligned around the spreads in the secondary trades for comparable outstanding Illinois bonds. In other words, the Illinois 'premiums' observable in the over-the-counter broker-dealer transactions were reflected in Illinois true interest costs and serial bond yields for new issues.

In order to test this secondary vs. primary market dynamic, we evaluated whether secondary market information is a useful factor for issuer borrowing costs for a sample of competitively sold state general obligation

securities issued between 31 January 2005 and 1 January 2011. We identified 448 competitive issues (consisting of over 6100 serial bonds) in
Bloomberg market platform for this period. We then obtained borrowing
cost estimates from *IPREO* (true interest costs, TIC, and net interest costs,
NIC) for this sample. Of the 448 competitively sold state general obligation
issues, 403 provide estimates of TIC, with the remaining 45 reporting NIC.
Due to major weaknesses of NIC (see for example Simonsen et al., 2005),
we focus solely on TIC as a measure of issuer borrowing costs. Complete
secondary market transactions data for competitively sold state GO
issues are collected from the EMMA of MSRB. Other relevant primary
and secondary market condition variables are from *The Bond Buyer* and
Bloomberg. Due to missing values for secondary market measures, we omit
three additional bond issues from our analyses. The final sample in this
work is based on 400 state general obligation bonds issued during the six
years under focus.

One of the biggest concerns for the underwriters is their ability to
resell the underwritten debt in the secondary market. Generally, when the
underwriters face difficulties in reselling the bonds they must absorb all the
risks associated with illiquidity. Therefore, if the underwriters expect such
difficulties, they may require greater levels of compensation. If the issuers
or the underwriters (or both) observe higher levels of aggregate secondary
market transactions dollar volume for debt issued during the 12 months
prior to issuing new money, they may move towards lower levels of TICs.
Furthermore, it is reasonable to expect that higher frequencies of transactions, similar to aggregate transactions dollar volume, may signal information about future levels of liquidity for new issues. Therefore, greater levels
on this measure of secondary market liquidity may result in lower levels of
TIC for new debt.

To estimate the effects of secondary market liquidity measures, we rely
on a two-stage maximum likelihood estimation method for the covari-
ates of true interest costs. The first stage corrects for self-selection in the
method of sale (Kriz, 2003) and insurance selection (Moldogaziev, 2012).
The second-stage regression model includes the liquidity test variables, and
a set of control measures related to individual bond characteristics and
municipal primary market condition factors. Our results suggest that the
number of secondary market transactions for debt issued during the past
12 months (a measure for secondary market liquidity width) has a significant inverse association with the newly issued bonds' true interest costs. All
held equal, a unit (natural log) increase in this variable is associated with
a decrease in borrowing costs of about seven basis points. As expected,
liquidity width for recently issued debt appears to result in significant
savings for the issuers.

However, we do not find enough evidence that aggregate secondary market dollar volume of transactions for debt issued during the past 12 months has any significant association with true interest costs. Thus, we conclude that the number of secondary trades matters for issuer borrowing costs, while the liquidity depth does not. This echoes the 'puzzle' and the incentives that the underwriters may have in pursuing frequencies of trades rather than dollar volumes of trades. Prior empirical research suggests that larger dollar transactions involve institutional investors (Downing and Zhang, 2004; Green et al., 2007b, 2010; GAO, 2012b) or informed investors (Green et al., 2007a). These larger transactions, however, appear to result in much narrower broker-dealer mark-ups and lower yields, which limits profits in the secondary trades. Therefore, true interest costs appear to be adjusted for liquidity width, which is good news for the issuers, yet may potentially be discomforting to smaller investors that are embedded in trade frequencies rather than volumes. Therefore, there appears to be a clear economic rationale to follow secondary market dynamics. Issuers that have greater levels of liquidity width for their outstanding bonds are more likely to benefit from lower borrowing costs for new issues.

7. SUMMARY

Secondary market disclosure is important for price discovery in both secondary and primary transactions. For municipal bond issuers as well as underwriters, their primary market transactions will be affected by the dynamics in secondary trades. The OTC market structure and the resulting prices are associated with true interest costs, competition among underwriters for municipal bonds, and an overall efficiency in the allocation of capital resources. Therefore, there appears to be a clear economic rationale for primary market issuers to follow secondary market dynamics. As we found, issuers that have greater levels of liquidity width for their outstanding bonds are more likely to benefit from lower borrowing costs for their new issues.

At the same time, issuers and underwriters may wish to supply the markets with timely and accurate financial data. In particular, Kioko et al. (2012) find that price dispersion or volatility is sensitive to information on measures of position and performance reported in the government-wide statements. Therefore, again there appears to be a clear economic gain in providing the secondary market with relevant government-wide fiscal measures. This would be the best tool for municipal issuers to help them manage pricing on their debt obligations, especially in the absence of pre-trade transparency in the secondary trades and the overarching OTC market-wide opacity. Finally, if the SEC becomes involved more intimately with regulating broker-dealer gross mark-ups as well as bid–ask spreads, market efficiency may improve significantly. However, one of the trade-offs would be greater involvement by the federal government in the municipal secondary market directly, and perhaps the primary market indirectly through tighter oversight of financial intermediaries.

NOTES

1. EMMA also provides access to official statements for a bond issue, any continuing disclosures, credit ratings and ratings actions.
2. The Municipal Securities Rulemaking Board (MSRB) makes secondary market trade information available through the Electronic Municipal Market Access (EMMA) portal in a format similar to the one provided in Table 8.1.
3. The MSRB maintains a list of registered broker-dealers on its webpage. This list can also be useful to investors as they can find registered broker-dealers in their own states or geographic regions to buy or sell (or compare bid prices) prior to making investment decisions.
4. Round-trip price is the midpoint of the buy–sell spread in the broker-dealer transaction, such that: $Midpoint = \frac{Price_{CB,t} - Price_{CS,t}}{2}$.
5. Green et al. (2007a) measured gross mark-ups as the percentage of the reoffering price, such that: $Markup = \frac{P_{transaction\ price,i} - P_{reoffering\ price}}{P_{reoffering\ price}}$
6. An alternative measure of gross mark-up is a spread between the average daily transaction price and individual transaction price normalized by the average daily transaction price.
7. Another point of interest for all municipal secondary market participants is price volatility. Downing and Zhang (2004) have estimated the measure of scaled price or price volatility using weekly data aggregation to mitigate the issues of scarcity of municipal secondary trades. Scaled price is the differential between the maximum observed price and the minimum observed price during any given week scaled by the inverse of the mean price for that same week, such that: $S_i(t) = \frac{100[P_i^{max}(t) - P_i^{min}(t)]}{P_i(t)}$ These authors discover that price volatility of secondary trades is associated with both the frequency of trades for any given bond as well as the average transaction size. However, it appears that the number of trades has a positive association with scaled price while the average transaction size is negatively associated with bond price volatility. This, they argue, happens in the relatively illiquid markets due to large transactions among informed institutional investors. A recent study by Kioko et al. (2012) finds that price dispersion or volatility is sensitive to information on measures of position and performance reported in the government-wide statements. However, information based on fund-based measures does not appear to add any additional value to price discovery in the secondary trades.

PART III

Financial structure and the risk/reward trade-off

The demands on state and local government financial managers have grown increasingly complex over the last few decades. No longer do government debt managers just sell debt and wait for the semi-annual principal and interest payments to come due for processing. The debt management portion of a financial manager's portfolio involves overseeing many complicated financial tasks including: managing a large fixed rate and variable rate bond portfolio, executing complex financial derivatives, trying to time the market for debt refinancing opportunities, evaluating arbitrage opportunities in the government's non-bond indebtedness portfolio, analyzing a multitude of credit enhancement products, and assessing and executing non-traditional capital financings such as public–private partnerships. In all of these financial management domains, the risk–reward trade-off is magnified and, thus, the debt managers' role is fundamental to the financial operations and well-being of the government. As such, a solid knowledge of financial markets, instruments and strategies is needed on the part of the debt manager.

However, the risk–reward trade-off is not just relegated to pure financial outcomes. Subnational governments need to understand some of the trade-offs associated with federal intervention in some of the financial management areas mentioned above. The federal government has enhanced its regulatory hand in certain financial management areas, such as derivatives and financial market transparency, and has tried to lend a hand in other capital financing ways, such as through the provision of low-cost federal loans and enhanced tax-exempt private activity bond volume cap. However, this 'help' has allowed the federal government to have more influence in subnational debt administration and capital financing decisions. This has sometimes resulted in capital finance decisions most preferred by the federal government and, in certain areas, has produced a much greater administrative burden on subnational governments in managing their financial affairs.

Part III of the book explores the various risks and rewards associated with the myriad complex financial structures and products subnational governments utilize. It starts with a discussion of the use of financial derivatives, potentially the most risky (and thus most potentially rewarding) and controversial debt management decision. It then provides a debt refinancing policy framework for prudently refinancing bond and non-bond liabilities. Next is a case study on the municipal action rate securities market that encapsulates the benefits and costs of the use of 'innovative' financial products. It then delves into the credit enhancement market that nearly completely collapsed during the recent Financial Crisis, illustrating the benefits and need for a robust bond insurance market. Finally, this part concludes with a discussion of non-traditional capital financing mechanisms that state and local governments are increasingly exploring in the light of huge capital financing needs and insufficient financing capacity from the traditional sources.

9. Financial engineering

This chapter details the ways state and local governments utilize financial derivatives in conjunction with their municipal securities to manage their borrowing costs. The chapter begins by discussing financial derivatives in general and then detailing the most prevalent type of derivative used by state and local governments, the interest rate swap. It proceeds to provide a technical analysis related to the use, valuation and risks associated with interest rate swaps. It then offers some best practices for the use of financial derivatives as advocated by the Government Finance Officers Association and as informed by a case study of a municipality's use of interest rate swaps. The chapter concludes with an overview of the impact of Dodd–Frank on the use of financial derivatives by subnational governments.

Over the last couple of decades, state and local governments have increasingly engaged in financial engineering to optimize their debt management programs. Financial engineering refers to the use of mathematical analysis to develop innovative financial products or strategies to address financial challenges. One of the most popular financial engineering techniques has involved the use of financial derivatives. A financial derivative is a financial instrument whose value is derived from another asset or an index of an asset value. The most common types of financial derivatives in municipal finance include futures, forwards, options, caps, floors, collars, rate locks and interest rate swaps.

One creative way in which to understand derivatives was explained by President Obama's former economic advisor, Austan Goolsbee. Goolsbee described a derivatives contract as similar to a taco coupon given out to a sporting event attendee that entitles the attendee to a free taco if one of the teams accomplishes some sort of goal as it relates to the game (e.g. the home team scores a certain number of points). Thus, the coupon only has value if the stated goal in the game happens. The taco coupon is not part of the game and does not affect the game but it does derive value from some aspect of the game (Javers, 2010). Financial derivatives are like the taco coupon in that they derive value from other transactions but they do not affect the value of the transaction they are derived from.

Interest rate swaps are the most common financial derivatives utilized by state and local governments (Luby and Kravchuk, 2013). An interest rate swap is an agreement between two parties to trade interest payments based on different indices on a notional amount of debt. Interest rate swaps can be beneficial to both parties exchanging payments based on the principle of comparative advantage. Comparative advantage is accessed by exploiting imperfections in the national and international capital markets.

Bicksler and Chen (1986) detailed the principle of comparative advantage in analyzing how a US corporation and foreign bank can use interest rate swaps to their mutual advantage. This comparative advantage emanates from the fact that US corporations often pay lower short-term interest rates but higher long-term interest rates than foreign banks. Foreign banks often pay higher short-term interest rates but lower long-term interest rates than US corporations. Given these parameters, both the US corporation and foreign bank could lower their borrowing costs if the US corporation issued short-term variable rate securities and the foreign bank issued long-term fixed rate securities. The two parties would then enter into an interest rate swap interest agreement to exchange interest rate payments on their underlying debt: the US corporation will effectively pay the foreign bank's long-term fixed rate and the foreign bank will effectively pay the US corporation's short-term variable rate (Bicksler and Chen, 1986).

1.   TYPES OF FINANCIAL DERIVATIVES

Since this book focuses on debt management, the financial derivatives we describe will be 'debt-related derivatives' or derivatives connected to the outstanding debt portfolios of subnational governments. Stewart and Cox (2008) classify debt-related derivatives as interest rate swaps, swaptions, forward delivery swaps and interest rate caps. An interest rate swap consists of a contract to synthetically exchange interest payments with a counterparty as a way to mitigate interest rate risk. A forward delivery swap is an interest rate swap executed now that comes into effect sometime in the future. A swaption is an interest rate swap that provides a counterparty with the option, but not obligation, to execute an interest rate swap some time in the future. An interest rate cap is a contract between a government and a counterparty whereby the government pays the counterparty an up-front premium to pay the excess interest payment on the government's variable rate bonds if the interest rate exceeds some predetermined rate. Interest rate swaps are the most utilized type of financial derivatives by subnational governments. For example, over 90 percent of all state government debt-related derivatives outstanding as of 2009 were interest rate swaps of some type (Luby and Kravchuk, 2013). The rest of this chapter will focus on interest rate swaps given this type of derivative's prominence in governmental debt portfolios.

2. INTEREST RATE SWAPS

States, local governments, public higher education institutions, hospitals and non-profit cultural institutions all have utilized different types of interest rate swaps. Swaps are structured financial products that entail a contractual exchange between a debt issuer and a financial institution (the 'counterparty', usually an investment bank), where the issuer can convert one interest rate basis to a different basis (say, from a floating rate or variable rate determined on one index to one based on another index, or from a variable rate to a fixed rate of interest, or vice versa). An example of a common interest rate swap is a floating-to-fixed interest rate swap whereby two parties agree to exchange payments, either floating rate or fixed rate, at future dates as specified in the derivatives contract.

In a floating-to-fixed interest rate swap, the fixed swap rate is set on the date that the swap is priced, and is often set as a spread or percentage of a similar type of treasury maturity. The floating rate is determined and reset according to some index such as LIBOR (London Interbank Offered Rate), or the SIFMA (Securities Industry and Financial Markets Association). The floating rate paid to bondholders is based on bond market conditions and the general credit quality of the government as enhanced by bond insurance or letters of credit. This potential mismatch between floating rates is known as basis risk and will be discussed below.

2.1 Swap Uses and Advantages

Subnational governments can use swaps to synthetically change floating rate debt into fixed rate debt (as in the case of floating-to-fixed rate swaps) so as to 'fix' their interest costs over the life of a bond issue. Governments may also employ swaps to synthetically change fixed rate debt into floating rate debt. This is known as a fixed-to-floating rate swap whereby the state or local government receives a fixed payment from a counterparty and makes a floating payment to the counterparty. The fixed payment is structured to cover the fixed interest payment on the bonds leaving the floating rate payment as the net result of the transaction from the perspective of the bond issuer. A fixed-to-floating rate swap attempts to take advantage of the historical borrowing cost advantage of variable rate debt without paying the normal liquidity and letter of credit fees often necessary to sell variable rate debt.

Governments may also utilize derivatives to take positions on future changes in bond market conditions related to the overall level of interest rates or relationships between securities indices (e.g. municipal market and US Treasury market). An example of this type of strategy is the use of a basis swap whereby the state or local government may agree to pay an interest rate based on a municipal bond market index and the counterparty agrees to pay an interest rate based on the US Treasury bond market. In this case, the state or local government will receive a net benefit from the derivative transaction if the US Treasury market-based swap produces payments that are in excess of the municipal bond market-based swap. These types of swaps can be problematic, though, in that they basically represent speculation on the future direction of interest rates; such activity is not an essential function of state and local governments nor is it one that governments are most equipped to engage.

2.2 Swap Risks to Issuers

Interest rate swaps carry serious financial risks that have to be understood and actively managed by state and local governments. The negative impacts of interest rate swaps can include significantly higher than expected swap payments, huge collateral postings and large termination payments to exit the swap. Swaps should not be used by issuers for speculation or to achieve the lowest interest rate in the short-term. In contrast, the prudent use of financial derivatives seeks to balance a significant amount of financial reward with a level of risk that is tolerable to the state or local governments. The major risks to be managed are basis risk, credit risk (also called counterparty risk), tax risk and termination risk. Luby and Kravchuk (2013) identified and discussed these risks:

1. Basis risk: this risk refers to the possibility that there may be mismatch between the interest payments exchanged under the interest rate swaps. In the case of a floating-to-fixed rate swap, the variable rate payment received from the counterparty may be less than the variable rate payment on the bonds. If the state and local government is relying on this variable rate payment from the counterparty to completely offset their variable bond requirements, such mismatch could cause fiscal stress.
2. Credit risk: this risk relates to the concern that the swap counterparty may not be able to satisfy the terms of the swap agreement over the entire term of the transaction. Since the bondholders are to be paid from the counterparty's payments, the government entity has exposed itself and bondholders to the credit of such counterparty. However,

it is the ultimate responsibility of the government entity to meet the principal and interest requirements of the underlying bonds even if the counterparty is not able to fulfill its requirements under the agreement.

3. Tax risk: this risk refers to potential long-term changes in the relationship between the exchange payments due to federal income tax changes. For example, the federal government could change marginal income tax rates that affect the long-term relationship between municipal interest rates and treasury interest rates. In this type of event, interest rate swaps where one party pays an interest rate based on a municipal securities index and the other party pays a rate based on a treasury securities index could have much different economic outcomes than if the bond index relationships stayed the same.

4. Termination risk: this risk concerns changes in the value of the interest rate swap agreement before its final maturity. If either counterparty desires to terminate the swap in advance of maturity, the swap will be valued at fair market value. Fair market value is impacted by the change in market interest rates since the swap's execution. It is also affected by changes to the government entity or counterparty's general credit. As such, one of the parties to the swap may have to make a significant payment to 'terminate' the swap if the aforementioned fair market value factors did not move in their favor since the swap's execution. Termination issues are discussed in more detail in the next section.

2.3 Swap Valuation

Like traditional municipal securities, the technical value of an interest rate swap is the present value of the net cash flows under the swap. The rate used to discount these future cash flows is based on the future floating rate payments based on a forecast of forward rates (e.g. LIBOR forward rates) for several years. Technically, swaps are valued based on US Treasury yields, the LIBOR rate spread and a SIFMA percentage (e.g. 67 percent of the one-month LIBOR rate). The calculation is based on the US Treasury yield representing the risk-free rate, LIBOR rate spread representing the risk premium and SIFMA percentage representing the historical relationship between LIBOR and SIFMA indices. Based on these inputs, the SIFMA swap rate is represented in equation (9.1):

SIFMA Swap Rate = Yield on US Treasuries of Similar Maturity   (9.1)
+ LIBOR Swap Spread + SIFMA Percentage

Table 9.1   Swap value to issuer as a function of interest rate changes

	Relative rates have risen	Relative rates have fallen
Government pays fixed rate	Increased value (+) (Government receives termination payment)	Decreased value (−) (Government makes termination payment)
Government pays floating rate	Decreased value (−) (Government makes termination payment)	Increased value (+) (Government receives termination payment)

In the event that the swap needs to be terminated for any reason by either party (i.e. the state or local government or the counterparty), the swap rate is recalculated based on current and future market conditions related to interest rates at the time of the swap termination. This can result in a sizeable termination payment from/to either party. Table 9.1 indicates that the government can end up a 'winner' or 'loser' relating to termination payments, depending on how interest rates have changed since the swap was initially executed. For example, if the subnational government executed a floating-to-fixed rate swap and then interest rates rose, the government would receive a termination payment from the counterparty as the fixed rate it was currently paying would be more valuable in a rising rate environment. On the other hand, if the government executed a floating-to-fixed rate swap and interest rates subsequently fell, the government would have to pay a termination payment to the counterparty as the fixed rate it was currently paying would be less valuable in a declining interest rate environment.

3.   INTEREST RATE SWAPS 'GONE AWRY'

There has been increased interest in financial derivatives in recent years given the fiscal stress these instruments caused many state and local governments as a result of the Financial Crisis. This section of the chapter provides a case study of a large municipality involving an interest rate swap 'gone awry' to better illustrate the potential risks of these financial instruments.[1]

A large municipality issued $500 million in revenue bonds in 2004. The bonds were sold to refinance outstanding bonds of the municipality. The transaction was designed to produce economic savings in excess of $31 million representing 6.72 percent of the bonds being refunded. To achieve such savings, the municipality used a floating-to-fixed interest rate swap.

The government would pay the counterparty a fixed rate, issue variable rate bonds and use the counterparty payment to offset the payment on the underlying bonds, thus leaving the fixed rate payment to the counterparty as the net payment on the transaction. The government opted for a blended credit enhancement structure with monoline bond insurance and a liquidity facility.

From closing until about January 2008, the interest rate swap performed effectively. That is, the variable rate swap receipt mostly matched the underlying variable rate bond interest, resulting in the municipality having an effective borrowing cost of the fixed swap rate plus liquidity and remarketing fees. Unfortunately, the effectiveness of the interest rate swap would not last due to the global Financial Crisis' effect on the municipal securities market. By late 2007, credit market participants became concerned with the financial health of most monoline bond insurers and many bank letter of credit providers that enhanced many of the municipal variable rate securities due to their exposure to the sub-prime mortgage crisis. As these insurers and banks began to be downgraded, the value of the variable rate debt insured by these companies plummeted. This resulted in significantly higher variable rate bond interest rates for such 'insured' or 'enhanced' paper.

The large municipality's variable rate refunding bonds were no exception. The downgrade of the municipality's bond insurer in May 2008 resulted in a general lack of investor appetite for the bonds, which produced several failed attempts at remarketing. Such remarketing caused the city to draw on its liquidity facility and pay much higher interest rates on these draws. This increased variable rate interest paid on the bonds produced significant basis mismatch whereby the municipality was paying substantially more on its variable rate bonds than the rate it was receiving from their swap counterparty. Since the economics of the bond refinancing assumed minimal basis mismatch, the savings on the bonds evaporated as the basis mismatch increased. The municipality addressed this basis mismatch by refunding a portion of the variable rate bonds with fixed rate bonds, terminating that portion of the swap. The government also purchased new letters of credit from higher-rated banks. However, the fees on these letters of credit were much more expensive than the 'replaced' credit enhancement fees.

Eventually, the basis mismatch from January 2008 to November 2008, the higher interest cost fixed rate refunding, the swap termination payment and the higher annual LOC fees effectively wiped out all of the economic savings from the refinancing. In fact, the municipality would have been better off not executing the refinancing in the first place since the expected additional costs of the new bonds now exceeded the debt service that would have been paid on the refunded bonds if they were kept in place.

4. FINANCIAL DERIVATIVES BEST PRACTICES (GFOA)

Given the potential risks associated with the use of financial derivatives, the Government Finance Officers Association (GFOA) has offered policy guidance for state and local governments in the use of these instruments. While the GFOA acknowledges that financial derivatives can be 'important interest rate management tools that, when used properly, can increase a governmental entity's financial flexibility, provide opportunities for interest rate savings, alter the pattern of debt service payments, create variable rate exposure, change variable rate payments to fixed rate and otherwise limit or hedge variable rate payments', it also recognizes the significant financial risks associated with these instruments (GFOA, 2010). These risks need to be systematically analyzed and managed in a rigorous and comprehensive manner.

Specifically, the GFOA recommends that state and local governments employ financial derivatives only if the following policy and activities are put in place. First, the state and local government should have a thorough understanding of the mechanics and risks of any financial derivative instrument under consideration. Second, the government should have the requisite staffing and expertise in-house or procure outside expert advisors to manage, monitor and evaluate the financial derivative. This expertise refers to evaluating and managing the major, specific derivatives risks described above (basis, credit, tax and termination), selecting derivative products and derivatives vendors, putting in place robust disclosure policies related to derivatives, and assigning specific personnel to monitor and evaluate the outstanding financial derivatives portfolio. Third, state and local governments that contemplate financial derivatives should have a comprehensive derivatives policy. At a minimum, this policy should include the following elements: description of the legal authority to execute derivatives, a list of allowable types of derivatives, conditions for derivative use, maximum allowable derivate instrument exposure, and procurement guidelines for derivatives vendors (GFOA, 2010).

5. FINANCIAL DERIVATIVES AND DODD–FRANK

A portion of the Dodd–Frank law was an attempt by Congress to protect subnational governments and their taxpayers from abuses and misuse of financial derivatives in the capital markets. The law allows the Securities and Exchange Commission to regulate, for the first time, the use of over-the-counter derivatives by subnational government entities. Some of the specific requirements of the law include swap counterparties acting in the best interest of the government and disclosing prevailing market rates to better inform governments of the fees associated with their derivative transactions. As of 2013, the Securities and Exchange Commission has not promulgated the final rules of Dodd–Frank as it relates to derivatives. However, some of the proposed rules have been released and include: (1) swap providers must report all swaps and state and local governments must maintain records on these swaps; (2) state and local governments must have a 'qualified independent representative' to advise on any swap before execution and that the state and local government have written policies in place regarding selection and monitoring of the advisor; and (3) counterparties must provide 'scenario analyses' of swaps to state and local governments prior to execution.

As it relates to the regulation of financial derivatives, Dodd–Frank represents a paternalistic policy approach towards subnational governments. It was an attempt to minimize the information asymmetries between swap counterparties and governments. Such reduction in the informational disadvantage was an attempt by the federal government to promote more prudent debt management practices by subnational governments. However, while most observers have noted the need for some sort of regulation of derivative instruments, the Dodd–Frank law may have an adverse impact on the municipal financial derivatives market. There is a serious concern that the heavy requirements leveled on swap counterparties could result in many of these firms exiting the municipal derivatives business. Such exits could hurt state and local governments by reducing the amount of service provider competition in these markets, making advice more limited, possibly less creative, and financial derivatives more expensive. This could also result in sub-optimal debt portfolios since these governments may not be able to avail themselves of financial advice that could help them manage their interest rate risk and lower their borrowing costs.

6. SUMMARY

The risks and rewards of financial derivatives as employed by subnational governments can be great. As such, the appropriate use of financial derivatives requires a government entity that is relatively sophisticated in managing complex financial instruments. This is not to say that state and local governments should always avoid the use of derivatives. Financial derivatives have been effectively used by many corporations and many state and local governments as a way to manage their liabilities. However, significant initial analysis, comprehensive formal policy prescriptions and diligent oversight are needed to ensure the most prudent use of financial derivatives. The case study detailed in this chapter evinces the need for such strategies. The federal government attempted to remedy the potential abuse and/or misuse of these financial products through the Dodd–Frank Act. Time will ultimately tell how this federal legislation impacts the use of financial derivatives in the subnational government sector in the United States.

NOTE

1. Bergstresser and Cohen (2012) provide an excellent analysis of a prominent example of an 'interest rate swap gone awry' in the case of Jefferson County, Alabama.

10. Reducing debt service by refunding debt

This chapter provides an overview of one of the major purposes of the sale of municipal securities: to refinance bonded and non-bonded indebtedness. The chapter begins with a discussion of the purposes and types of debt refinancing. It proceeds to detail the basic analytics behind debt refinancing, and examines four principles that undergird prudent debt refinancing strategies. The chapter concludes by offering some policy recommendations for subnational governments in their debt refinancing practices.

The primary reason subnational governments sell debt is to provide capital financing for projects such as the construction of roads, schools, government buildings, airports, water and wastewater systems, to name just a few typical capital projects. This debt is often structured such that the final maturity on these bonds can be decades into the future with the subnational government retiring the debt incrementally each year. Between the issuance date and final maturity on the bonds, economic conditions, operational position and policy/political preferences can change, necessitating the need to consider refinancing outstanding debt obligations.

There are three reasons for a state or local government to refinance or refund its bonded indebtedness (Wood, 2008). The most common reason is to take advantage of lower interest rates, which produces interest cost savings compared to the interest paid on the previously issued bonds. This type of refunding is known as an economic refinancing whereby the government replaces higher interest rate bonds with lower interest rate bonds. This strategy is very similar to an individual refinancing his home when interest rates have dropped from the time of the property's original purchase, which results in a decrease in the monthly mortgage payment.

The second reason for a bond refinancing is to 'restructure' the outstanding indebtedness of a state or local government. A debt restructuring involves the government replacing existing debt with new debt that is amortized over a longer time period than the existing bond debt service schedule. This provides debt service savings in the near term but at a cost of larger debt service in the future. Debt restructuring generally aims to provide near- and medium-term budgetary relief or to provide operating budget flexibility for additional future borrowing. As such, debt restructuring is known as a non-economic refinancing.

The third major reason for debt refinancing is to remove restrictive bond covenants in a state or local government's revenue bond program. Revenue bonds are usually issued under a master legal document (bond indenture) that includes the legal constraints of the revenue bond program related to such areas as pledged revenues, permissible financing purposes, additional bond tests, allowable future debt amounts, and permitted bond structures. However, the operational characteristics and/ or bond market conditions may change over time, which would incentivize state and local governments to issue future revenue bonds under different legal constraints. In this case, the state or local government could refund the existing bonds with new bonds that are sold under a different bond indenture. Like debt restructuring, this is known as a non-economic refinancing.

Many observers often think of debt refinancing only in the context of refinancing a state or local government's bonded debt, that is, the refinancing of municipal securities sold previously by the subnational government. This type of bonded debt sold by state and local governments to bond investors is known as a 'hard' liability. It is considered a hard liability because the subnational government has entered into a legally enforceable contract with its bond investors for the full and timely payment of principal and interest on the debt. In this type of refinancing the government is issuing a 'hard' liability (the new debt) to replace another 'hard' liability (the refinanced debt). However, state and local governments also can refinance 'soft' debt. Such debt may include pension liabilities, loans from the federal government for unemployment trust fund benefits or unpaid vendor bills.

This type of debt is classified as 'soft' because the liability can only be estimated and it may vary based on a number of factors such as investment performance and the life expectancy of retirees, as is the case for pension fund liabilities. These liabilities may also not be considered 'hard' in that their repayment terms are much more flexible than bonded debt. One such liability is unpaid vendor bills whereby the state or local government has more flexibility in the timeliness of the repayment to its vendors for goods and services provided to the government. An example of state or local government refinancing soft liabilities with hard liabilities is the use of pension obligation bonds. Governments use the pension obligation bond proceeds (hard liability) to replace the unfunded accrued actuarial liability (soft liability) in the pension system.

1. TYPES OF REFUNDING: THE FEDERAL GOVERNMENT VIEW

From a federal tax expenditure perspective, there are two types of municipal bond refundings. A current refunding is a refinancing of existing debt that is paid in full within 90 days of the refinancing. In contrast, an advance refunding is a refinancing of existing debt that is not paid in full within 90 days of the refinancing. Call protection (i.e. limitations on the ability to call and retire the bonds early) on existing bonds makes advance refundings common in the municipal securities market. In an advance refunding, the state or local government deposits the refinancing bonds proceeds in an escrow, and then the proceeds are invested to match the debt service requirements of the refunded bonds.

According to federal tax regulations, state or local governments are only allowed one advance refunding of an original bond issue but an unlimited amount of current refundings. The advance refunding restriction reflects the federal government's desire to limit tax expenditures related to the tax exemption of municipal securities. In the case of an advance refunding, there can be a significant amount of time where two bond issues (the refunded bonds and refunding bonds) sold to finance the same purpose are both outstanding due to call protection on the refunded bonds. The federal government does not want to engage in the double-subsidizing of capital projects which is the case when both the refunded and refunding bonds are outstanding at the same time. As such, the federal government's tax restriction on bond refinancing makes a state or local government's refinancing decision critical since they are limited in the number of times they can refund bonds in advance of maturity.

2. BOND REFINANCING ANALYSIS

The actual mechanics of structuring and analyzing a potential bond refinancing entails basic comparative analysis. That is, the state or local government performs an analysis that compares the debt service on their existing bond portfolio as currently structured against the debt service on its bond portfolio assuming a debt refinancing at current bond market interest rates for the government's debt. Such analysis usually concludes that some individual bonds will produce debt service savings and other individual bonds will not. The government 'sizes' the refunding by targeting the bonds that produce the expected debt service savings based on a predetermined savings metric as further detailed below.

Once the government targets the existing bonds for refinancing, it decides on a refinancing savings structure that will produce the annual timing of interest cost savings preferred by the government. There are three basic types of refinancing savings structure: up-front, equal annual and deferred. In an up-front savings structure all the savings occur in the first few years, with subsequent years yielding little or no debt service savings. An equal annual savings structure produces the same level of debt service savings in each year throughout the term of the refinancing. A deferred interest savings structure produces greater savings in later years compared to earlier years.

Table 10.1 visually illustrates this comparison between bond refinancing structures for a hypothetical bond issue that has $100 million in debt service coming due over the next 10 years. As shown in the table, the equal annual savings structure provides $5 million in savings each year over the 10-year period. The up-front refinancing savings provides $15 million in savings in each of the first three years and then provides zero savings thereafter. The deferred savings structure provides some savings in the first three years ($5 million per year), zero savings in years 4 to 7 and $15 million in savings in years 8 to 10. On an aggregate gross savings basis, the deferred interest savings structure provides the most savings while the up-front savings structure provides the least savings.

Even on a present value basis, the up-front refinancing savings structure is least efficient because it usually includes bonds that do not produce great amounts of present value savings (Luby, 2012b). However, this structure provides the greatest short-term budgetary relief, which is often attractive to elected officials who want to minimize tax increases (or maximize tax cuts) and maximize spending in the short-term. Equal annual savings and deferred savings structures are often more efficient than an up-front savings structure with the added benefit of providing more uniform and long-term budgetary benefits. However, these types of structures require elected officials and their debt managers to be patient until the savings are realized into the future, which often may not be in the short-term interest of elected officials.

From a budgetary perspective, the major problem with the up-front savings structure is that it can cause or exacerbate structural budget deficits. By taking all of the refinancing savings up-front (or over the first couple of years), the government is effectively utilizing a one-time revenue 'shot' to fund its budget. In the example of Table 10.1, after year 3, the government entity will have to either find additional revenues or cut spending to replace the $15 million in debt service savings that it had been enjoying over the first three years after the refinancing. Starting in year 4, the debt service on the refinancing bonds goes back to the same level as the refinanced bonds, $100 million. In addition, from the theoretical perspective of fiscal illusion,

Table 10.1 Refinancing savings structure comparison: equal, up-front and deferred (000s)

Year	Refinanced bonds P&I	Refinancing bonds P&I (Equal Annual Savings Structure)	Refinancing bonds P&I (Up-front Savings Structure)	Refinancing Bonds P&I (Deferred Savings Structure)	Annual savings (Equal Annual Savings Structure)	Annual savings (Up-front Savings Structure)	Annual savings (Deferred Savings Structure)
2011	$100 000	$95 000	$85 000	$95 000	$5 000	$15 000	$5 000
2012	$100 000	$95 000	$85 000	$95 000	$5 000	$15 000	$5 000
2013	$100 000	$95 000	$85 000	$95 000	$5 000	$15 000	$5 000
2014	$100 000	$95 000	$100 000	$100 000	$5 000	$0	$0
2015	$100 000	$95 000	$100 000	$100 000	$5 000	$0	$0
2016	$100 000	$95 000	$100 000	$100 000	$5 000	$0	$0
2017	$100 000	$95 000	$100 000	$100 000	$5 000	$0	$0
2018	$100 000	$95 000	$100 000	$85 000	$5 000	$0	$15 000
2019	$100 000	$95 000	$100 000	$85 000	$5 000	$0	$15 000
2020	$100 000	$95 000	$100 000	$85 000	$5 000	$0	$15 000
Total	**$1 000 000**	**$950 000**	**$955 000**	**$940 000**	**$50 000**	**$45 000**	**$60 000**

the up-front savings of $15 million per year provide the 'illusion' that the government has more money to spend (or to reduce taxes) than it will actually have in the near-term future. Thus, the up-front savings may provide an artificial incentive to increase spending from the operating budget in the short-term or to reduce taxes. However, neither budgetary action is sustainable based on the savings structure of the refinancing.

In a non-economic refinancing, the refinancing decision is usually based on political factors, short-term budgetary needs, or expected future borrowing needs. In the case of economic refinancings, the decision is purely a financial one based on present value savings analysis. Specifically, subnational governments evaluate the refinancing in terms of the amount of savings the refinancing produces on a present value basis using the true interest cost of the bonds as the discount rate. It then divides this present value amount by the size of the refunded bonds to get a scale as to the size of the present value savings, and then often uses a rule of thumb metric to determine whether to go forward with the refinancing. For example, they may have a 3 percent threshold that states that as long as the refinancing provides 3 percent present value savings as a percentage of the refunded bonds, the government should consider executing the transaction.

Table 10.2 details an actual bond refinancing for the County of Cook, Illinois issued in 2004 that produced over $16.5 million in debt service savings. The present value savings as a percentage of the bonds refunded was over 5.12 percent. Also, note that this type of refinancing would be classified as using an up-front refinancing savings structure as most of the savings accrued in the first three years.

However, the use of present value savings benchmarks can be a short-sighted way to make such a crucial decision as to when to refinance a bond. Because this type of analysis does not consider the opportunity cost of not being able to execute the refinancing in the future, it leaves a critical determinant out of the refinancing decision. That is, if interest rates declined further, the government could realize greater savings in the future if it waited on the refinancing. In bond finance terms, there is value to exercising the call option today (i.e. its intrinsic value) and there is value to exercising it later (i.e. time option value). By executing a refinancing today, the government is gaining the intrinsic value but forfeiting the value of its time option. Without expressly analyzing the time option, the government has not really fully assessed the refinancing. However, there are financial models that calculate the time option based on historical and projected interest rate forecasts. In fact, some governments have begun to use these time option models to help better optimize their refinancing decisions.

Table 10.2   Present value savings analysis: The County of Cook, Illinois General Obligation Refunding Bonds, Series 2004A ($000s)

Year	Refunded debt service	Refunding debt service	Debt service savings
2005	12048	6931	5116
2006	21273	11090	10182
2007	16507	15515	992
2008	15736	15713	23
2009	18532	18481	51
2010	10685	10686	−1
2011	21775	21779	−4
2012	10130	10125	5
2013	10130	10131	−1
2014	10130	10132	−1
2015	22520	22506	15
2016	33987	33956	32
2017	33957	33921	35
2018	43724	43682	42
2019	27495	27469	26
2020	27482	27455	28
2021	13819	13819	0
2022	13836	13836	0
2023	13854	13854	0
2024	13865	13865	0
	391483	**374945752**	**16538**

Note: Present value savings as a % of refunded bonds = 5.127% using the TIC as the discount rate.

Source: The County of Cook, Illinois General Obligation Series 2004A Bonds Official Statement.

3.   DEBT REFINANCING PRINCIPLES

Chapter 5 detailed the various principles that undergird debt management generally. The debt refinancing decision can be assessed using these same principles (Luby, 2014). Taxpayers and other stakeholders need to recognize that not all refinancings are the same. Specifically, some refinancings are more prudent than others as evaluated by the fundamental debt management principles. Moreover, state and local governments employ many different refinancing strategies that differ on a number of factors including the type of debt refinanced and transaction structure. While a government will commonly evaluate both the short-term and long-term aspects of a debt refinancing transaction, it is important for officials to take a longer-term perspective regarding the impact of the refinancing on the government. This chapter uses the principles previously described in Chapter 5 to assess the relative prudence of debt refinancing strategies. These principles are also discussed in more depth in Luby (2014).

3.1 Intergenerational Equity

Intergenerational equity in refinancing mainly involves the timing of the interest cost savings. That is, did the state or local government structure the savings on an up-front, equal annual or deferred basis? Intergenerational equity in debt refinancing is achieved when one generation is not burdened more than another. The idealized interest cost savings structure would be 'equal annual' as the savings are spread equally throughout the term of the bonds. The structure that most undermines intergenerational equity is the up-front savings structure where the current generation receives all of the benefits. Interestingly, deferred interest cost savings structures would also seem to violate intergenerational equity as the future generation benefits much more than the current one. However, this type of structure might be appropriate in the context of other tax and spending decisions in the case where such decisions benefit the current generation over future ones.

3.2 Economic Efficiency

In the context of bond refinancing, economic efficiency refers to minimizing the opportunity cost of refinancing the bonds at a later date when market conditions are different. This opportunity cost concept is known as the time value option in a particular refinancing. A completely economically efficient refinancing is one in which this opportunity cost is zero, that is, a refinancing where the interest cost savings approximates the expected savings in the future if the state or local government were to wait on executing the transaction (Kalotay and May, 1998; Zhang and Li, 2004; Kalotay et al., 2007). For municipal securities, the decision to refinance bonds is critical since the Internal Revenue Service generally limits subnational governments to only one advance refunding of a bond issue. While calculating the economic efficiency of a debt refinancing is complicated, time value option models are available to state and local governments and many of their municipal advisors are familiar with this type of sophisticated analysis as well.

3.3 Measurability/Certainty

In the context of debt refinancing, measurability refers to whether the interest cost savings of a refinancing can be measured, and certainty refers to whether such savings are 'locked in' throughout the term of the transaction. Fixed rate refinancings of fixed rate bonds satisfy these principles as the state or local government can measure and know with certainty what the interest cost savings will be over the course of the term of this type of transaction. In contrast, refinancing unfunded pension liabilities with pension obligation bonds (POBs) and hoping to earn more in the investment of the POB proceeds than the debt service, would undermine this principal as such savings are not measurable or certain at the time of the transaction's execution.

3.4 Management Flexibility

Management flexibility refers to the degree that a refinancing has constrained or freed up the future budgetary flexibility of a state or local government. For example, the use of pension obligation bonds to convert a 'soft' liability into a 'hard' liability compromises management flexibility as the government generally has much more control in the timing of payment of its pension liabilities than it does with municipal bond payments to investors.

4. DEBT REFINANCING RECOMMENDATIONS

Based on the principles described above, state and local governments should consider the following policy recommendations as they evaluate their debt refinancing strategies. A further discussion of these recommendations can be found in Luby (2014).

1. Avoid or be completely transparent with debt restructuring and up-front savings strategies
    Debt restructurings are inefficient because they do not maximize interest cost savings. Debt restructurings also burden future taxpayers for the benefit of current taxpayers, which undermines intergenerational equity. In the event that a debt restructuring is executed, subnational governments should be completely transparent regarding the additional burden such a transaction will place on future taxpayers. This should be clearly disclosed in any public discussion of the transaction so the taxpaying public is aware of the short- and long-term trade-offs

of the transaction. Along these same lines, subnational governments should also fully disclose the beneficiaries of economic refinancings that are structured so the savings are taken up-front. Taxpayers should know the generational benefits of these transactions as well as be aware of the degree they lead to or exacerbate a structural budget deficit, and should be empowered to veto such transactions if that is their preference.

2. Calculate the time value option for all economic bond refinancings

State and local governments should evaluate the opportunity cost of executing a refinancing today. These governments should avoid relying on static present value rules of thumb (e.g. 3 percent present value savings) in making their debt refinancing decisions. Time value option analysis allows such analyses and makes taxpayers aware of the economic efficiency of such transactions. By analyzing such opportunity costs, taxpayers will be made aware of the trade-off associated with executing a refinancing today compared to the savings level possibility of waiting until some time in the future. If the government does not have the in-house expertise to make such evaluations, it should demand that its municipal advisors or underwriters provide such an analysis prior to executing the transaction.

3. Avoid refinancings that do not provide measurable and certain savings

Debt refinancings should generally be executed only when the state or local government has 'locked in' the savings throughout the term of the transaction. As such, governments should avoid pension obligation bonds whose benefits are very much uncertain at the transaction's execution. In addition, state and local governments should avoid using financial derivatives in bond refinancing transactions as the borrowing cost is effectively 'variable' when the state or local government uses a derivative in connection with the transaction. If governments do consider such POBs or refinancings with financial derivatives attached, they should make their decision based on a risk-adjusted cost of capital of the transaction. In calculating the risk-adjusted cost of capital, the government examines hundreds (if not thousands) of possible interest rate scenarios that could occur in the future to determine the likelihood of specific scenarios that would present extreme fiscal stress to the government.

4. Weigh the loss in managerial flexibility under certain refinancing strategies

The use of municipal securities to refinance non-bond liabilities may be based on a quantitative rationale related to expected budgetary savings. However, there are qualitative factors that should also be weighed in such a transaction. Specifically, converting a soft liability into a hard liability limits managerial flexibility in future years. In recent years, some state and local governments have used bonds to refinance liabilities related to unpaid vendor bills, pension fund payments and unemployment trust fund loans outstanding to the federal government. All of these transactions, while possibly making sense from a borrowing cost perspective, have 'tied the hands' of future financial managers in dealing with budgetary pressures. Since soft liabilities usually have more flexible repayment terms, such conversion of these liabilities to 'hard debt' basically limits the financing options of the state or local government in future years, unless it is willing to default on its outstanding bonds. Since such default would effectively freeze these governments' ability to borrow, at least for a period of time, most state and local governments would not consider such a default option. In addition, using bonds to refinance non-bond liabilities may constrain the government's borrowing capacity for capital projects in the future. Many state and local governments have statutory or constitutional constraints that limit borrowing, and using capacity to convert non-bond liabilities to bonded debt would 'use up' some of that capacity.

5. Consider creative strategies to enhance refinancing savings
The municipal securities market has undergone dramatic change since the global Financial Crisis of 2008 and 2009. Investor demands and issuer preferences for these securities have been ever-changing during and after the Financial Crisis. As such, subnational governments should continue to monitor the market for creative financing strategies that may take advantage of this tumult in the financial markets. For example, some issuers have used revenue bonds to refund general obligations bonds as these revenue bonds have provided more cost-efficient financing as the general credit of some subnational governments has deteriorated in recent years. Historically, revenue bonds often carry interest rates greater than general obligation debt but the Financial Crisis has altered investors' perceptions of credit such that some revenue debt of an issuer may be viewed as more 'secure' than its GO debt. Subnational governments, with the help of their advisors, need to regularly monitor the municipal securities market to try to take advantage of such unique market opportunities.

6. Avoid statutorily constraining the managerial flexibility of debt managers in refinancing decision making
There has been some anecdotal evidence that some debt managers have engaged in imprudent decision making as it relates to debt finance (see Petersen, 2003; Miller and Justice, 2012; Bifulco et al., 2012; Luby, 2012a; Denison and Gibson, 2013). However, there is not systematic

evidence that such decision making is commonplace. In fact, one study found that state governments generally avoided 'imprudent' debt refinancing measures (Luby, 2012b). In addition, some research has found that statutorily constraining the debt refinancing decision making of these financial managers may lead to sub-optimal financial outcomes (Luby, 2009). As such, a thorough debt management policy related to debt refinancing with demands for significant transparency is probably the best course to follow as it relates to debt refinancing oversight. If increased disclosure is not satisfactory in incentivizing prudent decision making, a state or local government could set up an oversight committee to monitor debt management activities, including activities related to debt refinancing.

5. SUMMARY

This chapter examined subnational debt refinancing. The decision to refinance debt for economic or non-economic purposes is an important one in that it can decrease or increase the future strain on a subnational government's operating budget. Moreover, debt managers have at their disposal considerable ability to develop and craft these transactions to realize the budgetary savings in the time period most desired. Because of the long-term implications of refinancing both bond and non-bond liabilities, debt managers should use caution and rely on sophisticated analytical techniques in making the refinancing decision. Finally, taxpayers must remember that not all refinancings are the same and demand greater transparency for all of the debt refinancing strategies employed by their financial managers.

11. Lessons learned from the birth, growth and collapse of the municipal auction rate securities (MARS) market[1]

Municipal auction rate securities (MARS) were increasingly utilized by subnational governments to raise capital over the last few decades and improve the efficiency of their capital financing activities. MARS were developed as a means of reducing borrowing costs vis-à-vis long-term fixed rate and traditional variable rate demand bonds. However, the recent Financial Crisis which extended into the municipal securities market in 2007 and 2008 severely impacted the MARS market to the detriment of many state and local debt issuers. We critique this subnational government financial innovation by analyzing the birth, growth and collapse of the MARS market, primarily from the seller side, highlighting what we have learned over the global Financial Crisis.

The chapter continues by providing a descriptive analysis of the important characteristics of the auction rate market including size of issues, bond insurance, credit ratings, underwriters, uses of proceeds, and default rates. Then, the chapter proceeds with a detailed exposition of the borrowing cost motivations that led to the explosive growth in the MARS market in recent years. This section utilizes a matched pair analysis to empirically examine expected borrowing cost benefits to debt issuers. Next, we analyze the impact of the recent Financial Crisis on the efficacy of MARS and the various responses by state and local governments to the disruption in the MARS market. Finally, we conclude with specific 'lessons learned' for subnational government debt issuers. This section aims to establish a framework for better balancing the inherent tension between efficiency, risk-taking and market stability associated with capital market financial innovations as utilized by state and local governments in the United States. In sum, this chapter clearly illustrates both conceptually and through actual case study the risk–reward trade-offs in the municipal securities market as discussed throughout Part III of this book.

1.   MARS BACKGROUND

On 10 September 2008 Bank of America Corp. agreed with regulators to buy back $4.5 billion in auction rate securities it sold to over 5000 customers. The Bank of America 'buy-back' brought the total to over $50 billion in bank settlement agreements between regulators and some of the most prestigious banking firms: Citigroup Inc., UBS AG, Morgan Stanley, Wachovia Corp., J.P. Morgan Chase & Co., Merrill Lynch & Co., Goldman Sachs Group Inc. and Deutsche Bank AG (Kardos, 2008). The settlements were based on state attorneys general and Securities and Exchange Commission (SEC) allegations that the banks improperly sold auction rate securities to individuals, small businesses and other investors (Quigley, 2011).[2]

Municipal auction rate securities or 'MARS' are subnational government, variable-rate debt instruments sold to finance capital activities. MARS have been issued, rated and insured as long-term bonds, but priced, traded and marketed as short-term securities. From the investor perspective, auction rate securities were viewed as more liquid (i.e. could be sold quickly without a loss in principal value) than traditional variable rate debt instruments since the interest rate was reset at auction, and investors had historically been able to liquidate their positions at par value if needed. Due to the tax exemption and the large block size of many MARS ($25 000), investors in municipal auction rate securities were generally high net worth individual investors and institutions who wanted a cash-like investment for liquidity purposes but with a greater yield (Anderson and Bajaj, 2008). From the issuer perspective, municipal auction rate securities were viewed as having lower transaction costs since they could be sold without a put option (i.e. the option of the investor to 'put' the security back to the issuer and receive the principal back at certain predetermined regular intervals) and liquidity supports (i.e. third parties, usually banks, that provide liquidity to the investor in the event that the bond cannot be immediately resold to another investor), which was typical with traditional variable rate instruments after 1987 (California Debt and Investment Advisory Commission, 2004).

Since the first recorded MARS issue in 1988, over 3000 auction rate bond issues have been sold in the municipal securities market totaling over $280 billion (*The Bond Buyer Yearbook,* Thomson Reuters, various years). Annual issuance peaked in 2004 with the sale of $42 billion in auction rate securities. Issuance in 2004 shows evidence of the unbridled growth of auction rate securities in the municipal market. In 1990, they accounted for 2.1 percent of variable rate debt, and only 0.17 percent of the entire market. By 2004, they grew to an astounding 85 percent of variable rate

Table 11.1   *Municipal auction rate securities (MARS) 1988–2008*

Year	Total MARS new issuance (dollars, millions)	Total MARS new issues (number)	MARS as percent of total market volume	MARS as percent of VRDO debt
1988	25.00	1	0.02	0.13
1989	90.00	1	0.06	0.71
1990	283.00	5	0.17	2.11
1991	2 770.20	49	1.28	18.98
1992	3 686.90	59	1.33	17.01
1993	6 329.00	107	1.86	24.17
1994	4 772.90	78	2.12	21.51
1995	2 068.10	39	1.05	6.92
1996	2 832.20	56	1.25	10.21
1997	2 807.00	42	1.05	6.91
1998	4 376.60	74	1.36	12.52
1999	5 364.20	82	2.03	15.48
2000	9 892.60	137	4.09	20.74
2001	12 771.20	151	3.71	25.46
2002	32 893.90	251	7.63	63.12
2003	41 115.80	433	9.07	83.32
2004	42 921.00	438	10.30	85.65
2005	33 295.10	337	7.26	51.04
2006	32 968.80	321	7.62	56.89
2007	38 743.20	322	7.94	73.80
2008	–	0	0.00	0.00

Source: Thomson Reuters.

debt issuance and 10 percent of the entire municipal market, as shown in Table 11.1. But in February 2008 all that changed when the MARS market completely collapsed. Since December 2007, there have not been any new municipal auction rate securities sold (Securities Industry and Financial Markets Association, 2010).

However, for almost two decades prior to the 2008 collapse, the process of resetting interest rates through the auction process was mostly successful (Lee, 2008).[3] That is, borrowers were able to continue paying a low interest rate that reflected a truly liquid, short-term security, and investors were able to receive a reasonable return or liquidate their investment at face value. But in September 2007, faced with a credit crunch from the mortgage sector meltdown, banks started to back out of auctions, and auctions began to fail. This happened slowly at first, at a rate below 6 percent, but then on 13 February 2008, 82 percent of auctions failed, and most auctions continued to fail throughout the month (Lee, 2008). When auctions fail, borrowers and investors are both adversely affected. Investors that bought securities are unable to liquidate them at or near face value, having to absorb substantial losses to get out of their investments. For borrowers, an auction failure means that their bonds go unsold at short-term rates, and they are required to pay the default rate, which has been as high as 20 percent. Needless to say, persistent auction failure has left both issuers and investors seeking relief and redress from state and federal regulators.

2.   EVOLUTION OF MARS MARKET

The auction rate securities market emerged in the mid-1980s as a way for corporations, mutual funds, and state and local governments to issue long-term debt instruments but pay short-term interest rates. The auction rate securities market originated in the corporate finance world with the first sale of an auction rate corporate preferred stock. However, it did not take long for municipal governments to express interest in auction rate securities and enter the market. According to *The Bond Buyer* (Thomson Reuters) the first long-term municipal auction rate bond was issued by the San Diego Hospital Association in June 1988 for $25 million. As shown in Table 11.1, only one MARS issue was sold in 1988 and 1989, and five in 1990. But by 1991 MARS new issuance shot up to 49, worth $2.77 billion. At that point, MARS established itself as an important segment of the municipal market, roughly 19 percent of variable rate (short-term with put option) securities issued in 1991. Most of the early MARS issues were hospital revenue bonds supporting general acute care hospitals, with Lehman Brothers as the managing underwriter on almost half of MARS issues.

The MARS market grew in 1992 with 59 new issues, and in 1993 found its highest level in the 1990s with 107 new issues valued at $6.32 billion. After 1993, sales leveled off and fluctuated between 39 and 82 per year until 2000, when the market took off. From 2001 to 2002 MARS issues went from 25 percent of variable rate demand obligation (VRDO) debt to 63 percent. VRDO debt is the other prominent type of floating rate security used in the municipal market. In 2003 MARS debt issuance was almost 83 percent of VRDO issues. But MARS debt issues were on average much larger than VRDO issues: $96 973 000 compared to $31 844 000. Such large amounts of MARS paper floating in the market having to be reset regularly enhanced the gravity of the problem once liquidity dried up in 2007.

The market peaked in 2004 with 438 new MARS issues, totaling $42.921

billion in principal value. At this point MARS issues accounted for a 10 percent share of the entire municipal market, and 85 percent of the dollar amount of variable rate bonds sold. The years 2005, 2006 and even 2007 saw robust MARS sales at which point almost half the total size of the auction rate securities market (both municipal and corporate) was accounted for by MARS (Han and Li, 2008). By late 2007, the bottom dropped out of the market with zero new MARS sold since December 2007. Indeed, in the brief span of 20 years we have seen the birth, growth and death of the MARS primary market. Moreover, as of the end of July 2010, the amount of MARS outstanding was $66.8 billion, with approximately $1.2 billion being retired on average per month since January 2009. With such a retirement rate and assuming no additional issuance, the MARS market will be fully retired by 2015, thus spelling the death of the secondary MARS market as well (Securities Industry and Financial Markets Association, 2010). The drop in the MARS secondary market is also evinced by its collapse in trading activity. Between January and May 2010, monthly ARS trading volume averaged $4.5 billion, with 3246 trades compared to a monthly average in 2008 of $113.6 billion with 113 225 trades (Municipal Securities Rulemaking Board, 2010).[4]

For the first decade, 87 percent of the MARS market was limited to three types of revenue bonds sold by non-general governmental units involved in secondary education, primary health care and housing. The secondary education issues were sold to finance student loans and higher education general capital improvements. Health care MARS debt financed general acute care hospital facilities, and the housing debt was largely for single-family mortgage bonds. Over time MARS debt gained legitimacy as a safe and liquid security from the perspective of both issuers and investors, and issuance expanded from important but niche segments of the municipal market, health care, housing and secondary education, to the mainstream financing of public and general-purpose facilities (from 0.05 percent in 1999 to 10 percent in 2007). The vast majority of public facility and general-purpose MARS proceeds were generated from 2003–07. What began as a financial innovation used in the non-general governmental parts of the municipal market crept over into the more traditional, general governmental arena.

Many observers feel that it was unlikely that the MARS primary market would have achieved such mainstream success so quickly without the help of credit rating agencies and bond insurers (Preston, 2011). MARS market growth was made possible because bond insurers were willing to insure most MARS debt with the guarantee of timely principal and interest payments. Prior to the fall of 2008, all the major bond insurers were rated AAA so MARS debt issued with bond insurance carried a long-term, triple-A rating from the credit rating agencies Standard & Poor's, Moody's, and often Fitch. Since most MARS debt was rated triple-A, major investors such as high net worth retail investors and corporate treasurers were willing to purchase large amounts of MARS debt without much credit quality due diligence. In 1999, almost half of the 46 MARS debt issues were insured. In 2004, almost $30 billion of MARS paper, 78 percent of 2004 issues, was insured. Between 2004 and 2007, over 70 percent of the entire new issue market was insured, peaking at 80 percent in 2007. As a result, financial market participants had engineered an insured market of weekly reset (and therefore short-term) debt.

Because bond insurance was so prevalent in the municipal market, neither issuers nor investors were paying attention to the inherent interest rate reset risk from auction failure. The bond insurer's guarantee had nothing to do with liquidity. Bond insurers guaranteed timely payment of principal and interest. Bond insurers never guaranteed investors that their investment would remain liquid, nor did they assure issuers that all auctions would succeed and their maximum default rates would never go into effect. But what bond insurance did do, along with the associated long-term, triple-A ratings, was to lull investors and issuers to sleep as to the full risks inherent and explicitly stated in their MARS debt indentures.

Which brings up a basic question: why is debt with an interest rate reset either weekly or monthly considered by the rating agencies to be long-term debt? Almost all rated MARS debt has a long-term, not a short-term rating. Since the high interest rates of the late 1970s and early 1980s bankers have been trying to convert or engineer, long-term bonds into short-term debt, bringing the interest rate down to the short-term end of the yield curve and generating additional fees without a complete remarketing. The rating agencies apparently bought into the argument that since a MARS debt issue has a long-term 'final' maturity date, it is a long-term bond. This may be true in terms of 'final' payment. But it is not true in terms of what is the most important, fundamental aspect of a debt instrument – the interest rate on which interest payments are based and market value is largely determined. Moreover, it is clear from the legal fall-out from the auction failures that the long-term triple-A rating was assumed by investors to imply excellent 'short-term' credit quality, which it does not. Long-term ratings are based on long-term ability and willingness of an issuer to repay. Short-term ratings are substantially based on short-term liquidity. The problems in the MARS market are a consequence of the lack of short-term liquidity, not long-term inability or unwillingness to pay.

3. MOTIVATION BEHIND MARS GROWTH

In examining the primary motivation that fueled the explosive growth of
auction rate securities in the municipal bond market over the last decade,
a comparison of MARS with the other competing financial instrument
that also offers the advantage of short-term pricing with a long-term
dated maturity is needed. That is, auction rate securities are one type of
long-term floating interest rate instrument that are intended to function as
cash-like, short-term investments.[5] The other prominent type of floating
rate security used in the municipal market is the variable rate demand obligation (VRDO). VRDOs are tax-exempt instruments in which the yield is
reset on a daily, weekly or monthly basis based on a remarketing process or
according to an index. While VRDOs are issued with long-dated maturities of 20 to 40 years, they have short-term 'put' features that allow bond
investors to demand repurchase of their bonds at par plus accrued interest
on a short-term basis. This put feature often requires issuers to purchase
liquidity support devices like standby bond purchase agreements or letters
of credit in order to protect the issuer and investor in the event the bond
cannot be remarketed in a timely fashion once it is 'put'.

Prior to the growth in the auction rate securities market, VRDOs were
the dominant floating rate debt instrument used by state and local governments for the period of 1988 to 2001. The use of variable rather than
fixed rate debt in either the auction rate or variable rate demand mode is
generally based on two different justifications. First, variable rate debt can
serve as a hedge to an issuer's interest rate risk on its short-term cash-like
assets. However, this justification is weak for many state and local governments because of their lack of liquid assets. That is, unlike many corporations and some universities and hospitals, most subnational governments
do not possess large amounts of cash invested in short-term securities
that could and should be hedged with short-term variable rate debt in
order to produce a better match between the structure of its assets and
liabilities. Thus, for most issuers the use of variable rate demand bonds is
justified based on the expectation of achieving a lower cost of borrowing
(Government Finance Officers Association, 1997). That is, the short-term
nature of these securities as provided by the 'put' feature allowed these
bonds to be priced at the short end of the yield curve. Since the short
end of the yield curve produces lower interest rates in most interest rate
environments (i.e. at times when the bond market has a 'normal' upward
sloping yield curve), issuers of variable rate instruments usually enjoy
lower borrowing costs compared to similarly dated fixed rate maturities
that do not possess such a 'put' feature.

This borrowing cost advantage is evidenced in Figure 11.1. Between

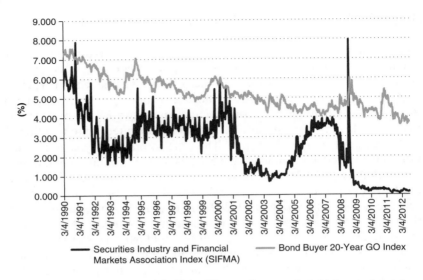

Source: Board of Governors of the Federal Reserve System, selected interest rates, state and local bonds; Thomson Reuters.

Figure 11.1   Historical trends in interest rates (long-term vs. short-term municipal bond interest rates, 1990–2012)

March 1990 and March 2009, the Securities Industry Financial Market Index (SIFMA) (formerly the PSA and BMA indices), an index of high grade variable rate municipal bonds, has produced lower interest rates in almost all periods compared to the Bond Buyer 20-Year GO Index (BBI 20 GO), an index of high grade 20-year fixed rate general obligation munici-pal bonds. The average interest rate for the SIFMA index for this period was 3.11 percent compared to 5.45 percent for the BBI 20 GO, a 233 basis point advantage for short-term floating rate securities. Recognizing this historical borrowing cost advantage, the Government Finance Officers Association advocated the use of a modest amount of variable rate debt in certain circumstances for some issuers, claiming that 'variable rate debt can be an important tool in managing a government's debt program and can help lower the cost of borrowing and provide a hedge against interest rate risk' (GFOA, 1997).

Unlike VRDOs, the interest rate on auction rate securities is reset through a Dutch auction process at predetermined and frequent intervals, commonly 7, 28 or 35 days.[6] Thus, auction rate securities have been issued, rated and insured as long-term bonds, but priced, traded and marketed as short-term securities. Owners of MARS have the option to hold their securities at each auction regardless of the new rate, bid to hold an existing position at a specified rate, or request to sell at the rate set by the auction. Therefore, provided an auction does not fail, investors view MARS as short-term securities and bid on them as such. Consequently, MARS securities have enjoyed similar pricing advantages as variable rate demand obligations since they are also able to take advantage of the historical interest rate benefit of the short end of the yield curve. Based on this cost of borrowing advantage, several public policy groups advocated for the potential efficacy of auction rate securities. For example, the California Debt and Investment Advisory Commission stated, 'MARS can be a valuable alternative and complement to fixed rate debt in a government borrowing program' (California Debt and Investment Advisory Commission, 2004).

The attraction of auction rate securities compared to variable rate demand obligations for government issuers was mainly twofold. First, the use of auction rate securities allowed issuers to expand and diversify their investor base. MARS investors were typically high net worth retail investors and corporate cash managers (Anderson and Bajaj, 2008; California Debt and Investment Advisory Commission, 2004). Money market funds were ineligible to hold MARS due to Securities and Exchange Commission Rule 2a-7 restricting them to securities with a final maturity of 397 days or less (a true short-term instrument) (California Debt and Investment Advisory Commission, 2004). Conversely, investors in tax-exempt variable rate demand obligations are mainly money market fund portfolios (in addition to high net worth investors and corporate cash managers) because these securities qualify under the federal regulatory rule that mandates the maturity and quality standards for money market funds and also due to the high minimum investment requirement, often $100000 (Municipal Securities Rulemaking Board, 2010; California Debt and Investment Advisory Commission, 2004). The relative diversity of investors between VRDOs and MARS allowed for an expansion of a government entity's investor base, which could, theoretically, lead to reduced overall borrowing costs.

The second attraction of auction rate securities to subnational government issuers was more directly related to the immediate borrowing cost benefits associated with such debt. MARS have fees associated with facilitating the auction (auction agent fee), credit enhancement fees to elevate the credit to levels acceptable to its targeted investor base (bond insurance), and relatively high remarketing fees because of the greater need to solicit investors compared to VRDOs. In addition, it was expected that MARS would carry slightly higher interest rates than VRDOs to compensate investors for the risk that the remarketing agent would not be able to locate another investor and thus the current investors would have to hold

Table 11.2   General cost comparison – MARS versus VRDO

	MARS	VRDO
Interest rate	+/– SIFMA index	+/– SIFMA index
Letter of credit	N/A	+65 basis points
Bond insurance	+7 basis points	N/A
Cost of issuance	+5 basis points	+3 basis points
Remarketing fee	+25 basis points	+9 basis points
Auction agent fee	+1 to +3 basis points	N/A

Source: California Debt and Investment Advisory Commission, 'Auction Rate Securities' (2004).

the bonds (this is known as a failed auction). VRDOs do not carry this risk because liquidity is guaranteed to these investors through a standby bond purchase agreement or letter of credit.

However, because MARS do not have this 'put' feature, they do not require the often-expensive third party liquidity facility required by VRDOs. It was expected that the cost savings from the absence of purchasing such a credit facility would make the total cost of auction rate securities cheaper than their VRDO counterparts, even taking into account the additional service costs and higher interest rate resets expected from MARS. The California Debt and Investment Advisory Commission detailed the expected borrowing cost advantage in their 2004 report, which is reproduced in Table 11.2.

The borrowing cost efficiency of auction rate securities can explicitly be seen through a matched pair analysis comparing two similar credit securities sold by the same government, one an auction rate security and the other a variable rate demand obligation. The Chicago Public Schools (hereinafter referred to as the CPS) sold several series of floating rate debt in both auction rate and variable rate modes under their unlimited tax general obligation bond indenture for the purpose of funding their capital improvement program. In February 2003, the School District sold $95 325 000 million in weekly reset auction rate bonds carrying bond insurance by MBIA and maturing on 1 March 2033. In November 2004, CPS issued $48 910 000 of weekly reset variable rate demand obligations with a standby bond purchase agreement from DEPFA Bank, bond insurance from FSA, and maturing on 1 March 2035. A comparison of the borrowing cost of these two bond issues is appropriate since they are matched in all respects (issuer, security, reset frequency and purpose) except for the variable of interest: security type (VRDO or MARS). Table 11.3 provides a summary comparison of these two securities.

Table 11.3   *Bonds description: Chicago Public Schools select floating rate issues*

	Unlimited Tax GO Bonds Series 2003B-3	Unlimited Tax GO Bonds Series 2004C-2
Type of security	MARS	VRDO
Issue date	2/13/03	11/10/04
Size	$95 325 000	$48 910 000
Maturity	1 March 2033	1 March 2035
Purpose	Capital improvements	Capital improvements
Security	General Obligation	General Obligation
Interest rate reset	Weekly	Weekly
Remarketing agent	Morgan Stanley	Goldman Sachs
Auction agent	Bank of New York	N/A
Liquidity facility/LOC	N/A	DEPFA Bank
Bond insurance	MBIA	FSA

Source: Bond Official Statements.

Comparing the all-in borrowing costs (taking into account all support costs) of these two matched pair securities provides anecdotal support for why MARS were attractive to government bond issuers as an alternative to VRDOs. First, Figure 11.2 compares the primary component of the all-in borrowing cost of the two securities, the weekly interest rate resets, for the time period that both securities were simultaneously outstanding (i.e. from the issuance of the 2004C-2 bonds, 10 November 2004, up to and including the date the 2003B-3 bonds were refunded and paid in full, 25 April 2008). From the beginning of the period until the auction rate market began to fail in October 2007, the MARS usually reset at lower rates than the VRDOs. After late October 2007, CPS' VRDOs significantly outperformed its MARS securities as investor demand for MARS dropped precipitously in light of the collapse of the MARS market. Prior to the MARS market collapse, the average interest rate reset on the VRDOs was 3.08 percent while the average interest rate reset for the MARS was 2.95 percent, 13 basis points less. While this finding seems to refute the commonly held notion that auction rate securities would carry slightly higher interest rates than VRDOs to compensate investors for the risk that the auction remarketing agent would not be able to locate another investor, it is in keeping with some recent research that found, on average, MARS yields were approximately 10 basis points less than yields of VRDOs. These researchers speculate that the efficacy of MARS may be due to the possibility that a competitive auction is a more efficient pricing

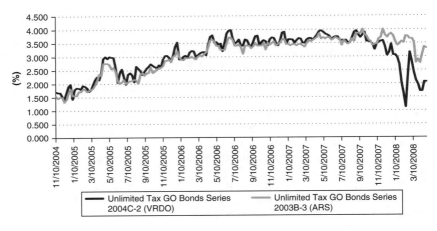

Source:　*Bloomberg.*

Figure 11.2　*Chicago Public Schools floating rate securities comparison*
(VRDO weekly interest rates versus ARS weekly interest
rates)

mechanism than the periodic VRDO yield resetting by the remarketing
agent (McConnell and Saretto, 2010).

While the interest rate resets are its primary component, the all-in borrowing cost also includes the various other bond support fees (auction
agent, remarketing, liquidity and insurance) that need to be calculated
before making a comparison of the cost efficiency of the two types of securities. Table 11.4 details these various costs for CPS' MARS and VRDO
bond issues.

Similar to what the California Debt and Investment Advisory
Commission described, the aggregate support costs for the MARS issue
were substantially less than the VRDO issue mainly due to the absence of a
liquidity facility for the MARS. Based on the average interest rate of both
of these securities (during the period that they were both simultaneously
outstanding but prior to the auction rate securities market collapse) and
their particular support costs, CPS realized an annual interest cost savings
of 47 basis points by selling its 2003B-3 bonds in an auction rate mode
compared to the borrowing cost it would have achieved selling its bonds
in a variable rate demand obligation mode as proxied by CPS' 2004C-2
bonds. This basis point spread translates into over $686000 in borrowing
cost savings for the period 10 November 2004 to 25 October 2007. If this
annual 47 basis point borrowing cost spread persisted for the entire life
of the 2004C-2 bonds from issuance on 10 November 2004 through to

Table 11.4   *Cost comparison MARS versus VRDOs, Chicago Public Schools unlimited tax series 2003B-3 and Series 2004C-2 (for the period 10 November 2004 to 25 October 2007)*

	Unlimited Tax GO Bonds Series 2003B-3	Unlimited Tax GO Bonds Series 2004C-2
Type of security	MARS	VRDO
Average interest rate reset	2.95%	3.08%
Letter of credit and or liquidity fee	N/A	0.55%
Bond insurance	0.18%	0.18%
Remarketing fee	0.25%	0.05%
Auction agent fee	0.01%	N/A
Total average all-in borrowing cost	**3.39%**	**3.86%**

Source: Chicago Public Schools and *Bloomberg*.

maturity on 1 March 2035, CPS would have saved over $6.8 million dollars in borrowing costs if it sold auction rate securities rather than variable rate demand obligations on its $48 910 000 2004C-2 bonds. Moreover, this bond amount, $48 910 000, is a relatively small amount of bonds in today's municipal market. In fact, by the end of 2007, CPS itself had about $1 billion of auction rate securities in its debt portfolio.

Given its rather sizable amount of floating rate debt outstanding, one can clearly conceive the magnitude of borrowing cost savings CPS envisaged as it accelerated its use of auction rate debt and reduced its reliance on variable rate demand obligations. Based on the scale of expected borrowing cost savings provided in this single example, it is not surprising that over the previous few years many state and local governments turned to auction rate securities as a means of more efficiently managing their capital finance programs. Unfortunately, these expected efficiencies never fully materialized as the auction rate securities market effectively imploded in early 2008.

4.   THE IMPACT OF THE MARS MARKET IMPLOSION AND SUBNATIONAL GOVERNMENT RESPONSES

As early as September 2007, there were signs of trouble in the auction rate securities market as several auctions failed. By late 2007, as the sub-prime mortgage crisis began to fully reveal itself, the bond markets began to question the financial soundness of many of the monoline bond insurers that insured many of the municipal auction rate securities due to their exposure to the sub-prime mortgage crisis. As previously mentioned, since 1999, half of all new MARS debt was insured. As these insurers began to be downgraded, the value of the MARS debt insured by these companies dropped, as indicated by higher auction clearing prices. In many cases, these higher clearing prices exceeded the maximum interest rate specified in the bond documents, thus leading to auction failures. By February 2008, as the sub-prime mortgage crisis deepened substantially, exacerbating the problems of the monoline insurers, the auction rate market effectively ground to a halt as over 1000 auctions failed over the course of only three days (Lee, 2008).[7]

The general effects on subnational government finances from the implosion of the MARS market can be observed from a different matched pair analysis for the period October 2007 and into 2008. Figure 11.3 details the interest rate resets on CPS' $71 450 000 2003D-4 MARS issue sold on 12 December 2003 and insured by XL Capital, one of the monoline insurers with the most exposure to the sub-prime mortgage crisis. The graph shows how these bonds basically traded flat or lower to SIFMA prior to October 2007 (like CPS' 2003B-3 ARS) while trading significantly higher than SIFMA after this time period. In fact, for several weeks in February 2008, these securities experienced failed auctions, thus having their bonds reset at 9 percent, the maximum rate under state law. From its issuance date of 12 December 2003 to 17 October 2007, the MARS average interest rate was 2.45 percent compared to the average SIFMA interest rate of 2.58 percent, a 13 basis point lower interest cost. However, for the period 17 October 2007 to 7 May 2008 (i.e. the date the bonds were refunded and paid in full), the MARS average interest rate was 5.17 percent compared to the SIFMA rate of 2.79 percent, a 238 basis point difference. This basis point spread increase translates into over $991 000 in additional borrowing costs over what would have accrued if the MARS issue traded 'flat' to SIFMA during this time period. In addition to the comparison with the SIFMA index, Figure 11.4 graphically shows how CPS' 2003D-4 MARS issue significantly underperformed its VRDO counterpart (the 2004C-2 bonds) during this time period, further evidence of the reduction in interest costs that CPS could have realized if it had issued VRDOs rather than MARS. Once again, this example is based on a relatively small bond par amount, $71 450 000, and, thus, one can envision how this 'spike up' in MARS interest rate resets had the potential of substantially impacting aggregate subnational government finances and operations had actions not been taken to reduce exposure to the MARS market. This adverse impact was

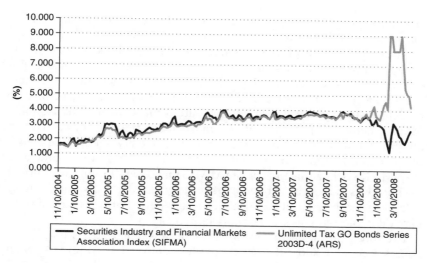

Source: Bloomberg.

Figure 11.3   Chicago Public Schools auction rate securities comparison to SIFMA

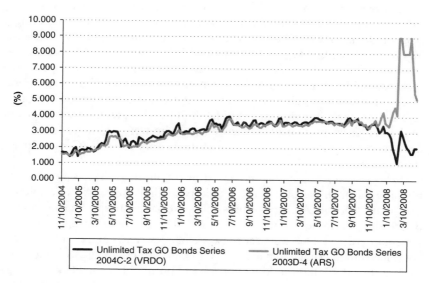

Source: Bloomberg.

Figure 11.4   Chicago Public Schools floating rate securities comparison (VRDO weekly interest rates versus ARS weekly interest rates)

especially troubling for a governmental issuer like CPS, which had about $1 billion of MARS in its bond portfolio (Shields, 2008).

Given the gravity of the situation, government issuers immediately began working towards solutions to minimize or eliminate their exposure to the MARS market. The 'cleanest' solution identified by issuers was to convert their MARS bonds to another interest rate mode or type of debt instrument such as a variable rate demand bond (Wells Capital Management, 2008). With a variable rate demand bond, investors have an additional layer of liquidity due to the liquidity facility put in place as part of the bonds and thus these bonds were generally much more marketable than MARS debt at the time of the MARS market implosion. In addition, the hope was that once the bond markets normalized, issuers would still be able to realize the interest cost benefits of long-term bond instruments that have their interest rates set like short-term debt.

Two problems immediately arose with this approach. First, many issuers were not allowed to make such a conversion from MARS to VRDOs under their bond documents (Lee, 2008). Second, even if issuers could make this conversion, the increase in draws on existing liquidity agreements associated with VRDOs insured by the downgraded monoline insurers and the rush of issuers seeking liquidity facilities substantially drove up the prices of such credit devices and dried up capacity from banks in offering these products (Lee, 2008). Because of this huge surge in demand for and decrease in supply of liquidity facility products, highly rated banks like J.P. Morgan and Bank of New York essentially 'owned' the market in offering these products and thus set the terms to their general benefit. For instance, most new liquidity facilities and letters of credit were for much shorter periods than in the past, they were only offered to higher rated 'plain vanilla' credits, and preference was given to the bank's current clients or new clients who were willing to give business to other areas of the bank such as depository services (Cooke, 2008; Ward, 2008).

However, even many of the government entities that were able to procure reasonably cost efficient liquidity facilities were still not able to restructure their MARS portfolios on a long-term basis. That is, many of the short-term liquidity facilities and letters of credit obtained during the credit crisis in 2008 were set to expire in a few years and in light of the continued credit crunch, renewal was far from certain. Some estimated that there were $109 billion in letters of credit and liquidity facilities expiring in 2011 (Corkery and Dugan, 2011). Given that much of this variable rate debt would have interest rate swaps attached to it that were probably 'out of the money', subnational governments were having to choose between paying even higher fees for liquidity or refinancing this variable rate debt into more costly fixed rate debt while paying large termination payments to settle their interest rate swaps.

Another alternative is to convert to other short-term financial instruments that offer the same benefits as VRDOs but do not necessitate the need for a liquidity facility. In 2010 and 2011, many state and local governments employed one of these instruments, floating-rate notes (FRNs), to replace VRDOs in a second round of restructuring their MARS portfolios. FRNs are variable rate notes often sold directly to money market funds that pay a floating rate as a spread to LIBOR or SIFMA. The benefit of FRNs is that they do not rely on secondary market demand and, thus, do not entail a liquidity facility or remarketing agent (Wallace, 2011). However, these securities do not have a long-dated maturity and usually mature within seven years, thus making them fundamentally different from long-dated MARS and VRDOs. Hence, these notes reflect a short-term rather than long-term MARS restructuring solution, with state and local governments still exposed to rollover risk once these notes mature (Seymour, 2010b).

A second approach that some issuers utilized was to refund their MARS portfolio with fixed rate debt. Since long-term fixed interest rates were still at historical lows in 2008, many issuers saw this as an opportunity to eliminate any future interest rate fluctuations in their debt portfolio while locking in relatively low long-term interest rates (Preston, 2011). This approach also had a couple of downsides. First, and most obvious, the refunding of variable rate debt with fixed rate debt eliminated the issuers' ability to receive the historical borrowing cost benefit of short-term variable interest rates compared to long-term fixed rates. Second, as mentioned in the preceding paragraph, many of the MARS issuers had entered into floating-to-fixed interest rate swaps on their auction rate bonds as a way to hedge interest rates. If an issuer wanted to refund the MARS with fixed rate debt, they would in effect be forced to terminate the swap since it would no longer be serving as a proper hedge now that their underlying debt was in a fixed rate mode as opposed to a floating rate mode. Because the general interest rate environment was currently lower compared to when many of these interest rate swaps were executed, issuers often owed large termination payments to the counterparty. These termination payments could be paid out of issuer funds or from the proceeds of the fixed rate bond refunding although such termination payments made the economics of such fixed rate refundings much less attractive.

A third approach that some MARS issuers attempted was to convince a bank to purchase their MARS and then negotiate changes to the securities without having to undertake a potentially costly refunding. For example, CPS privately placed $500 million of its MARS with Dexia Bank. The private placement allowed for CPS to shift indexes on which the interest rates it pays are based and also to change the remarketing modes (Shields, 2008). This essentially allowed CPS to convert $500 million of MARS debt to variable rate debt based on a negotiated spread to SIFMA. This allowed the issuer to eliminate its exposure to the auction rate market, keep its debt in a variable rate mode and hopefully avail itself of the historical benefit of variable rate debt, and avoid having to procure a difficult to obtain and costly liquidity facility. While this may have been the most optimal restructuring solution, limited appetite by most banks made this solution unavailable to most issuers.

Even after employing the aforementioned approaches in restructuring their MARS portfolios, state and local governments were still reeling from the effects of the MARS market collapse. The most obvious effect relates to the threat of rollover risk associated with near-term expiring liquidity facilities and FRN maturities as discussed above. A more subtle impact associated with the disappearance of the MARS market relates to the incongruity between security maturity length preferences of buyers and sellers of municipal securities. That is, most retail investors of tax-exempt bonds prefer short and intermediate term bonds, whereas state and local governments favor long-term debt due to the long-lived assets such as bonds finance. ARS and VRDOs were a means of crafting a financial instrument that fitted the goals of investors and issuers alike: long-dated securities with short-term pricing for issuers and liquidity for investors. There is some evidence to show that the collapse of the MARS market may lead to higher borrowing costs for state and local governments. Specifically, in the absence of the MARS option, subnational governments will be forced to sell long-dated fixed rate bonds to investors who clearly prefer short-term maturities, and, thus, these bond buyers will demand a substantial risk premium for making such concession (Seymour, 2010a).

5. LESSONS LEARNED FOR FUTURE PUBLIC FINANCIAL MANAGEMENT PRACTICES

The failure of the auction rate market provides an opportunity to pause and reflect on the policies and administrative practices that have developed over the last 35 years or so in the municipal securities market. The modern municipal market is not only a larger and more diverse marketplace; it is also a much more complex place where fragile webs of complex contractual arrangements lie just beneath the surface. While the market has survived numerous singular crises over the last 30 or so years (New York City, Orange County, etc.), never has a sector of the market collapsed so abruptly and permanently. Below we provide some lessons learned for subnational government officials to help establish better frameworks and practices to balance the inherent tension between efficiency, risk-taking, and market stability associated with capital market financial innovations.

5.1 Short-Term Securities Should Not be Viewed as Long-Term Securities

Since the 1980s financial market participants (underwriters, rating agencies, issuers, etc.) have willingly engaged in the illusion that securities with a long-term final maturity date but interest rate resets at short-term intervals are long-term securities. They are not. The most immediate component of risk is short-term with the setting and resetting of the interest rate. This is short-term risk and it is more a function of liquidity risk than credit risk, and should be viewed as such by all market participants. Long-term credit ratings and bond insurance provide signals regarding credit and default risk, not liquidity risk. This lesson was succinctly stated by the Federal Reserve Bank of Chicago:

> Auction rate securities represented an ingenious attempt to square a particular financial circle: to create a funding instrument that appears long term from the borrower's perspective but short-term from the lender's perspective. We now see what should have been obvious before: Such an arrangement is impossible. If a funding instrument is long term for one party, it must also be long term for another party; any appearance to the contrary must be an illusion. (D'Silva et al., 2008).

5.2 Never Take Liquidity and Financial Market Stability for Granted

Participants on all sides of the auction rate securities market believed that the auction market would always remain liquid – sufficient cash would be available to ensure a successful auction. They were wrong! The credit markets seized and investors and investment banks didn't have the cash to bid on securities, bondholders could not liquidate their investments, and issuers were stuck paying the maximum interest rate. The liquidity premium can be expected to be the highest when you need liquidity the most. Financial markets will not always be strong and stable, and issuers should prepare for times of fragility and uncertainty.

5.3 Financial Intermediary Risk is Real

An implicit assumption underlying much of the success of many financial innovations over the last three decades, such as derivatives, swaps and bond insurance, was that large investment banks, commercial banks and bond insurers were 'too big' to fail. Clearly we all know now that such a notion is incorrect. Financial promises to pay are only as good as the financial viability of the entity making the promise. No institution is too big to fail 'on you'.

5.4 Shift Risks Permanently, not Temporarily

Make sure risks transferred at the time of sale stay shifted throughout the life of the contract. If you transfer a form of risk (i.e. interest rate risk) at the beginning, make sure it stays transferred until final maturity. Risks shifted only temporarily are likely to revert squarely back on your shoulders at the least opportune time.

5.5 Take Contracts Verbatim and Craft Bond Indentures with Flexibility

Do not agree to contract terms you don't understand or are told will never materialize. Public managers are responsible for understanding the contracts they sign. If there is a provision in the debt indenture that is not under your control, and if exercised will be especially harmful to you, do not agree to it. Agree to contract terms that you have control over. Do not believe anybody when they say, 'We know that this provision is harmful to you, but don't worry, it will never be exercised.' If that's the case, then tell them not to put it in the contract in the first place. The collapse of the MARS market and the challenges public financial managers faced in reducing their exposure to this market show the benefit of crafting contracts and bond indentures that provide for a reasonable amount of flexibility should dramatic changes occur in the market.

5.6 Utilize Independent Financial Consultants Before Utilizing Complex Financial Innovations

Anecdotal evidence seems to indicate that many state and local governments relied too heavily on the advice of their underwriters in deciding to sell MARS (Preston, 2011). Based on recent lawsuits and legal settlements, it appears that these vendors were often not forthright about the risks associated with MARS to both the buyers and sellers of these securities. While there is no guarantee that independent financial advisors would have necessarily advised against the sale of such instruments, the use of these types of consultants at least theoretically serves as a 'check' on the 'advice' given by bond underwriters. Ideally, such financial advisors would be compensated on a retainer basis as opposed to being paid based on the execution of the transaction, which, unfortunately, is often common in the municipal securities market. The interests of the municipal financial advisor must be aligned as closely to its principal as possible in order to receive advice that is as uncompromised as possible. Retainer rather than transaction-based compensation arrangements would achieve this alignment best in the case of municipal financial advisors.

5.7 Analyze the Efficacy and Risks of Innovative Financial Instruments Regularly

Public scrutiny of the decisions made by subnational government public financial managers is often non-existent given the lack of transparency and understanding of the municipal securities market and the various financial instruments such as MARS, derivatives, VRDOs and so on, that compose this market. Oftentimes, these decisions only get evaluated when it is too late, such as when a dramatic market event occurs as was the case with the collapse of the MARS market. With the MSRB's introduction of the Electronic Municipal Market Access system (EMMA), a comprehensive, centralized online source for free access to municipal disclosures, and market transparency data and educational materials about the municipal securities market, such evaluations and analyses should be more timely and robust. Post-bond sale examinations should be routinized so that stakeholders, including the public at large, are regularly made aware of the various risks to the financial stability of the state or local government associated with various capital market positions. Such disclosure of the sizable exposure of many state and local governments to the MARS market may have led some of these governments to reduce their positions in these securities prior to the market collapse.

6. SUMMARY

The task of effectively and efficiently managing subnational financial resources has become more important and more complicated in recent decades so financial managers have increasingly looked to financial innovations to meet resource challenges. One such innovation, municipal auction rate securities, had been used more and more by governments over the last few decades to finance their capital activities more efficiently. However, the sub-prime mortgage market crisis, which extended into the municipal bond market in 2007 and 2008, severely impacted the municipal auction rate securities market to the detriment of many state and local governments.

The birth, growth and collapse of the municipal auction rate securities market provides a lens to view what we have learned from the recent Financial Crisis about subnational government financial innovation. This chapter offers some specific suggestions for government financial administrators to help them balance this tension between efficiency and risk-taking as it relates to markets, financial contracts, risk-shifting, and debt security features. The conclusion from our analysis is not that public financial managers should be unnecessarily conservative in their financial management of public resources but that innovative financial products and approaches need to be completely understood by public managers and their risks fully accounted for before taxpayer resources are placed at risk.

NOTES

1. This chapter is based on the unpublished paper by Craig L. Johnson and Martin J. Luby, 'The Birth, Growth and Collapse of the Municipal Auction Rate Securities Market', 23 December 2011.
2. Bergstresser et al. (2011) provide an excellent case study of the SEC's lawsuit against UBS related to its activities in the municipal auction rate securities market.
3. We characterize the MARS interest rate resetting process as 'mostly successful' because while auctions were generally successful, the SEC did fine 15 broker-dealer firms over $13 million in penalties for securities law violations in their conduct of MARS auctions. See United States Securities and Exchange Commission (2006).
4. The variable rate demand obligation (VRDO) market has also declined since the MARS collapse but not nearly as much as the MARS market. In the first five months of 2010, monthly VRDO trading volume and trades averaged $123.4 billion and 20 644, whereas in 2008 the trading volume and trades averaged $200.4 billion and 69 514 per month (Municipal Securities Rulemaking Board, 2010).
5. As McConnell and Saretto (2010) empirically demonstrate, however, MARS yields were significantly higher than traditional cash-equivalent securities.
6. In general, the Dutch auction process begins with the auction agent asking a high price and then reducing the price until a bidder emerges. For MARS, a modified Dutch auction process is used whereby the auction agent receives orders to sell and orders to buy and determines the lowest interest rate at which all of the securities will find a buyer: this interest rate is known as the 'clearing rate'.
7. McConnell and Saretto (2010) show that most auction failures were associated with MARS containing floating (not fixed) maximum auction rates. Investors in those cases probably viewed themselves as better off letting the auction fail, and receiving the higher maximum default rate specified in the indenture, rather than the lower, maximum floating reset rate.

12. Enhancing municipal credit

Often issuers (and sometimes underwriters in competitive bid sales) purchase private, third-party credit enhancement or participate in credit 'pooling' programs for their bonds. Individual investors may also purchase separately credit enhancement (usually bond insurance) from private firms to protect their investments. In private credit enhancement contracts, a bond becomes 'wrapped' by the financial guarantee of a bond insurance firm or a bank. When this happens, the issuers are said to 'lease' the creditworthiness of the credit guarantor or liquidity support provider. Current evidence suggests that credit enhancements lower issuer borrowing costs, provide additional repayment security, and send an important signal to financial markets, all of which improve liquidity and pricing in secondary market trades.

This chapter primarily discusses bond insurance – the most widespread form of private third-party credit enhancement for municipal bonds. Though the bond insurance industry is a much smaller version of the industry that existed prior to the meltdown during the Great Recession, it still remains the only feasible credit enhancement option for most credit classes. Alternative credit enhancement mechanisms such as state sponsored credit pools[1] or bank letters of credit are generally reserved for only the strongest credit quality issuers or shorter-term obligations. We provide a discussion of current empirical evidence on the role of bond insurance in the municipal market, the bond industry regulatory framework and risk exposures, and the uses of bond insurance.

1. BACKGROUND ON ENHANCING CREDIT

For over three decades, since the inception of the municipal bond insurance industry with the establishment of the American Municipal Bond Assurance Corporation (AMBAC) in 1971, bond insurance has been by far the most widespread form of credit enhancement in the municipal market. Prior to the Great Recession, as shown in Figure 12.1, more than half of municipal bonds were 'wrapped' by guaranties from mostly triple-A rated bond insurance firms.

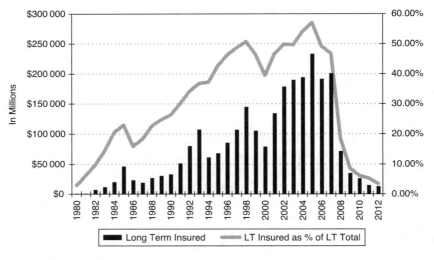

Source: Thomson Reuters.

*Figure 12.1   Municipal bond insurance volume and market penetration,
1980–2012*

The Great Recession, however, brought the meltdown of the entire bond
insurance industry and catastrophic change to the industry. The two lone
survivors of the 2008/2009 meltdown – Assured Guaranty Corporation
(AGC) and Financial Security Assurance (FSA) – consolidated in 2010
to create in essence a duopoly of the municipal bond insurance guarantee under one roof. In addition to US municipal bonds, the former (still
Assured Guaranty Corporation or AGC) currently insures structured
financial products globally, while the latter (now Assured Guaranty
Municipal or AGM) has only insured municipal bonds since the merger,
including municipal issues in countries abroad. The parent company for
both AGC and AGM – Assured Guaranty Ltd – set up a third insurance
firm called Municipal Assurance Corporation (MAC) in the summer of
2013 to insure exclusively US domestic subnational debt. These three
municipal bond insurance arms of Assured Guaranty Ltd were rated AA-
by Standard & Poor's in July 2013. The current municipal bond industry
landscape is dramatically different from the one dominated by several
triple-A rated firms prior to the Great Recession.

New entrants into the market have attempted to operate in the municipal bond insurance market. Berkshire Hathaway Assurance Corporation
(BHAC) was established in December 2007 to mitigate the bond insurance
industry's complete collapse. The firm started off slowly in 2008, mostly

reinsuring the portfolios of fallen firms, but through to 2012 still had underwritten very little business. In the summer of 2012, Build America Mutual (BAM) was launched to help fill the void left after the Great Recession. This firm was fully endorsed by the National League of Cities (NLC), which was concerned about limited credit enhancement mechanisms available to US cities of all sizes since the Financial Crisis (Cusick, 2012). Of the nine major monoline insurance firms that existed prior to the crisis, seven discontinued writing bond insurance contracts (ACA, Ambac, CIFG, FGIC, MBIA, Radian and XLCA) and are facing bankruptcy, regulatory administration, legal challenges, commutation disputes or reorganization. It is still unclear as to which of these firms, if any, will be able to rejoin the bond insurance industry.

Another form of credit enhancement involves bank letters of credit (that generally provide credit support) or 'stand-by' liquidity facilities (that generally provide liquidity support). Historically, letters of credit were mostly used for short-term debt obligations or variable rate municipal securities. However, two factors are likely to diminish the availability and use of letters of credit by municipal issuers. The first is the shrinking of the variable rate municipal market. Also, while municipalities continue to borrow for short-term purposes, short-term debt is a small fraction of the overall municipal debt market and is likely to remain so. As seen in Figure 12.2, short-term debt has remained at about 10–12 percent of the overall municipal debt market for the past several decades. Moreover, short-term debt is unlikely to solve the demand for municipal infrastructure projects that predominantly have multi-year horizons. At the same time, not all short- or long-term debt is necessarily protected by a letter of credit. Figure 12.3 shows that generally less than $20 billion was guaranteed by stand-by liquidity facilities until the mid-2000s.[2] This has changed dramatically since then, especially during the Great Recession when $77 billion was guaranteed by letters of credit in the municipal market in 2008. This volume has shrunk significantly to less than 2 percent of total municipal market penetration.

The second, perhaps more important reason, is a significant reporting change that banks are now facing after the Great Recession. The SEC writes in its 2012 report on the municipal securities market that banks are now required to maintain full liquidity coverage on their letter of credit lines. This may increase the costs of letters of credit or steer banks to more lucrative capital market products. Changes in banking regulations in Europe and the US are likely to require that commercial and investment banks show liquidity risk exposure on their accounting books. Therefore, stand-by liquidity facilities would now need to absorb the increased costs due to such extra capital requirements.

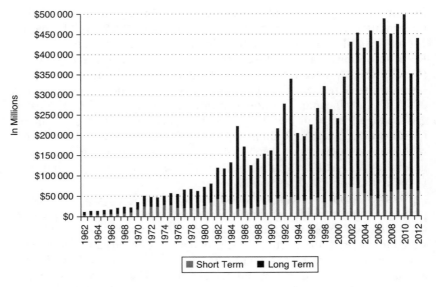

Source: Board of Governors, Federal Reserve.

Figure 12.2   Municipal short- and long-term debt issuance, 1962–2012

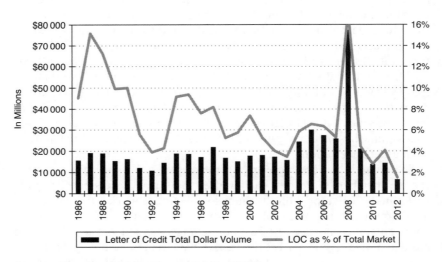

Source: *Bloomberg*; Moldogaziev and Johnson (2011).

*Figure 12.3   Letter of credit total municipal market dollar volume and
            market penetration, 1986–2012*

Finally, individual states may set up mechanisms to provide credit enhancement to their municipalities, such as credit pools or bond banks. However, these tend to be limited to certain purposes, such as school district infrastructure financing or transportation-related credit banks. In other words, the pools will be targeted at certain narrow policy areas. This may not give much flexibility to municipal issuers if their projects are outside of the selected areas. Moreover, states may have high entrance thresholds to their bond banks or credit pools, barring access to lower rated municipalities. In addition, unlike bond insurance, these tools are state-specific and are not sheltered from political and managerial interference from state authorities.

2.   BOND INSURANCE

Municipal bond insurance is a third-party guarantee by a private firm to pay coupon interest and principal on the insured bonds if the issuer fails to make timely payments. The standard insurance contract is irrevocable, unconditional and extends for the life of the insured bonds. The insurer guarantees to make principal and coupon interest payments to bondholders as they are scheduled to come due, and the payments remain tax-exempt and may not be legally accelerated. Most municipal bond insurance contracts are paid for at the time of sale by the issuer or underwriter in the form of an up-front premium. As such, the insured municipal borrowers would traditionally 'lease' the credit ratings of bond insurers for the duration of the contract.

Prior to the Great Recession, seven out of nine bond insurance firms were rated triple-A by Standard & Poor's (S&P), Moody's and Fitch. Ambac was by far the largest market leader in 2007, with firms such as MBIA, FSA and FGIC trailing it significantly as seen in Figure 12.4. The remaining two firms – ACA and Radian – specialized in niche sectors such as hospital, utility and other special-purpose debt issues and were rated single-A and double-A respectively by S&P before the recession in 2007.

Insured bonds, however, were not always rated triple-A. Bonds insured by MBIA have always been assigned triple-A ratings by S&P, but bonds insured by Ambac before 1979 received only double-A ratings from S&P. With improved claim-paying ability from the establishment of reinsurance support, S&P assigned triple-A ratings to the debt insured by Ambac. Before June 1984, Moody's Investors Service assigned ratings to insured debt based on only the intrinsic credit quality of the issuer, not the insurer. Hence, insured bonds came to the market from 1979–83 with a split-rating:

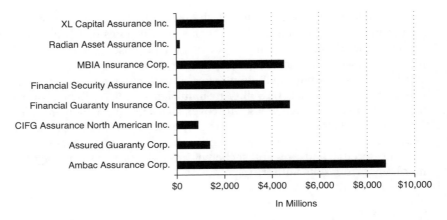

Source: Moldogaziev (2012).

Figure 12.4   Insured dollar volume by municipal bond insurance firms,
*   2007*

triple-A rating from S&P and a lower intrinsic rating from Moody's. Since
June 1984 insured bonds have carried the credit rating of the insurer for
both Moody's and Standard & Poor's. Therefore, the value of the guarantee was believed to be primarily, if not solely, based on the guarantor's
ability and willingness to pay in response to a default.

S&P started assigning intrinsic issuer ratings on insured bonds in 1995.
They refer to them as SPURs (Standard & Poor's Underlying Ratings)
(Peng, 2002). Other rating agencies now also assign intrinsic or underlying ratings on insured bonds, and empirical studies suggest that investors
use the underlying rating along with the insurer's rating in pricing bonds
(Peng, 2002). As the market became familiar with SPURs and underlying
ratings from other rating agencies, bond offering documents began carry-
ing underlying ratings along with the insurer's rating.

3.   EVIDENCE ON THE BOND INSURANCE NET
       BENEFIT

Most empirical bond insurance studies focus on the difference in interest
cost (TIC or NIC) between insured bonds and non-insured bonds rather
than the insurance premium (Joehnk and Minge, 1976; Cole and Officer,
1981; Braswell et al., 1982; Bland, 1987; Hsueh and Chandy, 1989; Hsueh
and Liu, 1990). Early research on bond insurance focused on the question

of whether or not bond insurance provided issuers with a net interest cost benefit and they found mixed results. Two empirical studies, Forbes and Hopewell (1976) and Braswell et al. (1982), for example, showed no positive benefit from bond insurance.

On the other hand, studies by Joehnk and Minge (1976) and Cole and Officer (1981) showed a net interest cost benefit from the purchase of bond insurance. They also determined that insurance guaranties were most efficient for lower rated municipalities. These studies further concluded that insurance remained beneficial regardless of economic volatility. Joehnk and Minge (1976, pp. 14–15) concluded that: 'The historical performance of guaranteed bonds suggests that the market recognizes enhancement of agency ratings, due to the addition of the guarantee, as a reflection of improved investment quality.' None of the above studies, however, explicitly analyzed bond insurance premiums.

The study by Kidwell et al. (1987) was the first to explicitly analyze bond insurance premiums as a component of the issuer's borrowing costs. Using a sample of 398 MBIA insured bonds sold from 1975–80, they found that most insured issues (except Aa rated bonds) did receive a net benefit. The reduction in NIC was greater than the cost of insurance. Furthermore, the net benefit to the issuer generally increased as the credit quality of the bond issue decreased. They concluded that either the presence of insurance enhanced market efficiency, or insurance companies, have, on average, set premiums too low. In their sample of MBIA bonds, however, the insurance premium did not vary monotonically over the rating distribution. According to the authors, it is 'evidence that MBIA and Moody's diverge in their estimates of default risk for insured issues'.

Kidwell et al. (1987) reported in their sample that the average premium was 11.7 basis points. Smith and Harper (1993) used a sample of 219 insured bonds sold in Florida from 1990–92 and found an average insurance premium of 6.58 basis points, a significant drop from what Kidwell et al. (1987) reported on MBIA-insured bonds sold from 1975–80. For a sample of 720 bonds sold in California from 2001–05, Liu (2012) found the average reported insurance premium was 3.72 basis points, which is 43.4 percent less than the 6.58 percent reported by Smith and Harper (1993) and 68.2 percent less than the premium reported by Kidwell et al. (1987). Moldogaziev and Johnson (2011) reported that insurance premiums grew from 4.1 basis points in 2008 to 29.8 basis points in 2009 for a sample of city and county bond issuers in Texas.

Average bond insurance premiums have decreased significantly over the years from the 1980s to 2007, but grew significantly in 2009. The insurance premium across underlying credit rating categories has changed as well. We can compare the Kidwell et al. (1987), Liu (2012), and Moldogaziev and

Johnson (2011) studies to get an idea of changes in the insurance premium credit spread from 1975 to 2005. The range in premiums across the first study and the latter two studies is stark. In Liu (2012), insured bonds with an underlying rating of AA have an average insurance premium of 1.89 bps and BBB+ and below bonds an insurance premium of 8.31 bps. In contrast, Kidwell et al. (1987) report an average Aa premium of 10.0 bps and Baa premium of 12.7 bps. The Kidwell et al. (1987) spread is much less (2.7 bps to 6.42 bps), indicating an increase in the overall premium rating spread over time. The majority of the change is from a steep premium drop on higher rated bonds.

Another distinction between Liu (2012), Moldogaziev and Johnson (2011), and Kidwell et al. (1987) is that in Liu (2012) the insurance premium is a strict increasing function of credit risk – as credit rating decreases, the insurance premium increases. In Moldogaziev and Johnson (2011) and Kidwell et al. (1987) it is not, since some higher rated bonds have higher insurance premiums than Baa1 bonds. Hence, from the data in Liu (2012) the function appears to be monotonic, whereas in Kidwell et al. (1987) it does not, and the break in the lower risk/lower premium relationship is between Baa1 and A rated bonds.

Moldogaziev and Johnson (2011) find consistent evidence that the choice of bond insurance and the size of insurance premiums contain information on the *ex ante*, intrinsic risk of the insured issuer. This has important public policy implications. Bond insurance information is not readily available in the market because it is not consistently disclosed in itemized detail at issuance like bank underwriting spreads and other issuance costs.[3] Bond insurance premium information is important to the marketplace and should be disclosed on every bond issue in the official prospectus. Disclosing bond insurance premium information has the potential to make the municipal market more transparent and efficient since it provides a distinct perspective on the differential risk of the insured debt. Furthermore, Moldogaziev and Johnson (2011) find that the Financial Crisis has had a significant effect on the utilization of bond insurance and the size of insurance premiums. The number of insured issues in their sample dropped 49 percent from 2007 to 2008 and another 46 percent from 2008 to 2009; while the insurance premium increased dramatically from 2007 to 2008, and was well over double the previous high in 2005. As a result, they argue that the Great Recession has left a smaller, and more costly, municipal bond insurance market in its wake.

Denison (2001) builds on empirical research on municipal bond insurance by evaluating the association between aggregate quarterly insured municipal bond volumes and risk premiums. Using the theory of market segmentation, he finds that the supply side of the market has a significant association with the yield differential between triple-A vs. Baa securities. Denison concludes that his

> results demonstrate that ceteris paribus, a 1% increase in the percentage of new issue municipal bonds using insurance decrease the average yield spread ratio by nearly 0.01. A 0.01 decrease in the spread ratio combined with a yield of 6% on Aaa bonds translates to a reduction in the yield spread differential of approximately six basis points. (Denison, 2001, p. 407).

Bond insurance, Denison (2009) states, provides the municipal bond market with high investment grade securities while the supply of natural, high investment grade securities is limited.

Nanda and Singh (2004) also find that bond insurance provides greatest benefits for the lowest rated municipal bond issuers. More importantly, they argue that bond insurance provides tax arbitrage in case of a default by the issuer of a tax-exempt bond. Municipal bond investors demand securities with a tax-exempt status. Nanda and Singh (2004) state that the tax arbitration powers of municipal bond insurance are of particular significance for longer-duration bonds. Indeed, it is common practice for municipalities to issue debt broken down into a number of serial bonds, where the series with the longer maturities, generally greater than 10 years, are 'wrapped' by bond insurance. These authors argue that by agreeing to insure a bond, the insurance firms act as 'co-issuers' of tax-exempt securities. In other words, insurance firms become suppliers of tax-exempt bonds for the remaining maturities when municipalities default on their debt. Nanda and Singh (2004), similar to Kidwell et al. (1987) and Moldogaziev and Johnson (2011), find that the distribution of bond insurance in the municipal bond market is not monotonic. Only a small number of very high- and very low-rated bonds are 'wrapped' by bond insurance in their sample of municipal bonds. Most bond insurance, they discover, involves debt rated with the double-A to triple-B range of credit quality.

A number of studies have also assessed the role of bond insurance in secondary trades. Bond insurance, via its credit enhancement role, is generally expected to improve bond liquidity and price discovery. It is also said that bond insurers play an important monitoring role and serve as an extra quality signaling tool in the market. Green et al. (2007) have found that insured bonds tend to result in higher gross mark-ups for informed institutional investors but lower gross mark-ups for relatively uninformed retail investors. Another study by Green et al. (2010) discovered that insured bonds tend to depress ask- and bid-side half spreads. Marlowe (2007) and Moldogaziev et al. (2013) find that bond insurance decreases reoffering yields. At the same time, Harris and Piwowar (2006) and Hong and Warga (2004) suggest that bond insurance is positively associated with transaction costs and effective bid–ask spreads. Therefore, bond insurance is very rarely insignificant in empirical studies and it has important effects on both liquidity and price discovery.

4. BOND INSURANCE INDUSTRY REGULATION

Every state has its own regulatory environment that governs municipal bond insurance. Though the 1986 'Financial Guaranty Insurance Model Act' of the National Association of Insurance Commissioners (NAIC) calls for harmonization of monoline industry regulation in the US states, significant variation still remains (Moldogaziev, 2013; Drake and Neale, 2011; Perkins and Quinn, 2001). In order to write business, insurance firms have to register and become licensed in the state in which they want to operate. Perkins and Quinn (2001) have reviewed insurance industry laws in the US states and provided details for select states that had one of the largest volumes of insured bonds. They argue that of all the states, the New York insurance department (NYID) is the de facto monoline insurance industry regulator. They draw upon the Appleton Rule of 1989 in Article 69 of 'Financial Guaranty Insurance Corporations' (FGICs) that requires any bond insurance firm wishing to operate in the State of New York to abide by the rules of the state. This rule does not consider the domicile status of insurance firms. Furthermore, bond insurance companies were required to remain 'monoline' within the definition adopted by the State of New York. As such, if a bond insurance firm operating in New York wrote multiline business outside of New York it would lose its license in the State of New York (e.g. §6904 Article 69; and Drake and Neale, 2011). Moldogaziev (2013) argues that since all of the firms in the bond insurance industry operated in New York, the insurance department of the State of New York was de facto the main regulator of the industry prior to the Great Recession.

However, it appears that the definition of 'monoline' was fairly broad as reflected in New York's insurance department rules. Moldogaziev (2013) and Drake and Neale (2011) question whether insurance contracts in structured finance products in asset backed securities, and investments in these products, were justifiably similar to the risks in the municipal bond market. It is now clear that the non-municipal finance portion of the portfolios of bond insurance firms (Moldogaziev, 2013), as well as their asset investment decisions (Drake and Neale, 2011), exposed the municipal bond insurance industry to risks that led to its meltdown in 2008. Moldogaziev (2013) writes about the increased exposure to non-public finance risks in monoline portfolios and notes that:

Article 69 defines monoline beyond the municipal bond market securities and includes a variety of asset-backed securities (ABSs) and collateralized debt obligations (CDOs). Consequently, Article 69 permits industry exposure to risks beyond the traditional municipal bond market and widens the definition of monoline to include structured non-municipal finance products. In 1997, monoline firms received permission to underwrite credit default swaps (CDS) based on the opinion of New York Department of Insurance subject to a few relaxed rules [see NY Circular Letter No. 19, 2008, p. 6; Drake and Neale, 2011, p. 34]. (This line of business was also becoming a staple product of the mainstream multi-line insurance firms.) Finally, insurance guaranties for CDO-squared products were permitted in 2004. (p. 210).

States generally require capital reserves or 'collateral' for bond insurance firms based on levels and types of risk in their insured portfolios. These capital reserves must provide sufficient liquidity to cover potential claims should the underwritten entities default on their obligations. Hence, the requirements are based on the default assumptions on underwritten securities. Table 12.1 shows the levels of statutory capital requirements for the top four bond insurance firms, who amongst themselves had accounted for over 80 percent of all insured municipal bonds in the US. This period covers the decade preceding the Great Recession. These municipal industry leaders had statutory reserves that were around (sometimes below) 1 percent of total insured exposures. Their total insured exposures, however, did not consist solely of municipal bond insurance contracts. As discussed in the sections below, municipal insurance firms were also insuring non-municipal finance and non-domestic securities, for which statutory reserve requirements should have been more stringent.

Table 12.1   Statutory capital reserve requirements, top-four firms, 1998–2008

Year	AMBAC	FSA	FGIC	MBIA
1998	0.81	0.99	1.44	1.04
1999	0.88	1.02	1.45	1.08
2000	0.86	0.93	1.27	1.08
2001	0.86	0.73	1.12	1.09
2002	0.88	0.71	1.09	1.09
2003	0.99	0.71	0.89	1.12
2004	1.15	0.70	0.85	1.02
2005	1.18	0.69	0.80	1.12
2006	1.23	0.68	0.80	1.06
2007	1.22	0.63	0.27	0.94
2008	0.80	0.47	0.62	0.07

Source: Form SEC-10K and quarterly financial reports.

Prior to the Great Recession, the State of New York required minimum capital of $75 million and a policyholders' surplus equal to $65 million for monoline firms to maintain their business operations and license. NY Circular Letter No. 19 (New York Insurance Department, 2008) describes statutory capital requirements in the following manner:

> 'Capital' is defined by Insurance Law § 107(a)(12) to mean, when used in reference to a stock insurance company, the aggregate par value of all classes of shares of capital stock issued and outstanding. 'Surplus to Policyholders' is defined by Insurance Law § 107(a)(42) to mean the excess of total admitted assets over the liabilities of an insurer, which is the sum of all capital and surplus accounts minus any impairment thereof. (p. 4).

Furthermore, Section 6903 (paragraphs 1 to 4) in Article 69 specifies contingency reserves, in addition to excess capital and surplus to policyholders' rules. For public finance securities portfolio exposure, the range of contingency reserves is 0.55–2.5 percent depending on risk category, as measured by credit quality. In terms of structured finance securities portfolio exposure, the range of contingency reserves is 1–2.5 percent. While it appears that structured finance products are assumed to be riskier, the contingency reserves certainly fall far short of the actual rate of defaults in structured finance products such as mortgage and other non-public finance asset-backed securities. According to Standard & Poor's (2012a), default rates for triple-A structured finance were 1.89 percent and 0.85 percent in 2008 and 2009 respectively. At the same time, default rates for investment grade structured finance were 6.26 percent and 8.24 percent during the same years. Finally, speculative grade structured finance defaults were 16.25 percent and 56.03 percent respectively in 2008 and 2009. These two years also coincide with the complete collapse of the bond insurance industry due to insured risk exposures (Moldogaziev, 2013) and the decision to invest in structured products by bond insurance firms (Drake and Neale, 2011).

Certainly, many have argued that the true levels of risk in structured securities were misunderstood even by the most able analysts because these products were very new. Indeed, a study before the Financial Crisis by Lucas et al. (2004) reported on levels of historic defaults in structured finance products, finding they were comparable to municipal market default rates. The term 'historic' though is somewhat problematic as the structured finance securities were relatively new and not well known to many capital market participants, and they had not been tested through major economic upheavals such as the Great Depression. Klein (2009) argues that when the nature of investment products is unknown due to 'newness' in the market, statutory requirements initially must be very conservative. While average statutory requirements may have been satisfied by the bond insurance firms, as evidenced in Table 12.1, it is still hard to understand why structured financial products were assumed to have levels of risk similar to public finance products. Therefore, the definition of 'monoline insurer' was clearly overstretched beyond its original meaning. This situation creates a paradoxical situation where one fiscal sovereign, that is the State of New York Insurance Department, was de facto responsible for regulating the bond insurance industry in the US. The SEC became more interested in the insured portfolios of monoline firms after the Great Recession through greater regulation of derivative securities. This action enhances the federal government's role by regulating one aspect of the portfolio of municipal bond insurance firms, but does not further strengthen or change the overall role of the states in regulating the monoline industry.

5. RISK EXPOSURE OF BOND INSURANCE FIRMS

In the mid-1990s bond insurers diversified their insured portfolios away from municipal finance products to mortgage- and collateralized asset-backed securities (Moldogaziev, 2013). Bond insurers also appear to have kept their investment capital in mortgage- and asset-backed securities (Drake and Neal, 2011). Therefore, the risk exposure of monoline firms was both in their insured portfolios and investment portfolios. With the meltdown on mortgage and structured finance markets during the Great Recession, seven out of nine existing bond insurance firms failed.

Prior to the industry's collapse in 2007, almost 60 percent of long-term municipal bonds coming to the market were insured. The deterioration of the bond insurance industry caught many people by surprise. Markets were extremely confident in the financial soundness of monoline firms. For example, bond insurance experts Godfrey and York wrote that:

> Insured bonds seem to have suffered unfairly from various degrees of skepticism about their ability to perform as well as natural Triple-A's. For example, they have endured the capital-adequacy allegation that insurers do not have sufficient resources to meet their obligations when the economic chips are down. [. . .] Insured bonds are even stronger than natural Triple-A's because of the extra measure of protection. [. . .] We proved that by applying *severe economic pressure* to both naturals and insured bonds. A diversified portfolio of natural Triple-A bonds probably would not make it through a Great Depression without defaults. Insured bonds, on the other hand, should do so without any ultimate defaults. (Godfrey and York, 1994, p. 124, italics added).

Even credit rating agencies stood by the bond insurance firms as late as October 2007 and maintained triple-A ratings with stable outlooks for most of the insurance firms (Green and Smith, 2007, 29 October). Only a few months later, the bond insurance industry went through the most catastrophic events in the history of monoline insurance. What explains the incongruence between expectations and actual events? Moldogaziev (2013) reports that scholarly research on bond insurance firms was mostly concentrated on the public finance side of the bond insurance business (Justice and Simon, 2002; Godfrey and York, 1994; Satz and Perry, 1992; Feldstein, 1983). Prior to the Great Recession, only Hirtle (1987) and Kotecha (1998) even mentioned anything about the structured finance exposure in bond insurance firm portfolios.

This lack of empirical attention is puzzling as the financial industry was aware of structured finance insurance contracts that municipal bond insurance firms were involved in well in advance of the Great Recession. Greenwald reported in a business insurance practitioners' periodical that in the first three quarters of 1999 'bond insurers guaranteed $104 billion in asset- and mortgage-backed securities, collateralized bond and loan obligations, and international transactions; compared with the $95 billion insured in the municipal market' (2000, p. 3). Since the mid-1990s to 2007, 'anywhere between 10%–50% of total insured portfolios of financial guarantee firms were in the structured finance products at any given time'(Moldogaziev, 2013, p. 202). One could multiply (1) the proportions of insured structured finance portfolios of monoline firms reported in Moldogaziev (2013), and (2) the proportions of investments in structured finance securities by monoline firms discussed in Drake and Neale (2011), by the default rates in structured finance securities reported by Standard & Poor's (2012a) and see why the entire muni bond industry collapsed in 2008.

6.   DOES THE MARKET NEED BOND INSURANCE?

Bond insurance became a fundamental part of the municipal securities market in the 1980s. The annual use of insurance on long-term bonds went from 6 percent in 1981 to 22 percent in 1988 to a peak of 57 percent in 2005, prior to the recent Financial Crisis. It plunged to 18.52 percent in 2008 and stood at 6.20 percent in 2010. In 2010, the two arms of Assured Guaranty insured about 1700 issues, a combined volume of about $27 billion. Since 2010, bond insurance has remained around 5 percent of total newly issued long-term bonds. The 2007/08 Financial Crisis is a major turning point in the history of the municipal bond insurance industry. In light of these recent trends, a natural question is whether the municipal securities market requires such high levels of bond insurance, now or in the future.

There are several factors that will keep bond insurance important to municipal issuers. It is still the only third-party long-term guarantee that a municipality can purchase from the private sector. It is unlikely that the volume of insured bonds will be anywhere near the levels prior to the Great Recession when more than half of the new issues arrived to the market 'wrapped' by monoline guarantee. Nevertheless, S&P reports that 2013 is likely to be a profitable year for existing and active bond insurance firms (S&P, 2012b). While the cost of bond insurance has significantly increased after the Great Recession (Moldogaziev and Johnson, 2011), an introduction of more competition in the industry and growth in insured volumes are likely to bring those costs down (S&P, 2012b).

The National League of Cities (NLC) recommended the creation of a mutual insurance company in 2008 amidst the bond insurance industry's meltdown. The logic in favor of such an entity was that many municipalities were unable to access capital markets without credit enhancement. In the end, NLC chose to endorse BAM as the bond insurer of choice. In return, BAM announced that it would stick to insuring only fixed rate domestic bonds and remain truly monoline. One of the fallen bond insurance firms – MBIA – has been attempting since 2009 to set up a uniquely US public finance firm by spinning off its domestic portfolio under a new arm called National Public Finance Guarantee Corporation (NPFG). Considering the low default rates of municipal issuers during the past several decades, such a monoline focus may help to stabilize the bond insurance industry in the long run.

Assured Guaranty Ltd, the biggest player in the bond insurance market in 2013 (dominant since 2009), has now set up a third arm, MAC, that exclusively insures domestic fixed income securities. However, Assured Guaranty Ltd continues to insure non-US public finance as well as non-public finance asset-backed securities, including structured finance securities originating outside the US. It does so through its two arms – AGM and AGC respectively. There is sufficient evidence today that asset-backed securities on average have default risks that greatly exceed the previously assumed default rates of 1–2.5 percent. S&P (2012b) reports that in 2009, 2010 and 2011 respectively about 16.63 percent, 10.77 percent and 12.27 percent of structured finance securities in the market have defaulted. Consequently, the statutory reserve requirements for structured finance products as well as international public finance products must be adjusted upwards in line with existing knowledge on recent default rates. Indeed, Rajan (2005) and Acharya et al. (2009) maintain that some products that municipal bond firms had been insuring prior to the Great Recession, such as credit default swaps (CDS), have elements of catastrophic risk events that are associated with severe losses. Therefore, products such as CDS could be regulated as catastrophic risk products and become the exclusive domain of catastrophic risk insurers, not municipal bond insurers.

Most importantly, we find that despite the significantly higher costs of bond insurance after the Great Recession (see Moldogaziev and Johnson, 2011), certain municipal issuers still appear to receive a net benefit from purchasing bond insurance. In this section we analyze a sample of over 800 competitively sold city and county debt issues for Texas municipalities during 2000–10. We first estimated the measure of insurance cost following the method in Kidwell et al. (1987). The insurance premium cost is estimated using equation (12.1).

$$Insurance\ Cost = \frac{Insurance\ Premium}{(Par\ Value\ of\ Issue) \times (Average\ Maturity\ of\ the\ Issue)}$$

(12.1)

Since bond insurance premiums are almost always paid up-front, this measure of insurance cost is also a present value cost of bond insurance. Information on bond insurance was collected from the Texas Bond Review Board. We then subtracted the bond insurance cost from individual issue true interest costs (TICs), which we obtained from IPREO.[4] This step provides the adjusted cost of borrowing, which excludes insurance cost. Kidwell et al. (1987) argued that issuers will purchase bond insurance if and only if the benefits of bond insurance are greater than the cost of such insurance. After subtracting the cost of bond insurance, we estimated a model of adjusted-TICs for a set of issue, issuer and market variables, which we collected from Bloomberg.

Figure 12.5 shows that significant benefits of bond insurance occurred for issuers rated between AA- and BB+; with the greatest benefits for A- and BBB+ rated bond issues. For an issuer with an average credit quality in the sample, which is a single-A rated city or county, there is a 10 basis point benefit from purchasing vs. not purchasing bond insurance, even after subtracting the cost of insurance. Therefore, in line with findings from extant research, our most recent empirical evidence suggests that, all else held equal, bond insurance is still beneficial to investment grade issuers below AA- (as well as BB+ rated issuers). Issuers rated AA (AA2) and above do not benefit from bond insurance. However, there appear to be non-monotonic benefits beyond the cost of insurance to single-A and BBB+ rated issuers, which Thakor (1982) attributed to the signaling informational role of bond insurance.

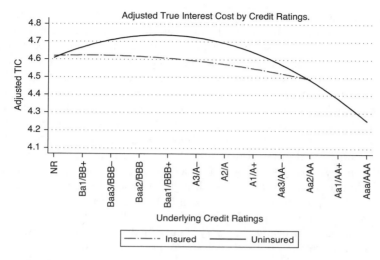

Source: Authors' estimates.

Figure 12.5   Benefits of bond insurance, Texas city and county issuers, 2000–10 (N = 816)

7.   SUMMARY

There are a number of tools that state and local governments can employ in order to enhance their credit and receive lower borrowing costs. Bond insurance is a third-party credit enhancement mechanism that is still available to municipal issuers despite the meltdown of the bond insurance industry during the Great Recession. Bond insurance market penetration since 2010 has remained at 6 percent or less, which is far lower than the 51 percent penetration in 2005. Nevertheless, bond insurance may be the only private party credit enhancement mechanism that many municipal issuers can turn to. At the same time, bond insurance costs have increased significantly since the Great Recession. It appears, however, that even with these higher insurance costs bond insurance remains beneficial to investment grade municipal bond issuers rated below AA-/Aa3 through to BBB-/Baa3.

With time more bond insurance firms may be established to join the few firms that have been operating since the Great Recession. A couple may even re-emerge from bankruptcy and vie for bond insurance business. But it is not likely that market penetration will return to pre-recession years, nor should it. If bond insurers are to remain truly monoline, then bond insurance costs should not be expected to drop significantly without the entry of new firms. In the past, monoline firms argued for non-public finance business because their earnings in the public finance sector were allegedly inadequate as insurance fees were relatively low. If, however, bond insurers continue insuring non-public finance securities, their capital reserve requirements must be adjusted to reflect much higher default rates in structured financial securities. Some sophisticated products that have features of catastrophic risk exposure, such as credit default swaps, may need to be banished from municipal bond insurance portfolios altogether.

Currently, existing bond insurance firms appear to be practicing self-regulation by mostly sticking to public finance insurance contracts. Self-regulation may not always work though. Individual states may need to exercise their powers of fiscal sovereignty to reign in the monoline insurance industry in the future. The de facto role of the State of New York as the major bond insurance industry regulator does not fit the traditional definition of autonomous 'fiscal sovereigns'. Other states clearly have a stake in the health of the municipal bond industry, and therefore they should not shirk their regulatory responsibilities. The enhancements in the Dodd–Frank Act as related to derivatives and structured financial securities favor a greater role for the federal government in monitoring financial intermediaries in the municipal bond market. This potential encroachment of federal regulators can only be at the expense of state fiscal sovereignty, however uncertain the final outcomes of such an infringement may be.

NOTES

1. Credit pools can also be set up and run by private entities. However, these privately run credit pools still may have stringent eligibility requirements allowing only the strongest credit quality issuers to join their pools.
2. It is not unusual to see debt issues with both a letter of credit and a stand-by credit facility.
3. Bond insurance premium information is not typically disclosed in the official statement with other issuance costs (i.e. credit ratings, attorneys, financial advisors, etc.). A few states, for example Texas, make bond insurance fees freely available to the public. But states such as these are exceptions rather than widespread occurrences.
4. IPREO is a company that provides a number of market-related data and services on the municipal market sector. More about this company and about the range of their services is available on their webpage: http://www.ipreo.com/home.

13. 'Non-traditional' capital financing mechanisms

This chapter details some of the evolving capital finance mechanisms beyond traditional municipal securities that subnational governments have begun to utilize in recent years. Given the sizeable capital needs at the subnational level, governments have turned to other 'innovative' financing strategies such as federal loans and credit support, public–private partnerships and infrastructure banks. The federal government has encouraged the use of these financial measures and made it easier and more attractive for subnational governments to use them as a way to more efficiently access capital. This chapter discusses these strategies in depth and details some of the trade-offs associated with their use especially as it relates to issues of fiscal federalism.

As described in previous chapters, state and local governments have historically funded their capital activities either on a pay-as-you-go basis or a pay-as-you-use basis. Pay-as-you-go refers to funding capital with government taxes and fees as such revenues are realized. Pay-as-you-use financing entails the use of debt finance in leveraging future fiscal resources for payment of capital costs in the current period. Historically, state and local governments employed debt finance via the selling of tax-exempt municipal bonds to raise capital on an up-front basis. These bonds were primarily repaid with the state or local government's own-source revenues. However, state and local governments have recently begun to turn to other 'non-traditional' financing mechanisms to raise capital for two distinct reasons. First, due to the dwindling resources for debt repayment and their overall weak creditworthiness, subnational governments have begun to exhaust their existing municipal debt capacity limiting their market access. Such capital market capacity depletion has forced some governments to look elsewhere beyond the municipal bond market for financing.

Second, state and local governments have begun to assess whether the traditional municipal bond financing mechanism is optimal in managing the risks of certain projects. That is, in a municipal bond financing, state and local governments bear all of the risk as it relates to the project's expected benefits, initial construction costs and ongoing capital and maintenance costs. Municipal bond investors do bear risk as it relates to the timely repayment of bond principal and interest but this risk is relatively muted given the historical scarcity of municipal bond defaults. Some claim that the private sector would be better at evaluating and bearing some of the afore-mentioned risks, which would justify greater levels of private sector involve-ment in the financing, constructing and operating of such capital projects. Given these two reasons, some state and local governments have begun to consider two general types of alternative financing mechanisms: (1) federal credit support and loans; and (2) public–private partnerships. Within these general types, there are various financing mechanism sub-types. Moreover, some governments have combined these two general non-traditional financ-ing mechanism types to more efficiently and effectively finance their infrastructure capital needs. The rest of this chapter details these non-traditional capital finance mechanisms and concludes with two case studies of government projects that have combined these financing approaches.

1.   FEDERAL CREDIT SUPPORT AND LOANS

Due to scarce resources for infrastructure projects at all levels of govern-ment in the United States, the federal government has tried to facilitate subnational capital-raising by offering loans and credit support for specific types of infrastructure projects. The Federal Highway Administration (FHWA) has taken the lead in these efforts through its Office of Innovative Program Delivery. From a financing perspective, the Federal Highway Administration provides various financing mechanisms designed to increase state and local governments' ability to deliver transportation projects, accelerate project construction and reduce project costs. These programs include Section 129 loans, state infrastructure banks, GARVEE bonds, private activity bonds and TIFIA loans.

Section 129 loans use federal-aid highway apportionments to fund loans for transportation projects. Since the starting repayment of the loan can be delayed up to five years, state governments can use the loans to complete construction of a project and delay repayment until revenues associated with the project are realized. However, there have been only two projects to date that have relied on Section 129 loans: (1) $135 million for President George Bush Turnpike in Dallas; and (2) $45 million for the Blue Water Bridge in the State of Michigan. State Infrastructure Banks (SIBs) also use federal-aid apportionments to establish a revolving infrastructure bank that provides low-cost loans and credit assistance for highway and transit projects. Once repayments are made back to the SIB, the bank then loans out those repayments to other government entities for infrastructure projects. As of September 2012, 32 states and territories have executed 700 SIB loan agreements for a total financing amount of $6.5 billion.

GARVEE bonds are traditional tax-exempt municipal securities with special features tied to the federal government. GARVEE bonds are grant anticipation revenue vehicles where the state or local government pledges repayment of such debt from future federal transportation grants. As such, GARVEEs are not repaid with state and local own-source revenue but from future resources provided by the federal government. The creation of a new bond issue through GARVEE allows state and local governments to diversify their bond repayment sources. This bond repayment diversification reduces the burden on their existing general obligation and revenue bond credits and allows these governments to retain debt capacity for other projects. However, it should be noted that GARVEEs are a debt obligation of the subnational government selling the bonds, not the federal government. As such, GARVEEs are subject to significant federal appropriation risk and reauthorization risk associated with the funding of the federal transportation program. Consequently, some investors view these securities as more risky than traditional municipal government general obligation bonds. As of April 2013, 25 states and three territories have issued over $14.5 billion in GARVEEs.

Transportation private activity bonds (PABs) are also traditional tax-exempt securities with significant federal involvement. In the most recent reauthorizations of the multi-year federal transportation law (SAFETEA-LU and MAP-21), there has been at least $15 billion allocated for private activity bonds for transportation projects. Subnational governments can issue these tax-exempt PABs in a public–private partnership to provide a private entity access to lower cost financing in developing transportation infrastructure. The government issues the bonds and the private entity uses the proceeds to help build the infrastructure project. The private entity is responsible for the repayment of the debt service on the PABs. The advantage of PABs is the ability to procure low-cost financing for projects that have substantial private sector involvement. As of April 2013, over $3 billion in PABs has been issued for seven projects and PAB allocations have been approved for eight projects totaling $5 billion.

The Transportation Infrastructure Finance Innovation Act (TIFIA) was created to leverage federal resources and stimulate private capital investment in transportation infrastructure through credit assistance in the form of direct loans, loan guarantees and standby lines of credit to large projects of national or regional significance. Like the other federal financing mechanisms, the TIFIA program does not represent new funding for transportation through grants but rather a new financing mechanism. These projects generally have to be greater than $50 million with the

TIFIA financing not exceeding 33 percent of project costs. As such, state or local governments are obligated to combine this financing mechanism with other financing types in funding the project.

TIFIA credit assistance is available for highways and bridges, intelligent transportation systems, intermodal connectors, transit vehicles and facilities, intercity buses and facilities, freight transfer facilities and passenger rail vehicles and facilities. The benefits of the TIFIA financing program are improved access to capital markets, flexible repayment terms and potentially lower cost financing than can be found in private capital markets for similar securities. The interest rate on a TIFIA loan is comparable to the rate on US Treasury securities of similar maturity on the day of the TIFIA loan closing. As of 29 October 2013, the 35-year TIFIA direct loan rate was 3.62 percent. As shown in Figure 13.1, the federal government has provided over $11.8 billion in TIFIA assistance for projects totaling $46.4 billion up to September 2013 dispersed throughout the nation.

As stated above, the general benefits of the various federal credit support and loan programs are improved access to capital markets for both the private and public sectors in public infrastructure projects, flexible repayment terms, relief of pressure on existing bond credits through creation of new bond credits, and potentially lower cost financing. These are significant benefits that underscore some of the primary reasons state and local governments have increasingly turned to these mechanisms for financing their capital activities. However, there are several drawbacks associated with these financing mechanisms. Federal loans based on taxable treasury securities rates may carry higher interest rates than tax-exempt municipal bonds. Historically, the relationship between municipal bond yields and treasury bond yields have been between 75 and 90 percent, although this ratio has been above 100 percent in recent years. The longer term historical relationship levels imply a lower potential financing cost for highly rated governments that issue municipal bonds using a federal repayment source.

Also, there are many restrictions related to the type, size and structure of federal loan and federal guarantee financings that complicate and/or preclude the availability of these instruments for many types of projects. Connected to this concern are the transaction costs associated with these financings due to the increased staff time and expertise devoted to executing the transactions. Compared to traditional municipal revenue bond financings, federal financial instruments require more staff time and resources due to their relative novelty and the increased federal government regulations associated with them.

Finally, there is an overarching concern related to the loss of financial autonomy for subnational governments in the use of federal financial instruments. This loss in autonomy spans several dimensions including,

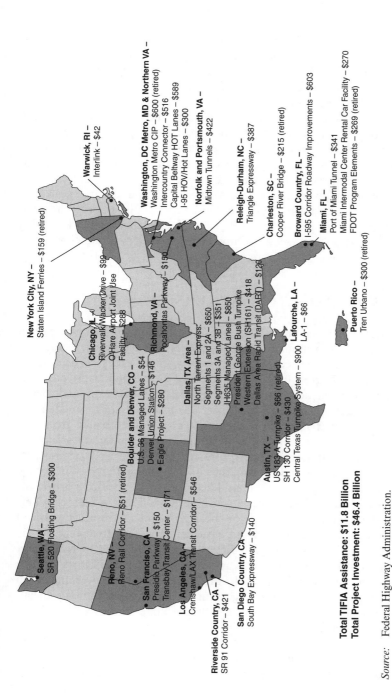

New York City, NY –
Staten Island Ferries – $159 (retired)

Warwick, RI –
Interlink – $42

Washington, DC Metro, MD & Northern VA –
Washington Metro CIP – $600 (retired)
Intercountry Connector – $516
Capital Beltway HOT Lanes – $589
I-95 HOV/Hot Lanes – $300

Norfolk and Portsmouth, VA –
Midtown Tunnels – $422

Raleigh-Durham, NC –
Triangle Expressway – $387

Charleston, SC –
Cooper River Bridge – $215 (retired)

Broward Country, FL –
I-595 Corridor Roadway Improvements – $603

Miami, FL –
Port of Miami Tunnel – $341
Miami Intermodal Center Rental Car Facility – $270
FDOT Program Elements – $269 (retired)

Puerto Rico –
Tren Urbano – $300 (retired)

Lafourche, LA –
LA-1 – $66

Austin, TX –
US 183-A Turnpike – $66 (retired)
SH 130 Corridor – $430
Central Texas Turnpike System – $900

Dallas, TX Area –
North Tarrant Express:
Segments 1 and 2A – $650
Segments 3A and 3B – $351
IH635 Managed Lanes – $850
President George Bush Turnpike
Western Extension (SH161) – $418
Dallas Area Rapid Transit (DART) – $120

Richmond, VA –
Pocahontas Parkway – $150

Chicago, IL –
Riverwalk/Wacker Drive – $99
O'Hare Airport Joint Use
Facility – $288

Boulder and Denver, CO –
US-36 Managed Lanes – $54
Denver Union Station – $146
Eagle Project – $280

Seattle, WA –
SR 520 Floating Bridge – $300

Reno, NV –
Reno Rail Corridor – $51 (retired)

San Francisco, CA –
Presidio Parkway – $150
TransbayTransit Center – $171

Los Angeles, CA –
Crenshaw/LAX Transit Corridor – $546

Riverside Country, CA –
SR 91 Corridor – $421

San Diego Country, CA –
South Bay Expressway – $140

Total TIFIA Assistance: $11.8 Billion
Total Project Investment: $46.4 Billion

Source: Federal Highway Administration.

Figure 13.1 Transportation Infrastructure Finance Innovation Act (TIFIA) use by geographic area, 2013

191

but not limited to: (1) the exposure to the federal government's budget and legislative process in the appropriation of federal grants for bond repayment of GARVEEs; (2) the federal preference for specific types of projects in the determination of eligibility for TIFIA loans; (3) the application and approval by the Department of Transportation for private activity bond authority; and (4) the ongoing federal servicing and monitoring of the use of loan proceeds for TIFIA loans. These concerns represent a significant encroachment by the federal government into the financing activities of subnational governments compared to the substantial autonomy enjoyed by these governments in the issuance of tax-exempt municipal bonds. As such, subnational governments need to carefully weigh the potential benefits and drawbacks from these various federal credit support and loan devices in determining if these types of 'non-traditional' capital financing mechanisms are advantageous compared to traditional municipal bond financing.

2.   PUBLIC–PRIVATE PARTNERSHIPS

Public–private partnerships (P3s) are the other non-traditional capital financing mechanism subnational governments increasingly use in addressing their infrastructure needs. P3s come in two general types: (1) brownfield financings; and (2) greenfield financings. The use of public–private partnerships in the construction of new infrastructure is often referred to as a greenfield project P3. Brownfield project P3s involve public–private partnerships related to existing infrastructure. In most contemplated greenfield P3s, the private sector is tasked with designing, financing, constructing, operating and maintaining the new infrastructure asset. In return for performing such activities and bearing the risk of those activities, the private entity receives the right to collect and keep (all or a specified portion of) the revenues from the asset over a specified term. From a financing perspective, the benefit to the state or local government from a greenfield P3 is that it relieves the government entity of procuring financing for the project. In addition, in some greenfield P3s, the private sector entity may provide an up-front payment to the government or provide future revenue sharing from operating the asset. In those instances, the government can use the proceeds from the P3 arrangement to finance other capital projects. An example of a greenfield P3 project is the State of Texas $2.7 billion I-635 highway project which relies on a private operator to build, finance, maintain and operate a 17-mile road corridor in the Dallas-Fort Worth area. This is also an example of a greenfield project that potentially allows for the government entity to receive future revenues from the project. More specifically, should toll revenues on I-635 exceed specified levels, the Texas Department of Transportation will receive up to 75 percent of the excess toll revenues.

In a brownfield P3 project, the infrastructure asset is already in service so the private sector entity is only tasked with operating and maintaining (which may include significant future capital costs) the asset. In return for a one-off up-front payment to the government (and/or future ongoing revenue sharing), the private entity receives the right to collect and keep all the revenues from the asset over a specified term. From the perspective of the state or local government, a brownfield P3 financing relieves the government of financing future capital costs associated with the asset while realizing significant up-front and/or ongoing money to fund other capital projects. Of course, in receiving such up-front and/or ongoing funding, the government forfeits all or a portion of the future revenues associated with the asset. The City of Chicago has been an active participant in brownfield financings in recent years. Chicago has entered into long-term P3 agreements related to the Chicago Skyway ($1.8 billion, 2005), its parking meters ($1.2 billion, 2008) and its downtown parking garages ($563 million, 2006).

It should be noted that the level of value offered by the private sector as it relates to risk sharing and cost containment may be very different depending on the type of P3. That is, construction, revenue, operational, maintenance and environmental risks are much higher for new infrastructure assets and, as such, P3s may be a better arrangement due to the more appropriate risk-sharing arrangement between the public and private sectors in a greenfield project vis-à-vis a brownfield project. The City of Chicago has also been in the forefront in the development of greenfield P3s that try to achieve the proper balance of risk between sectors through the creation of its infrastructure bank. The City of Chicago created the Chicago Infrastructure Bank (CIT) in April 2012, the first local government infrastructure bank in the United States. According to its charter, the goal of the CIT is:

> to provide alternative financing and project delivery options for transformative infrastructure projects. To accomplish this, the Trust hopes to structure innovative financing strategies and attract capital from diverse types of investors. The Trust also hopes to achieve and demonstrate real risk transfer to third-party investors, and to stimulate cross-agency financing while creating efficient capital structures. (Chicago Infrastructure Trust, 2013).

As of November 2013, the first CIT project is currently in process. This project, entitled Retrofit One, attempts to provide funding for energy efficiency projects including lighting, windows, HVAC units and water pumping stations to reduce the City's and the Chicago Public Schools' consumption of electricity and the City's consumption of natural gas. This project seeks investors using the operating cost savings resulting from the Retrofit Projects to fund the payments that provide the return on investment. In addition, the city expects to structure the financing such that it could 'share' the resulting savings with the investors during the term of the financial agreement. The benefit of this type of project as financed by the CIT is twofold. First, the city does not need to use any of its traditional financing approaches either on a pay-as-you-go or pay-as-you-use basis to fund the project. Thus, it retains the resources of such financing approaches to, perhaps, fund other less risky projects. Second, the city transfers to the private sector future revenue risk in the event that the project's energy savings do not materialize at the levels expected.

Proponents of public–private partnerships in the financing, constructing and operating of infrastructure assets cite many benefits. The Reason Foundation (2011) states five potential benefits. First, P3s provide delivery of additional needed infrastructure that would not be built without private sector involvement given the constrained capital budgets of most subnational governments. Second, P3s offer the ability to raise large new sources of capital for projects since they are attractive to more types of investors compared to traditional municipal bond financing. Third, public–private partnerships shift risk from taxpayers to investors in such areas as construction costs and future revenues. Fourth, P3s may provide a more business-like approach in the financing and managing of infrastructure offering taxpayers greater cost savings and better customer service than the public sector. Finally, P3s may produce major innovations, such as value pricing in the context of toll road finance, that historically have not been provided by the public sector in its management of infrastructure.

However, there has been no shortage of critics of public–private partnerships based on the way these arrangements have been contemplated and used in the United States over the last several years. As state and local governments have considered tapping into additional funding and financing through P3s as a means to meet their growing infrastructure needs, some observers have noted how the short- and long-term public interest may be compromised by the use of such public–private partnerships. Bunch (2012) details several of these concerns related to policy and financial issues, the expertise of government officials, transparency, and long-range flexibility and resource availability. She specifically lists the following concerns: (1) creation of new toll roads; (2) potentially higher tolls with private operators; (3) failure to capture the true value of the project; (4) use of funds for short-term needs at the expense of long-term needs; (5) potential loss of control and future flexibility; (6) higher private sector financing costs;

(7) insufficient expertise/experience among government officials; and (8) lack of transparency and potential for corruption (Bunch, 2012). From an overarching perspective, similar to federal financing mechanisms, there is a concern of loss of financial autonomy in the use of public–private partnerships. In the case of federal financing mechanisms, state and local governments cede financial autonomy to the federal government. With respect to P3s, the private sector usurps financial autonomy from state and local governments. Bunch's aforementioned concerns reflect this loss of financial autonomy to the private sector.

In light of many of the concerns cited by Bunch, many government entities and policy groups have been developing guidelines for P3 transactions. One such framework offered by the academic community is by Vining and Boardman (2008). Vining and Boardman offer eight rules for governments in the evaluation and administration of public–private partnerships including: (1) establish a jurisdictional P3 constitution; (2) separate the analysis, evaluation, contracting/administrating, and oversight agencies; (3) ensure that the bidding process is reasonably competitive; (4) be wary of projects that exhibit high asset-specificity, are complex or involve high uncertainty, and where in-house contract management effectiveness is low; (5) include standardized, fast, low-cost arbitration procedures in all P3 contracts; (6) avoid stand-alone private sector shells with limited equity provided by the real private sector principals; (7) prohibit the private-sector contractor from selling the contract too early; and (8) have a direct conduit to debtholders.

3. COMBINING 'NON-TRADITIONAL' FINANCING MECHANISMS

Given the significant size of the infrastructure deficit in the United States, many observers believe that subnational governments will probably have to take an 'all of the above' approach in financing their capital needs. That is, these governments will need to rely on both traditional financing mechanisms such as municipal bonds and non-traditional traditional means such as federal loans/credit support and public–private partnerships to meet their capital needs. Virginia's Capital Beltway project and Texas' I-635 project evince this multi-financing approach as it relates to the combination of various non-traditional financing mechanisms. The rest of this chapter provides further details on both of these landmark infrastructure projects.

The Capital Beltway project was a $1.4 billion public–private partnership between the Virginia Department of Transportation (VDOT) and its private partners. The Capital Beltway P3 was a groundbreaking infrastructure public–private partnership for several reasons including: (1) it included the largest private-sector equity investment in a US greenfield public–private partnership; (2) it was the first US surface transportation project to use tax-exempt private activity bonds; and (3) it was the first transportation project to combine US Department of Transportation TIFIA funds and PABs in one financing transaction (Luby, 2009). The structure of this innovative financing arrangement produced a significantly lower cost of capital for the private sector partner. Without such beneficial financing terms, the level of private sector support would probably have been much less threatening to the viability of the project.

As part of the project, VDOT granted its private-sector partner the right to design, construct, finance and operate high occupancy toll (HOT) lanes on the Capital Beltway on I-495 in Virginia. The purpose of the project was congestion mitigation in Northern Virginia through the use of such electronically-controlled HOT lanes. The project added two new lanes in each direction over 14 miles of the Capital Beltway. HOT lanes can be used by buses, car pools and emergency vehicles but all other traffic must pay a fee for travel on the lanes. The tolls are set based on congestion levels: when congestion is high, toll rates increase and vice versa.

The Capital Beltway's private operator relied on two federally sponsored finance options, PABs and TIFIA funds, to help finance the project. PABs are tax-exempt bonds that retain their preferred tax status even with significant private sector involvement in the project, which is not normally allowable with traditional tax-exempt securities. The use of PABs lowers the financing cost for the private sector participant and, thus, more likely ensures their involvement in the project. The TIFIA program was designed to fill market gaps by providing projects with supplemental or subordinate debt at low-interest rates. Luby (2009) stated the following in describing how PABs and TIFIA were supposed to work in concert with each other:

> The United States Department of Transportation expected that applicants for PAB authority would, like in the Capital Beltway project, also apply for TIFIA credit assistance. Thus, TIFIA applicants that might previously have needed to consider senior-lien taxable financing could now combine the benefits of senior-lien tax-exempt financing with subordinate TIFIA debt. (Luby, 2009).

The Capital Beltway's private operator ultimately used $589 million of PABs and $525 million in TIFIA funds as its federally-subsidized financing. The rest of the financing came from private equity. The financing structure provided a low-cost financing alternative compared to financing this portion of the project using primarily corporate debt as described by Luby (2009):

The 40-year tax-exempt PABs cost the private entity 4.97 percent, while the TIFIA funds were borrowed at an interest rate of 4.45 percent. As such, the weighted average cost of capital of both PABs and TIFIA loans for the project was 4.71 percent. This debt cost of capital is likely much lower than what this private-sector entity could have procured in the corporate bond market at the same time. For example, in June 2008, 20-year BAA-rated corporate debt was being sold in the low-to-mid-7 percent range. Such low cost financing attracted private sector involvement in the project, which allowed the government to retain their financing capacity for other projects, while ensuring that the project was still completed efficiently. (Luby, 2009).

The $2.7 billion I-635 project involved a public–private partnership between the Texas Department of Transportation and the LBJ Infrastructure Group, a private operator of toll roads throughout the world, which consisted of a joint venture of Cintra, Meridiam Infrastructure, and the Dallas Police and Fire Pension System. The project agreement covers 52 years in which the LBJ Infrastructure Group will design, build, operate and maintain the road. At the end of the P3 agreement, operation and maintenance of the road reverts back to the Texas Department of Transportation. The significant increase in users on I-635 over the last few decades causing traffic jams at all times of the day necessitated the project. In its original build in 1969, the road's capacity was 180 000 cars per day. By 2009, the number of cars traveling the road was estimated at 270 000 per day, with projections showing 450 000 per day by 2020.

In light of such huge increases in traffic, the State of Texas explored expansion options as far back as 1987. However, such plans were scrapped as the estimated cost of the project was twice as much as the amount the Department of Transportation could finance. Consequently, the State of Texas determined that a private partner would be needed to provide the requisite financing to complete a project of this size and scope. The I-635 public–private partnership consisted of the design and building of a 17-mile expressway turning the LBJ/I-635 corridor from an eight-lane free expressway to an 18–20 lane expressway with priced and free lanes. Construction on this project was estimated to run from 2011 to 2014. Once completed, drivers can remain on the main lanes for free or opt for new express lanes which will be variably priced, managed toll lanes. The toll rates will depend on traffic conditions, vehicle size and number of vehicle passengers.

In addition to the sheer size and scope of the I-635 project, its financing characteristics were just as innovative and novel. The funding sources for the project were as follows: (1) $665 million in equity from LBJ Infrastructure Group including a portion from the Dallas Police and Fire Pension System; (2) $615 million in private activity bonds; (3)

$850 million in TIFIA loans; and (4) $496 million in Texas Department of Transportation funds. The $615 million in PABs was the largest private activity bond allocation in history for a US toll road transaction. The TIFIA loan was the second largest loan in history for such a project. Both of these funding sources illustrate the potential import of federal financing mechanisms in infrastructure development in the United States. The equity investment made by the Dallas Police and Fire Pension System represented the first direct investment in infrastructure by a pension fund in the United States. This funding source underscored the benefit of diversifying financial instruments for subnational government capital investment as pension funds generally do not purchase municipal bonds since these funds do not receive a benefit from tax exemption. Finally, the project's utilization of Texas Department of Transportation funds in concert with the federal financing and equity investment ensures that all parties (state, local, federal, private developer) have a stake in the project.

The revenue sharing arrangement in this project was also novel in that it was an attempt to address one of the primary concerns regarding P3s related to the future true value of the asset. That is, given the often long-term nature of P3 projects, there is a concern that the value of the infrastructure asset may increase substantially over time such that revenues may be much greater than expected over time. In the I-635 project, the State of Texas and the private developer structured the transaction such that if expected toll revenues are greater than a certain threshold, the LBJ Infrastructure Group will share up to 75 percent of the 'excess toll revenues' with the Texas Department of Transportation. With respect to flow of funds, the LBJ Infrastructure Group contracted with the North Texas Tollway Authority to collect tolls. After subtracting NTTA administrative costs, debt service, maintenance costs and operations costs, the remaining revenues will represent the private operator's profit. 'Excess toll revenues' are determined based on an agreed-upon internal rate of return on the equity investment, with revenues exceeding that internal rate of return subject to revenue sharing with the State of Texas. However, if the converse happens and toll revenues do not materialize as expected, the private developer, not the State of Texas, is liable for the revenue deficiency. As such, by using a public–private partnership structured like the I-635 project, the State of Texas shifted the construction and revenue risk from the taxpayer to the private sector while retaining the possibility of capturing higher than expected future revenue growth if such toll revenues materially exceed expectations.

4. SUMMARY

The use of non-traditional financing mechanisms is partly in response to the inadequacy of the municipal securities market to provide the requisite level of financing for the capital demands of state and local governments. It is also a response to the changing perceptions around proper risk-sharing among sectors with respect to sizeable public infrastructure projects. Clearly, the federal government crafted the federal financing mechanisms to facilitate subnational capital-raising. However, these financing mechanisms also allow the federal government to further insert itself into the financial affairs of state and local governments. In that sense, one can see how there is no 'free lunch' as it relates to these non-traditional financing mechanisms. State and local governments will ultimately have to decide whether the trade-off of greater access to efficient capital for reduced financial autonomy is worth it. One can speculate that, as in many areas of fiscal federalism, some state and local governments will see such value in that trade-off and others will not, thus producing even greater diversity in subnational financial policymaking.

14. Conclusion

This book has used the theories and methodologies that are a part of the second-generation theory of fiscal federalism described by Oates (2005). We have used financial economics, information economics, public choice and principal–agent theories to analyze how the municipal market operates, how the market should operate, the role and practice of financial intermediaries, and the appropriate level and type of state–local, and federal regulation. This book is written to systematically answer the question posed at the beginning of Chapter 1:

> Why is understanding the financial instruments sold by state and local governments in the United States of America important?

Part I provided an overview of the various aspects that make the municipal securities market 'special'. It also placed the municipal market in the greater constitutional, judicial and legislative context of fiscal federalism. We analyzed the tax status of municipal securities as a driving force behind the federal government's approach to the market, and the primary factor behind the tension between the national and subnational governments over the debt financing affairs of state and local governments in the United States. The federal tax exemption of municipal debt is fundamentally important to the USA's fiscal federalist framework, yet coupled with fiscal sovereignty, results in a segmented market with sufficient, but limited demand for municipal securities.

We have argued that state fiscal sovereigns have created rules and institutions that provide a solid, enduring foundation supporting the repayment of debt issued by subnational governments. We argue that these fiscal rules and institutions provide system-wide support, resulting in securities that are uniquely pre-selected prior to issuance, and layered with security once issued.

Part II delved into the technicalities of bringing a municipal debt issue to market as well as discussing the basic structure of these financing instruments. This part of the book also provided a primer in the mechanics of fixed income securities, concepts that must be understood by state and local government financial managers as they navigate and negotiate the complex and turbulent waters of the capital markets. Part III offered several illustrations of the risks and rewards of municipal securities, especially the more sophisticated instruments, products and strategies employed by subnational governments in recent years. This part set the stage for understanding some of the reasons the federal government has begun its recent encroachment into the municipal securities market related to state and local governments' (1) increased use of sophisticated financing strategies and (2) ever growing demands on the municipal securities market to meet the capital finance needs of subnational governments.

Our intention is that this book helps policymakers, practitioners and scholars develop policies and management practices that strengthen the municipal securities market in this new era of financial management and fiscal federalism. We also hope to have provided a broader view of the role of the municipal securities market in the fiscal relationship between the national and subnational levels of government in the United States. We believe a better understanding of the history, dynamics and current issues facing this relationship in the context of the municipal securities market can lead to better relations between levels of government, ultimately improving financial outcomes for all of the citizens they serve.

Improving financial management activities and decision making in the context of the municipal securities market is incredibly salient given the recent Financial Crisis and recession. The severe fiscal stress placed on Jefferson County, Alabama and Harrisburg, Pennsylvania, as examples, were the result of poor debt management decisions. In the case of Jefferson County, public corruption related to the debt management function also played a role. The subsequent municipal bankruptcy proceedings of both these local governments have shone a very large spotlight on the financial management activities of state and local governments across the United States. To the extent that subnational governments are deemed incapable of managing their own financial affairs, greater federal involvement in the form of more regulation is likely to be seen in the future.

The recent Dodd–Frank Act evidences this predisposition at the federal level. Dodd–Frank impacted the municipal securities market in several ways, including: (1) regulating municipal advisors and municipal derivative instruments for the first time; (2) increasing regulation of the credit rating agencies; (3) creating the Office of Municipal Securities with the SEC; (4) enhancing the responsibilities of the MSRB; and (5) providing a budget and more staff to GASB. All of these Dodd–Frank statutory provisions have given the federal government more control over the financing activities of state and local governments. To be sure, many municipal market participants agree that much of this regulation was long overdue and the intent was surely to make the subnational capital markets more transparent and, thus, more efficient for the general welfare of all market actors. However, it is still uncertain how these regulations will ultimately impact the market and whether state and local governments will eventually receive a net benefit from such increased oversight.

To the extent that greater federal involvement is inevitable, state and local governments need to weigh the benefits and costs of such federal 'support' in their financial affairs. There is no doubt that the federal government wants to facilitate efficient raising of capital at the subnational level. The sizeable current and expected future federal budget deficits are likely to preclude the federal government from significantly increasing its grant-making to subnational governments for infrastructure projects. Thus, one can expect future increased federal involvement to come in the form of 'financing' rather than 'funding'. However, state and local governments need to be keenly aware of the potential loss in financial autonomy, exposure to the uncertain federal appropriations process, and the greater regulatory and administrative burden that may result from greater federal involvement. Aspects of the TIFIA program, the Build America bond program and the Dodd–Frank Act, respectively, provide acute evidence of these concerns.

While TIFIA financing can provide low-cost financing, its limitations on project type and its administrative burden may mitigate some of the borrowing cost advantages. The Build America Bond program clearly provided a borrowing cost advantage over traditional tax-exempt securities. However, the recent federal budget sequestration that impacted the federal subsidy payments made under the Build America Bond program illustrates how subnational government finances are at significant risk through exposure to federal budgetary politics. Finally, the impact of the Dodd–Frank law is still uncertain. What we do know is that Dodd–Frank has changed the relationship between underwriters and issuers, placed a greater burden on the municipal advisors who advise state and local governments and, for better or worse, generally given greater regulatory 'teeth' to the SEC in municipal securities matters.

The upcoming years will surely witness even greater changes in the municipal securities markets as all market players adapt to evolving financial, economic and regulatory environments. Moreover, the capital financing needs of subnational governments are unlikely to recede given the severely aging infrastructure throughout the United States. Our hope is that this book contributes to the inevitable future discussions on improving subnational capital-raising, by assisting scholars, practitioners and policymakers utilize the municipal securities market in its singularly important role of meeting the capital financing and infrastructure needs of twenty-first-century Americans within the fiscal federalist framework.

Appendix A: review of time value of money

1.   REVIEW OF TIME VALUE OF MONEY

The idea that money has a time value is fundamentally important to modern finance and pricing debt instruments. Money has a time value because of the opportunities of investing money at a rate of interest. Interest is the cost to rent money and the interest rate is the return expressed as a percentage. A dollar in hand today is worth more than a dollar expected to be received in the future because you could invest the dollar today at a rate of interest and earn interest on your dollar. We need to understand time value of money from two perspectives: future value and present value.

2.   FUTURE VALUE

Future value determines the worth of all expected future cash flows at some known future date. The future value of any sum of money invested today can be determined by the future value formula:

$$FV_n = PV(1 + r)^n \qquad (A.1)$$

where:
FV_n = future value in dollars n periods from now, or the ending amount;
PV = original principal in dollars, or the beginning amount;
n = number of years, or more generally, periods involved in the transaction;
r = interest rate per period as a decimal.

The notation $(1 + r)^n$ means that $(1 + r)$ should be multiplied n times: the n is called the exponent of the expression. The exponential expression produces compound interest. Compounding is the process of earning interest on interest as well as on the principal amount. Compounding is a powerful concept in which the principal amount (PV) can grow rapidly – indeed, exponentially – over time and it reflects the true opportunity costs of funds over time.

The expression $(1 + r)^n$ represents the future value of $1 invested today

Table A.1 *Future Value (FV) of a $5 million investment, 10-year horizon, 12% interest compounded annually*

Years, (N)	Periods, ($N \times 1 = n$)	Investment, (PV)	Future Value of $1, $(1 + r)^n$	Future Value, $FV = PV(1 + r)^n$
1	1	$5 000 000.00	$(1+.12)^1 = 1.1200$	
2	2		1.2544	
3	3		1.4049	
4	4		1.5735	
5	5		1.7623	
6	6		1.9738	
7	7		2.2107	
8	8		2.4760	
9	9		2.7731	
10	10		3.1058	$15 529 241.04

Notes:
FVn: Future Value of an investment
PV: Present Value of an investment
N: Number of years, investment horizon
n: Interest compounding periods during the investment horizon
r: Interest rate
$(1 + r)^n$: Future Value of $1 at a compounding rate of r and period n

at a compounding rate of r for n periods. For example, assume that a treasurer invests $5 million in a debt instrument that promises to pay 12 percent per year for 10 years. Using the future value formula in (A.1), the future value of the $5 million is $15 529 241.04.

$$FV_{10} = \$5000000(1 + .12)^{10}$$
$$= \$5000000(1.12)^{10}$$
$$= \$5000000(3.1058)$$
$$= \$15529241.04$$

From equation (A.1) we see that $5 million invested now, earning interest at 12 percent with annual compounding, grows to $15 529 241.04 at the end of 10 years. Table A.1 shows the relationship between the original principal and future value of a one-off investment.

The example in Table A.1 shows how to calculate future value when interest is paid annually, or one time per year. When interest is paid more than once per year, both the number of periods and the interest rate must be adjusted by the number of times interest is paid. The interest rate becomes:

r = annual interest rate/number of times interest is paid per year;

And the number of periods becomes:

n = number of times interest is paid per year × number of years.

For an investment that pays interest every six months, or semi-annually, n is multiplied by 2, and r is divided by 2. For an investment that pays interest four times a year, or quarterly, n is multiplied by 4 and r is divided by 4.

If the treasurer in the above equation invested $5 million in a debt instrument that promises to pay interest semi-annually, rather than annually, then r would be 0.06 and n would be 20:

$$r = \frac{0.12}{2} = 0.06$$

$$n = 10 \times 2 = 20$$

And

$$
\begin{aligned}
FV_{10 \times 2} &= \$5000000(1 + 0.12/2)^{10 \times 2} \\
&= \$5000000(1.06)^{20} \\
&= \$5000000(3.2071) \\
&= \$16035677.36
\end{aligned}
$$

Notice that the future value of the $5 million when interest is paid semi-annually is greater than when interest is paid annually: $15 529 241.04 to $16 035 677.36.

Even though the annual interest rate is the same in both cases, 12 percent, semi-annual compounding results in a greater future value. The more frequent compounding, the more interest on interest is earned and the greater the future value. Another way of viewing it is that when interest is paid more frequently, the greater is the opportunity for reinvesting the interest. This relationship is seen in Table A.2. More frequent compounding results in higher future values being applied to the PV amount.

Table A.3 shows the future value of $1 for both annual and semi-annual compounding. Notice that for each year (i.e. 1.0, 2.0, 3.0, 4.0. . .) the future value factor is larger under semi-annual compounding than annual compounding, thus resulting in the greater future value amount.

Future value is a positive function of the interest rate (r), the maturity (n) and the current amount (PV). The more you invest today (PV), holding r and n constant, the higher the value will grow to in the future. In the

Table A.2   Future value (FV) of a $5 million investment 10-year horizon,
*   12% interest compounded semi-annually*

Years, (N)	Periods, (N × 2 = n)	Investment, (PV)	Future Value of $1, $(1 + r/2)^{\wedge}(n \times 2)$	Future Value, $FV = PV(1 + r/2)^{\wedge}(n \times 2)$
0.5	1	$5 000 000.00	$(1+.06)^1 = 1.0600$	
1.0	2		1.1236	
1.5	3		1.1910	
2.0	4		1.2625	
2.5	5		1.3382	
3.0	6		1.4185	
3.5	7		1.5036	
4.0	8		1.5938	
4.5	9		1.6895	
5.0	10		1.7908	
5.5	11		1.8983	
6.0	12		2.0122	
6.5	13		2.1329	
7.0	14		2.2609	
7.5	15		2.3966	
8.0	16		2.5404	
8.5	17		2.6928	
9.0	18		2.8543	
9.5	19		3.0256	
10.0	20		3.2071	$16 035 677.36

Notes:
FVn: Future Value of an investment
PV: Present Value of an investment
N: Number of years, investment horizon
n: Interest compounding periods during the investment horizon
r: Interest rate
$(1 + r/2)^{\wedge}(n \times 2)$: Future Value of $1 at a semi-annual compounding rate of $r/2$ and periods
$N \times 2$

future value equation the interest rate is referred to as the compounding interest rate. The higher the compounding interest rate, the greater the future value will be, holding PV and n constant. Therefore, higher interest rates lead to greater future value. Table A.4 shows the relationship between future value and interest rates of 5 percent, 15 percent and 25 percent. As the interest rate increases from 5 percent to 15 percent to 25 percent, the future value grows from $8 144 473.13 to $20 227 788.68 to $46 566 128.73.

Future value is also a positive function of maturity (n). The longer a principal value is invested, the greater the future value.

Table A.3   *Comparison of Future Value (FV) interest factors under annual and semi-annual compounding: 10-year horizon, 12% interest*

ANNUAL compounding: Years, (N)	SEMI-ANNUAL compounding: Years, (N)	ANNUAL compounding: Future Value of $1, $(1 + r)^n$	SEMI-ANNUAL compounding: Future Value of $1, $(1 + r/2)^{\wedge}(n\times 2)$
	0.5		$(1+.06)^1 = 1.0600$
1.0	1.0	$(1+.12)^1 = 1.1200$	1.1236
	1.5		1.1910
2.0	2.0	1.2544	1.2625
	2.5		1.3382
3.0	3.0	1.4049	1.4185
	3.5		1.5036
4.0	4.0	1.5735	1.5938
	4.5		1.6895
5.0	5.0	1.7623	1.7908
	5.5		1.8983
6.0	6.0	1.9738	2.0122
	6.5		2.1329
7.0	7.0	2.2107	2.2609
	7.5		2.3966
8.0	8.0	2.4760	2.5404
	8.5		2.6928
9.0	9.0	2.7731	2.8543
	9.5		3.0256
10.0	10.0	3.1058	3.2071

Notes:
N: Number of years, investment horizon
n: Interest compounding periods during the investment horizon
r: Interest rate
$(1+r)^n$: Future Value of $1 at an annual compounding rate of r and period n
$(1+r/2)^{\wedge}(n\times 2)$: Future Value of $1 at a semi-annual compounding rate of $r/2$ and periods $N\times 2$

From Tables A.4 and A.5 it is clear that as interest rate and maturity increase, the future value amount increases rapidly; this is a mathematical result of the fact that the future value formula is an exponential expression and an example of the power of compound interest.

Table A.4 Future Value (FV) of a $5 million investment: 10-year horizon, 5%, 15% and 25% interest rates compounded annually

Years, (N)	Investment, (PV)	Future Value of $1 at 5%, $(1+r)^n$	Future Value at 5%, $FV = PV(1+r)^n$	Future Value of $1 at 15%, $(1+r)^n$	Future Value at 15%, $FV = PV(1+r)^n$	Future Value of $1 at 25%, $(1+r)^n$	Future Value at 25%, $FV = PV(1+r)^n$
1	$5000000	$(1+.05)^1 = 1.0500$		$(1+.15)^1 = 1.1500$		$(1+.25)^1 = 1.2500$	
2		1.1025		1.3225		1.5625	
3		1.1576		1.5209		1.9531	
4		1.2155		1.7490		2.4414	
5		1.2763		2.0114		3.0518	
6		1.3401		2.3131		3.8147	
7		1.4071		2.6600		4.7684	
8		1.4775		3.0590		5.9605	
9		1.5513		3.5179		7.4506	
10		1.6289	$8144473.13	4.0456	$20227788.68	9.3132	$46566128.73

Notes:
FVn: Future Value of an investment
PV: Present Value of an investment
N: Number of years, investment horizon
n: Interest compounding periods during the investment horizon
r: Interest rate
$(1+r)^n$: Future Value of $1 at a compounding rate of r and period n

208

Table A.5 *Future Value (FV) of a $5 million investment, 5-year, 10-year and 15-year horizons, 15% interest compounded annually*

Years, (N)	Investment, (PV)	Future Value of $1 at 15%, $(1+r)^n$	Future Value at 15%, $FV = PV(1+r)^n$
1	$5 000 000	$(1+.15)^1 = 1.1500$	
2		1.3225	
3		1.5209	
4		1.7490	
5		**2.0114**	**$10 056 785.94**
6		2.3131	
7		2.6600	
8		3.0590	
9		3.5179	
10		**4.0456**	**$20 227 788.68**
11		4.6524	
12		5.3503	
13		6.1528	
14		7.0757	
15		**8.1371**	**$40 685 308.15**

Notes:
FVn: Future Value of an investment
PV: Present Value of an investment
N: Number of years, investment horizon
n: Interest compounding periods during the investment horizon
r: Interest rate
$(1+r)^n$: Future Value of $1 at a compounding rate of r and period n

3. PRESENT VALUE

The present value is the current value of cash flows expected to be received in the future. Present value is the value, now, of a payment or payments expected to be received or paid in the future. The concept of present value reflects the fact that $1 in hand now has greater value than a dollar expected sometime in the future. Present value is a very important concept because the value of any debt instrument is the present value of its expected cash flows.

The process of finding the present value is called discounting. Discounting is simply the reverse of compounding, and present value is the reverse of future value. In discounting, we know the value of the future payment, and we are trying to determine its value today; in other words, discount its value back to the present. In compounding, today's value is known, but its future value must be derived; the principal value and the interest it generates are compounded until it reaches its future value. The future value formula can be transformed into a present value formula:

$$FV_n = PV(1 + r)^n \tag{A.2}$$

When solved for PV the equation becomes:

$$PV = \frac{FV_n}{(1 + r)^n} = FV_n(1 + r)^{-n} = FV_n\left(\frac{1}{1 + r}\right)^n \tag{A.3}$$

Therefore, the present value formula is:

$$PV = FV_n\left(\frac{1}{1 + r}\right)^n \tag{A.4}$$

The equation provides the present value (PV) of a future cash flow (FV_n) received in period n discounted at interest rate r. Using the present value formula in equation (A.4), if a treasurer expects to receive a \$15 530 000 cash flow on his investments 10 years from now, and his interest rate (i.e. required rate of return) is 12 percent compounded annually, then the value of the investment now is \$5 000 244.36, which is the present value of the expected future cash flow.

$$PV = \$15\,530\,000\left(\frac{1}{1 + 0.12}\right)^{10}$$

$$= \$15\,530\,000(0.3220)$$

$$= \$5\,000\,244.36$$

This solution is also shown in Table A.6.

Present value is a function of the interest rate (r), the maturity (n), and the expected future value amount (FV_n). As r and n increase, the PV amount quickly decreases. For example, Table A.7 shows that the PV of \$1 discounted at 12 percent decreases over the 0–40-year time horizon. The PV of \$1 to be received 40 years from now is less than the PV of \$1 to be received 32 years from now, and so on. The longer it takes for you to receive your money in the future, the less value it has for you today, the lower its current or present value.

The higher the discount rate applied to a future value, the lower the present value. As shown in Table A.8, the PV of \$1 declines rapidly (holding maturity constant) as the interest rate increases from 0 percent to

Table A.6 *Present Value (PV) of expected $15 530 000, 10-year horizon, 12% interest compounded annually*

Years, (N)	Future Value, (FVn)	Present Value of $1, $[1/(1+r)]^n$	Present Value $(PV) = FVn[1/(1+r)]^n$
10	**$15 530 000**	**0.3220**	**$5 000 244.36**
9		0.3606	
8		0.4039	
7		0.4523	
6		0.5066	
5		0.5674	
4		0.6355	
3		0.7118	
2		0.7972	
1		0.8929	

Notes:
PV: Present Value of an expected cash flow
FVn: Expected cash value in the future
N: Number of years, investment horizon
n: Interest compounding periods during the investment horizon
r: Interest rate
$[1/(1+r)]^n$: Present Value of $1

Table A.7 *Present Value (PV) interest factors, 40-year horizon, 12% interest compounded annually*

Years, (N)	Present Value of $1, $[1/(1+r)]^n$	Years, (N)	Present Value of $1, $[1/(1+r)]^n$	Years, (N)	Present Value of $1, $[1/(1+r)]^n$	Years, (N)	Present Value of $1, $[1/(1+r)]^n$
40	0.0107	30	0.0334	20	0.1037	10	0.3220
39	0.0120	29	0.0374	19	0.1161	9	0.3606
38	0.0135	28	0.0419	18	0.1300	8	0.4039
37	0.0151	27	0.0469	17	0.1456	7	0.4523
36	**0.0169**	26	**0.0525**	16	**0.1631**	6	**0.5066**
35	0.0189	25	0.0588	15	0.1827	5	0.5674
34	0.0212	24	0.0659	14	0.2046	4	0.6355
33	0.0238	23	0.0738	13	0.2292	3	0.7118
32	0.0266	22	0.0826	12	0.2567	2	0.7972
						1	0.8929

Notes:
N: Number of years, investment horizon
n: Interest compounding periods during the investment horizon
r: Interest rate
$[1/(1+r)]^n$: Present Value of $1, interest factor

Table A.8   Present Value (PV) interest factors, 10-year horizon, 0%, 10%,
            20% and 30% interest rates compounded annually

Years, (N)	Present Value of $1 at 0%, $[1/(1+r)]^n$	Present Value of $1 at 10%, $[1/(1+r)]^n$	Present Value of $1 at 20%, $[1/(1+r)]^n$	Present Value of $1 at 30%, $[1/(1+r)]^n$
10	1.0000	0.3855	0.1615	0.0725
9	1.0000	0.4241	0.1938	0.0943
8	1.0000	0.4665	0.2326	0.1226
7	1.0000	0.5132	0.2791	0.1594
6	**1.0000**	**0.5645**	**0.3349**	**0.2072**
5	1.0000	0.6209	0.4019	0.2693
4	1.0000	0.6830	0.4823	0.3501
3	1.0000	0.7513	0.5787	0.4552
2	1.0000	0.8264	0.6944	0.5917
1	1.0000	0.9091	0.8333	0.7692

Notes:
N: Number of years, investment horizon
n: Interest compounding periods during the investment horizon
r: Interest rate
$[1/(1+r)]^n$: Present Value of $1, interest factor

10 percent to 20 percent to 30 percent. Present value and future value are equal when $r = 0$; or in other words there is no time value to money.

A $350 000 cash flow expected to be received five years from today has a lower *PV* if it is discounted at a 20 percent rate rather than a 10 percent rate, as shown in Table A.9. Stating that you require a 20 percent return on a $350 000 investment, rather than a 5 percent return, is equivalent to stating that its current or present value is lower to you. Evaluated at 20 percent, its present value is $140 657.15, whereas at 5 percent its present value is $274 234.16.

4.   FUTURE VALUE OF AN ORDINARY ANNUITY

An annuity can be simply defined as the same cash flow paid or received periodically. For an investment, it is the same amount of money invested periodically. The amount of money must be the same (e.g. $100 000); it must be invested at the same interval (e.g. annually) over a specified, definite number of periods (e.g. 10 years). In the equation of the future value of the cash flows below, unless otherwise stated, annuities are due in the beginning of each period. In other words, timing of the annuity matters,

Table A.9 *Present Values (PV) of $350000 at various rates, 5-year horizon, 5%, 10% and 20% interest rates compounded annually*

Years, (N)	Future Value, (FVn)	Present Value of $1 at 5%, $[1/(1+r)]^n$	Present Value at 5% (PV) = $FVn[1/(1+r)]^n$	Present Value of $1 at 10%, $[1/(1+r)]^n$	Present Value at 10% (PV) = $FVn[1/(1+r)]^n$	Present Value of $1 at 20%, $[1/(1+r)]^n$	Present Value at 20% (PV) = $FVn[1/(1+r)]^n$
5	**$350000.00**	**0.7835**	**$274234.16**	**0.6209**	**$217322.46**	**0.4019**	**$140657.15**
4		0.8227		0.6830		0.4823	
3		0.8638		0.7513		0.5787	
2		0.9070		0.8264		0.6944	
1		0.9524		0.9091		0.8333	

Notes:
PV: Present Value of an expected cash flow
FVn: Expected cash value in the future
N: Number of years, investment horizon
n: Interest compounding periods during the investment horizon
r: Interest rate
$[1/(1+r)]^n$: Present Value of $1

and care should be extended to account for such modifications in timing. The future value of an ordinary annuity formula is:

$$FV_n = A\left(\frac{(1 + r)^n - 1}{r}\right) \tag{A.5}$$

where:
A = amount of the annuity in dollars;
r = interest rate per period as a decimal;
n = number of periods.

The term in brackets is the future value of an ordinary annuity of $1. When you multiply it by the amount of the annuity (A), it results in the future value of an ordinary annuity (FV_n). For example, if $100000 is invested each year at 5 percent for the next 10 years, beginning one year from now, then:

$$A = \$100\,000$$
$$r = .05$$
$$n = 10$$

Therefore:

$$FV_{10} = \$100\,000\left(\frac{(1 + 0.05)^{10} - 1}{0.05}\right)$$
$$= \$100\,000(12.5779)$$
$$= \$1\,257\,789.25$$

The future value of the ordinary annuity of $100000 invested per year for 10 years at 5 percent is $1257789.25. This relationship is provided in Table A.10. Please note that one can adjust equation (A.1), which was used to estimate the future value of a single cash flow, to account for repeated cash flows. Since the ordinary annuity is fixed, we can factor it out and multiply it by the sum of interest factors for all periods. This is done in equation (A.6).

$$FV_n = A\sum_{i=1}^{N}(1 + r)^n \tag{A.6}$$

Consequently, mathematically $\left(\frac{(1 + r)^n - 1}{r}\right) = \sum_{i=1}^{N}(1 + r)^n$ as both produce an aggregate future value for $1 at future period, n, given rate r. Equation (A.6) allows seeing into the 'black box', where one can obtain detailed future values for $1 in each period. However, using formula (A.5)

Table A.10 Future Value (FV) of a $100 000 annuity, 10-year horizon, 5% interest compounded annually, using future value annuity formula

Years, (N)	Periods, (N×1 = n)	Annuity, (A) $100 000	Future Value of $1 Annuity, $[(1+r)^n-1]/r$	Future Value, $FV = A[((1+r)^n-1)/r]$
1	1		1.0000	
2	2		2.0500	
3	3		3.1525	
4	4		4.3101	
5	5		5.5256	
6	6		6.8019	
7	7		8.1420	
8	8		9.5491	
9	9		11.0266	
10	**10**		**12.5779**	**$1 257 789.25**

Notes:
FVn: Future Value of an annuity
A: Annuity
N: Number of years, investment horizon
n: Interest compounding periods during the investment horizon
r: Interest rate
$[(1+r)^n-1]/r$: Future Value of $1 annuity at a compounding rate of r and period n

is much easier because it will produce the same aggregate result in just one calculation. Review Tables A.10 and A.11 to see that the relationship exists.

5. PRESENT VALUE OF AN ORDINARY ANNUITY

The present value of an ordinary annuity is the value today of a series of future cash flows. In the present value of an annuity formula, unless otherwise noted, cash flows are due at the beginning of the discounting period (i.e. any cash flow in the current period is due at period zero; the present value of one dollar today is exactly one dollar):

$$PV = A\left[\frac{1 - \left(\frac{1}{(1+r)^n}\right)}{r}\right] \tag{A.7}$$

where:
A = the amount of the annuity in dollars;
r = interest rate per period as a decimal;
n = number of periods.

Table A.11   *Future Value (FV) of a $100 000 annuity, 10-year horizon,*
               5% interest compounded annually, using future value of a
               single cash flow formula

Years, (N)	Periods, (N×1 = n)	Investment, (PV)	Future Value of $1, $(1+r)^n$	Future Value, $FV = PV(1+r)^n$
1	1	$100 000.00	1.0000	$100 000.00
2	2	$100 000.00	1.0500	$105 000.00
3	3	$100 000.00	1.1025	$110 250.00
4	4	$100 000.00	1.1576	$115 762.50
5	5	$100 000.00	1.2155	$121 550.63
6	6	$100 000.00	1.2763	$127 628.16
7	7	$100 000.00	1.3401	$134 009.56
8	8	$100 000.00	1.4071	$140 710.04
9	9	$100 000.00	1.4775	$147 745.54
10	10	$100 000.00	1.5513	$155 132.82
		Σ	**12.5779**	**$1 257 789.25**

Notes:
FV_n: Future Value of an investment
PV: Present Value of an investment
N: Number of years, investment horizon
n: Interest compounding periods during the investment horizon
r: Interest rate
$(1+r)^n$: Future Value of $1 at a compounding rate of r and period n

The term in large brackets is the present value of an ordinary annuity factor. It is the present value of an ordinary annuity of $1 for n years at r interest rate. Using this annuity formula is merely a short-cut way of calculating the present value for a series of cash flows. In the example below you can see that the present value ordinary annuity factor equals the sum of the present value factors for each period. Assuming an investment is made annually for the next 5 years ($n = 5$), and the interest rate (r) is 8 percent, using the annuity formula the present value of the annuity factor is:

$$\frac{1 - \left(\dfrac{1}{(1 + 0.08)^5}\right)}{0.08}$$

$$= \frac{1 - 0.68058}{0.08} = 3.9927$$

which is equal to:

$$\frac{1}{(1 + 0.08)^1} + \frac{1}{(1 + 0.08)^2} + \frac{1}{(1 + 0.08)^3} + \frac{1}{(1 + 0.08)^4} + \frac{1}{(1 + 0.08)^5}$$

$$= 0.9259 + 0.8573 + 0.7938 + 0.7350 + 0.6806 = 3.9927$$

Thus,

$$\left[\frac{1 - \left(\frac{1}{(1 + r)^n}\right)}{r}\right] = \sum_{i=1}^{N}\left(\frac{1}{1 + r}\right)^n.$$

The advantage of equation (A.7) is that it reduces the number of intermediate calculations at the expense of finer detail. Using the present value of an ordinary annuity formula, if $200 000 is expected to be received annually over the next five years, and the interest rate (r) is 8 percent, the present value is:

$$PV = \$200\,000\left(\frac{1 - \left(\frac{1}{(1 + 0.08)^5}\right)}{0.08}\right)$$

$$= \$200\,000\,(3.9927)$$

$$= \$798\,542.01$$

Confirm in Tables A.12 and A.13 that the two equations are indeed related.

Table A.12 Present Value (PV) of a $200 000 annuity, 5-year horizon, 8% interest compounded annually, using present value annuity formula

Years, (N)	Annuity, (A) $200 000	Present Value of $1 Annuity, $[1-(1/(1+r)^n)]/r$	Present Value $(PV) = A[(1-(1/(1+r)^n))/r]$
5		**3.9927**	**$798 542.01**
4		3.3121	
3		2.5771	
2		1.7833	
1		0.9259	

Notes:
PV: Present Value of an annuity
A: Annuity
N: Number of years, investment horizon
n: Interest compounding periods during the investment horizon
r: Interest rate
$[1-(1/(1+r)^n)]/r$: Present Value of $1 annuity at a compounding rate of r and period n

Table A.13 *Present Value (PV) of a $200 000 annuity, 5-year horizon, 8% interest compounded annually, using present value of a single cash flow formula*

Years, (N)	Payment, (FV)	Present Value of $1, $1/(1+r)^n$	Present Value, $(PV) = FV[1/(1+r)^n]$
5	$200 000	0.6806	$136 116.64
4	$200 000	0.7350	$147 005.97
3	$200 000	0.7938	$158 766.45
2	$200 000	0.8573	$171 467.76
1	$200 000	0.9259	$185 185.19
	Σ	**3.9927**	**$798 542.01**

Notes:
FVn: Future Value of an investment
PV: Present Value of an investment
N: Number of years, investment horizon
n: Interest compounding periods during the investment horizon
r: Interest rate
$1/(1+r)^n$: Present Value of $1 at a compounding rate of *r* and period *n*

Appendix B: basic principles of valuing debt instruments

1. BASIC PRINCIPLES OF VALUING DEBT INSTRUMENTS

A bond is a financial obligation whereby the issuer promises to pay the bondholder a specified stream of future cash flows. A bond has two basic cash flows: (1) interest income, paid periodically throughout the life of the bond or coupon interest; (2) principal, paid once at the final maturity when the principal is redeemed. The value of the principal and interest cash flows is a function of the time value of money. The time value of these cash flows is an important determinant of how much the principal and interest cash flows are worth. The time value calculation is based on the interest rate, which is the cost of money to the borrower and the expected return to the lender.

2. COUPON INTEREST

To determine the interest payments on a bond you must first calculate the coupon interest (*CI*). Let's calculate the total coupon interest for a $1000 bond that pays a fixed 10 percent coupon interest rate for 20 years. The interest rate stated on the bond and payable to the bondholder is called the coupon interest rate. We calculate the coupon interest with the following formula:

$$Coupon\ Interest = Par\ Value \times \frac{Coupon\ Rate(CR)}{Compounding\ Periodicity} \quad (B.1)$$

where:
Par Value = $1000, the principal value of the bond that is redeemed at maturity.[1]
Coupon Rate = the interest rate stated on the bond; since municipal bonds pay interest semi-annually, the annual interest rate must be divided by 2, the compounding periodicity.

If the bond has an annual coupon rate of 10 percent, the semi-annual coupon rate is 5 percent (0.10/2), and the coupon interest payable every six months is $50 ($1000 × ($\frac{0.10}{2}$)). If the bond has a final maturity date of 20 years, indicating 40 semi-annual cash flows, the total coupon interest the bond would pay is:

$$Total\ Coupon\ Interest = CI \times Number\ of\ Cash\ Flows \qquad (B.2)$$

$$Total\ Coupon\ Interest = \$50 \times 40 = \$2000$$

The total coupon interest paid on a $1000 bond with a 10 percent coupon rate compounding semi-annually, and final maturity of 20 years is $2000. However, total coupon interest must be discounted to provide present values of the coupon interest flows.

3. PRINCIPAL

The second cash flow in deriving the value of a bond is the principal value that is redeemed at maturity. In our example the principal amount of the bond is $1000. This is a $1000 cash flow to be paid (to bondholder) in 20 years, or assuming semi-annual coupon payments, 40 periods from now. Thus, it is also discounted on a semi-annual basis based on compounding periodicity. Similarly to the coupon interest payments that are made on a semi-annual basis, all cash flows, including the principal, must be evaluated on a semi-annual basis.

4. DISCOUNTING PRINCIPAL AND INTEREST

The value of the bond is determined by discounting the stream of interest and principal to its present value. The discount rate is the required yield. The required yield is based on the yield or return on comparable bonds. We use the required yield to calculate the present value of the two cash flows: interest and principal. The final year of the bond is called the final maturity date. On the final maturity date there are two cash flows: the final interest payment and the principal payment. Interest is paid throughout the life of the bond, principal is paid only once on the final maturity date. Once these cash flows are discounted, that is, we calculate their present values, they are added and the result is the present value, or price, of the bond. A bond's price is the present value of the bond's future cash flows.

The present value calculation for a bond is referred to as the yield-to-maturity because the discount rate used to calculate the present values of the cash flows is the yield on the bond's cash flows until the final maturity date. The yield-to-maturity calculation combines the present value of the annuity formula for the coupon cash flows plus the present value formula for the principal payment. The yield-to-maturity (YTM) formula is:[2]

$$BP = \frac{C_1}{(1+y)^1} + \frac{C_2}{(1+y)^2} + \ldots + \frac{C_n}{(1+y)^n} + \frac{P_n}{(1+y)^n}$$

$$BP = \sum_{i=1}^{N} \frac{C}{(1+y)^n} + \frac{P_n}{(1+y)^n}$$

$$BP = PV(Ordinary\ Annuity) + PV(Single\ Cash\ Flow) \qquad (B.3)$$

where:
BP = bond price or the present value of the bond;
C = coupon interest payment, must account for compounding periodicity;
y = yield-to-maturity, must be adjusted by compounding periodicity;
P = principal paid at maturity (in dollars);
N = number of periods until maturity, must be adjusted by compounding periodicity.

The YTM is the rate of return on the bond assuming that the bond is held to maturity and all the cash flows received prior to maturity are reinvested at the YTM rate. If the bond price, coupon interest payments and principal value are known, then the YTM can be calculated. For an 8 percent fixed coupon bond with semi-annual compounding that matures in 20 years priced at par, the YTM can be calculated as follows:

$$\$1000 = \frac{\$40}{\left(1 + \dfrac{y}{2}\right)^1} + \frac{\$40}{\left(1 + \dfrac{y}{2}\right)^2} + \frac{\$40}{\left(1 + \dfrac{y}{2}\right)^3} + \ldots + \frac{\$40 + \$1000}{\left(1 + \dfrac{y}{2}\right)^{20 \times 2}}$$

Using a method of iteration, select r that satisfies the equality. For example, select $y = 0.08$ (adjusted for compounding periodicity) and confirm that:

$$\$1000 = \frac{\$40}{(1 + 0.04)^1} + \frac{\$40}{(1 + 0.04)^2} + \frac{\$40}{(1 + 0.04)^3} + \ldots + \frac{\$40 + \$1000}{(1 + 0.04)^{40}}$$

The answer, $y = 0.08$, is easily obtained from trial-and-error using a financial calculator or computer. Table B.1 is an excerpt from an Excel file that shows the above estimation in a table format.

The coupon interest cash flow of $40 was derived using the coupon

Table B.1   Yield-to-maturity for PV = $1000, coupon rate = 0.08, maturity = 20 years

Years	Period (y*2=N)	Cash flow per $1000 of par value	Present value of $1 at y/2 = 4%	Present value of cash flow (PVCF)
0.5	1	$40.00	$0.9615	$38.4615
1	2	$40.00	$0.9246	$36.9822
1.5	3	$40.00	$0.8890	$35.5599
2	4	$40.00	$0.8548	$34.1922
2.5	5	$40.00	$0.8219	$32.8771
3	6	$40.00	$0.7903	$31.6126
19	38	$40.00	$0.2253	$9.0114
19.5	39	$40.00	$0.2166	$8.6648
20	40	$1 040.00	$0.2083	$216.6206
Σ	**Total**			**$1 000.00**

interest formula in equation (B.2). The discounted maturity value is added to the discounted series of interest payments. In our example, the discount rate of 0.04 ($y/2$), equates the value of future cash flows of 40 interest payments ($N*2$) and one principal payment at maturity with the price of the bond. In other words, we calculate the present value of the coupon interest payments and the principal by using the annuity and single cash flow formulas in equations (A.6) and (A.3). Table B.1 can be summarized as:

$$\$1000 = PV(Ordinary\ Annuity) + PV(Single\ Cash\ Flow)$$

The YTM calculation incorporates the coupon income, the capital gain or loss from the difference between the principal value and the bond price, and the timing of the cash flows. Often, investors may be interested to know the yield-to-call (YTC). Bonds with call options can potentially disturb the investment decisions of bondholders if the issuer of the security chooses to exercise its call option. Generally, it will be known when and at what price the issuers can call their bonds. Therefore, yield-to-call can still be estimated using equation (B.3), where the left-hand side will be equal to a predetermined call price, but the right-hand side of the equality remains the same, as in the example above with time-to-maturity, of course, substituted with time-to-call. The iterative method of finding the YTC remains unchanged.

5. YIELD OF A ZERO-COUPON BOND

Not all municipal bonds pay coupon interest. A zero-coupon bond has a 0 percent coupon rate and does not pay interest. A zero-coupon bond has only one cash flow, that being at final maturity. Since there is only one cash flow, the price of a zero-coupon bond is found using the single cash flow formula, the same formula used to discount the principal value:

$$BP = \frac{P_n}{(1 + y)^n} \qquad (B.4)$$

For a 30-year zero-coupon bond priced to yield 5 percent, assuming semi-annual compounding, the bond price is $227.29, as calculated below:

$$BP = \frac{\$1000}{(1 + 0.025)^{60}} = \$227.29$$

Notice in Figure B.1 that the present value, or price, of the bond grows over time to the principal value at maturity. This is why the zero-coupon bond is also called a capital appreciation bond. The bond accretes in value from the initial purchase price to the principal value at maturity. The rate of appreciation is the yield rate.[3]

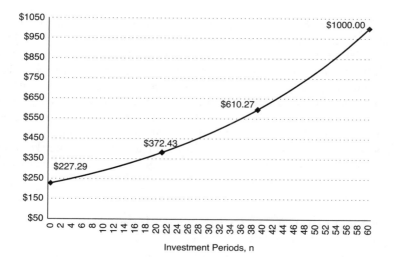

Figure B.1 *Present Value of zero-coupon bond, maturity = 30 years, y = 5%, par = $1000*

The YTM of a zero-coupon bond can be determined by rewriting equation (B.4) above:

$$BP = \frac{P_n}{(1 + y)^n}$$

$$(1 + y)^n = \frac{P_n}{BP}$$

$$y = \left(\frac{P_n}{BP}\right)^{\frac{1}{60}} - 1 \qquad\qquad (B.5)$$

Therefore, if you knew that the bond's price was $227.29 (from the zero-coupon bond example above), you could derive the yield:

$$y = \left(\frac{\$1,000}{\$227.29}\right)^{\frac{1}{60}} - 1$$

$$y = 1.025 - 1 = 0.025 = 2.5\%$$

6.   FACTORS AFFECTING BOND PRICE

This next section describes the relationship between bond prices and several variables that affect bond prices. We begin by describing the basic relationship between changes in market interest rates and bond prices. Since the present value of a bond changes simultaneously with exogenous (determined by external market forces) changes in interest rates, understanding the effect of interest rates on bond prices is fundamentally important to understanding bonds and other debt instruments. Next, we add additional layers to our discussion by describing the relationship between coupon rates, maturity and bond prices. Unlike changes in market interest rates, coupon rates and maturity are endogenous (determined by the issuer) characteristics of a debt instrument.

7.   BOND PRICE–YIELD RELATIONSHIP

A bond's price moves inversely with interest rates. In other words, the price of the bond changes in the opposite direction to the interest rate, or required yield. Since the bond price is the present value of its cash flows, if there is a change in the yield used to discount those cash flows, the price of the bond changes. As the required yield increases (decreases) bond price decreases (increases). Often the change in the required yield is based on changes in market interest rates. As the level of interest rates change, the investors' required yield is also likely to change. The cash flows are fixed, so the only way to change the compensation to investors to reflect the change in required yield is to change the bond's price.

The change in the required yield is literally a change in the discount rate used to discount the cash flows. At a lower discount rate, the cash flows have a higher present value, and therefore investors demand a higher bond price. On the other hand, at a higher discount rate the cash flows have a lower present value, and therefore investors accept a lower bond price. The required yield that investors demand may also change as a result of several other factors including changes in the credit quality of the bond, tax issues affecting the after-tax return on the bond, and the expected return on alternative investments.

Table B.2 and Figure B.2 show the price–yield relationship for a 5

Table B.2 *Relationship between required yield (ry) (2% to 20%) and bond price (BP), BP(CR=0.05), BP(CR=0.10), and BP(CR=0.15)*

ry	BP (CR=5%)	BP (CR=10%)	BP (CR=15%)
0.02	$1 587.94	$2 567.84	$3 547.75
0.03	$1 350.00	$2 224.99	$3 099.98
0.04	$1 157.12	$1 942.71	$2 728.30
0.05	**$1 000.00**	**$1 709.06**	**$2 418.12**
0.06	$ 871.35	$1 514.60	$2 157.84
0.07	$ 765.44	$1 351.83	$1 938.22
0.08	$ 677.77	$1 214.82	$1 751.88
0.09	$ 604.76	$1 098.81	$1 592.86
0.10	**$ 543.60**	**$1 000.00**	**$1 456.40**
0.11	$ 492.05	$915.34	$1 338.63
0.12	$ 448.33	$842.38	$1 236.43
0.13	$ 411.02	$779.13	$1 147.25
0.14	$ 378.97	$723.99	$1 069.00
0.15	**$ 351.26**	**$675.63**	**$1 000.00**
0.16	$ 327.16	$633.00	$938.83
0.17	$ 306.06	$595.20	$884.34
0.18	$ 287.49	$561.53	$835.57
0.19	$ 271.04	$531.38	$791.73
0.20	$ 256.39	$504.26	$752.13

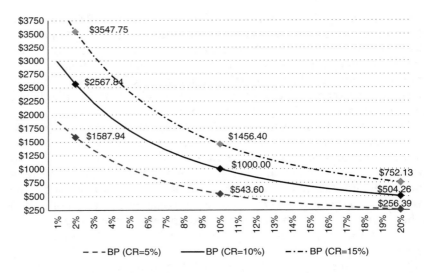

Figure B.2   *Relationship between required yield (ry) (2% to 20%)*
            and bond price (BP), BP(CR=0.05), BP(CR=0.10) and
            BP(CR=0.15)

percent, 10 percent and 15 percent coupon bond with a 25-year maturity. The first column in Table B.2 shows the required yield. The third
column shows the prices for a 10 percent coupon bond at various levels
of the required yield. As the required yield increases from 2 percent
to 20 percent, the price of the par bond decreases from $2567.84 to
$504.26. Why? The present value of a promised future cash flow is
inversely related to the discount rate. As the yield increases, the value of
each of the bond's cash flow components – the coupon interest and the
principal – decreases. The bond's price is decreasing because the price
is the sum of the present value of the cash flows; the higher (lower) the
discount rate, the lower (higher) the price of the bond. Also note that the
price–yield relationship in the graph is not linear. In bond terminology,
the price–yield relationship is referred to as curvilinear and is convex to
the origin.

8. RELATIONSHIP BETWEEN COUPON RATE, YIELD AND PRICE

The required yield used to discount the coupon cash flows affects the
price of the bond. The required yield relative to the coupon rate deter-

mines whether the bond is priced as a discount, par or premium bond. The relationship between coupon rate, yield and price can be observed in Table B.2 and Figure B.2. In the figure, we depict yield curves for bonds that pay coupon rates of 5 percent, 10 percent and 15 percent. Notice that as required yields increase, prices for all three bonds decrease. However, the prices are either above, equal or below the par value of $1000, depending on the coupon and yield rates.

For example, the column for the bond prices when the coupon rate is 10 percent in Table B.2 shows that when the coupon rate is equal to the required yield the price is equal to $1000. However, when the required yield is below 10 percent (which is below the coupon rate of 10 percent) the bond prices are greater than $1000. On the other hand, when the required yield is above 10 percent (which is above the coupon rate of 10 percent) the bond prices are less than $1000. The same dynamic is true for the bonds that have coupon rates of 5 percent and 15 percent, as seen from the remaining two columns in the table. Table B.3 summarizes these relationships between coupon rates, yields and bond prices.

From Table B.3 we learn that if a bond's price is set at the prevailing level of interest rates in the market, the bond's price will be approximately equal to par. If the bond is priced at par, the coupon interest rate equals the yield, and the bond is said to be a par (value) bond. If the coupon rate is greater than the yield, the bond is priced at a premium above par, and is a premium bond. If the coupon rate is less than the yield, the bond is priced at a discount below par, and is a discount bond. Finally, zero coupon bonds are deeply discounted bonds.

Prices are often quoted as a percentage of par. Table B.4 shows how a price quote is converted into a dollar price. (Discount > Par > Premium (95–105)). A discount bond with a quoted price of 96 and a par value of $1000 is priced at $960.00 (0.96 × $1000), or $960.00 per $1000. A par bond has a quoted price of 100, and a premium bond with a quoted price of 104 is priced at $1040.00 (1.04 × $1000), or $1040.00 per $1000.

Table B.3   Price expectations for coupon and yield rates, Pn = $1000

Relationship	Bond type	Expected price
Coupon Rate = Yield	Par	$1000
Coupon Rate > Yield	Premium	Above $1000
Coupon Rate < Yield	Discount	Below $1000
Zero Coupon Rate < Yield	Deep Discount	Below $1000

Table B.4   Price quote to dollar price, Pn = $1000

Price quote (PQ)	Conversion index (PQ/100)	Dollar price
95	0.95	$950.00
96	0.96	$960.00
97	0.97	$970.00
98	0.98	$980.00
99	0.99	$990.00
100	1.00	$1 000.00
101	1.01	$1 010.00
102	1.02	$1 020.00
103	1.03	$1 030.00
104	1.04	$1 040.00
105	1.05	$1 050.00

9.   RELATIONSHIP BETWEEN BOND PRICE AND MATURITY

Table B.5 and Figure B.3 show the relationship between bond price and final maturity for a zero-coupon bond with a required yield of 10 percent, assuming annual interest compounding. The longer the final maturity of a zero-coupon bond, the lower its price. The more distant a future cash flow of a given amount, the less value it has in today's dollars or present value.

10.   PRICE–TIME PATH OF A BOND

For coupon-bearing bonds, the bond's time path is dependent on the initial price of the bond. Figure B.4 shows the price–time path of premium, par and discount bonds. The time path shows the bond's price from the initial sale to final maturity, holding all else constant. Each bond has a 10 percent coupon rate with a 25-year final maturity; the premium bond is priced to yield 5 percent, the par bond is priced to yield 10 percent, and the discount bond is priced to yield 15 percent. At the final maturity each bond is redeemed at par value ($1000). For the premium and discount bonds, the time path shows the bond price movement from the initial sale price to par at maturity. As time increases (or as the time to bond maturity decreases) the value of a premium (discount) bond naturally decreases (increases) from market price to par value at maturity.

Table B.5   *Relationship between maturity (1 to 20 years) and zero coupon bond price, Pn = $1000, ry = 0.10*

Maturity	Bond price = $Pn(1/(1+ry)^n)$
1	$909.09
2	$826.45
3	$751.31
4	$683.01
5	$620.92
6	$564.47
7	$513.16
8	$466.51
9	$424.10
10	$385.54
11	$350.49
12	$318.63
13	$289.66
14	$263.33
15	$239.39
16	$217.63
17	$197.84
18	$179.86
19	$163.51
20	$148.64

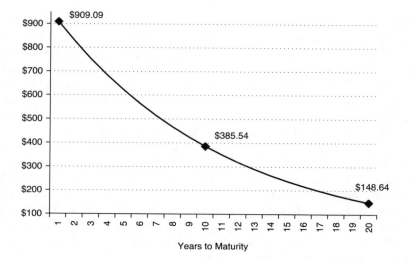

Figure B.3   *Relationship between maturity (1 to 20 years) and zero coupon bond price, Pn = $1000, ry = 0.10*

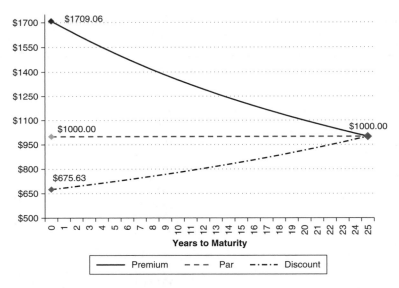

Figure B.4   Time path of premium (ry=15%), par (ry=10%), and discount bonds (ry=5%), CR = 0.10, maturity = 25 years

11.   BOND PRICES AND INTEREST RATE RISK

Debt can take dramatic swings in value from changes in interest rates. This is referred to as interest rate risk – the risk that changes in interest rates will affect the value of the debt. Risk involves the idea that expected returns will be different from actual returns. If interest rates change substantially over the life of a debt instrument, expected returns can be very different (greater or less) than actual returns. The relationship between changes in interest rates and changes in debt prices often results in bond price volatility. Price volatility is the change, usually measured as a percentage, in price.

We begin with the problem of reinvestment rate risk and the yield measure realized compound yield (RCY).[4] Reinvestment rate risk refers to the risk that the yield on reinvested coupon cash flows will be different from the yield-to-maturity (YTM) rate. Though YTM is the most often used measure of bond return, it assumes that all cash flows are reinvested at the YTM rate.[5] If the cash flows are not invested on average at the YTM rate, the YTM figure will not accurately reflect actual returns. The expected return may not be realized.

The RCY figure is the discount rate that equates the total future return of a bond investment to its current market price. The total future return

Table B.6 *Relationship between time to maturity (1 to 20 years) and bond prices, RCY at 2%, 8% and 14%*

Maturity	BP (RCY 2%)	BP (RCY=YTM 8%)	BP (RCY 14%)
1	$1078.82	$1018.86	$963.84
2	$1156.08	$1036.30	$932.26
3	$1231.82	$1052.42	$904.67
4	$1306.07	$1067.33	$880.57
5	$1378.85	$1081.11	$859.53
6	$1450.20	$1093.85	$841.15
7	$1520.15	$1105.63	$825.09
8	$1588.71	$1116.52	$811.07
9	$1655.93	$1126.59	$798.82
10	$1721.82	$1135.90	$788.12
11	$1786.42	$1144.51	$778.78
12	$1849.74	$1152.47	$770.61
13	$1911.81	$1159.83	$763.48
14	$1972.66	$1166.63	$757.26
15	$2032.31	$1172.92	$751.82
16	$2090.78	$1178.74	$747.07
17	$2148.11	$1184.11	$742.92
18	$2204.30	$1189.08	$739.30
19	$2259.39	$1193.68	$736.13
20	$2313.39	$1197.93	$733.37

includes the principal payment, coupon interest payments and the reinvestment of those cash flows at a rate of return.[6] The RCY can be calculated on an *ex ante* or *ex post* basis. On an *ex ante* basis, the reinvestment rate can be projected from expected changes in interest rates during the life of the bond to simulate what will happen to the bond's total future return if market interest rates change during the life of the bond. On an *ex post* basis, RCY is calculated using the rate of reinvestment return on actual coupon payments reinvested until the final maturity date. If the coupon interest payments are reinvested at the YTM rate, then the RCY will equal the YTM. If the coupon payments are not reinvested at the YTM rate, then the actual returns on the bond will be different from the expected returns. When the coupon interest payments are not reinvested at the YTM rate, the RCY is a better measure of actual return than YTM. A broader measure of return, however, is the total future return (TFR) relative to the same fixed coupon yield. TFR would account for RCY and any transactions costs or price adjustments along the way. These extra costs can be any transaction fees, taxes, yield changes, inflation, default losses and so on.

Table B.6 and Figure B.5 show bond prices for three conditions where RCY equals 2 percent, 8 percent and 14 percent. Only one of these

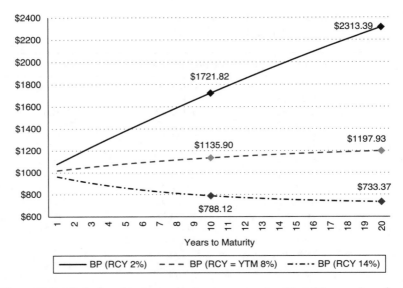

Figure B.5   Relationship between time to maturity (1 to 20 years) and bond prices, RCY at 2%, 8% and 14%

RCY at 8 percent happens to equal YTM at 8 percent. The coupon rate is 10 percent, meaning that the RCY at 2 percent and 8 percent are premium bonds, while the RCY at 14 percent is a discount bond. One can see that if the coupon interest cash flows are not reinvested at YTM rates, the expected losses or gains can be substantial for longer maturity bonds. In other words, when the RCY and YTM both are equal to 8 percent, one price curve would be on top of the other (the middle curve). However, when RCY is 2 percent, which is much less than YTM at 8 percent, the loss to the investor would be the difference between the two price curves (between the middle and top curves). Alternatively, when the RCY is 14 percent, greater than the YTM at 8 percent, the investor would gain funds equal to the difference between these curves (between the middle curve and the bottom curve). These differences in losses or gains when RCY deviates from YTM are greatest as time to maturity increases.[7]

12.   MEASURING BOND PRICE RISK

The following section examines the price volatility characteristics of municipal bonds. Price volatility is the change in price. The price of a bond changes in the opposite direction to the change in the required yield for the bond. Using the illustration provided previously in Table B.2 and Figure B.2 (5 percent, 10 percent and 15 percent/25-year, yields 2–20 percent), it is easy to see that as the yield increases, price decreases. Notice that as the yield changes from the origin, the slope is convex at a decreasing rate.

13. NON-SYMMETRIC CHANGES IN PRICE FOR CHANGES IN YIELD

This highlights the basic property that bond price increases are greater than decreases for a change in yield. Given a change in yield (e.g. 200 bps), the percentage increase in price is greater for a decrease in yield than the percentage decrease in price for an increase in yield. Table B.7 shows that increases in bond prices as yield decreases are greater than decreases in bond prices as yield increases. For a 200bps decrease in yield, the bond's

Table B.7   Interest risk exposure, $Pn = \$1000$, coupon rate $= 0.10$, maturity $= 25$ years; $ry = 1\%$ to 20%

Yield	$BP = C[\{1-(1/(1+ry)^n)\}/ry] + Pn(1/(1+ry)^n)$	Yield change from par	BP change from par	BP % change from par
0.01	**$2986.43**	**−0.09**	**$1986.43**	**198.64%**
0.02	$2567.84	−0.08	$1567.84	156.78%
0.03	$2224.99	−0.07	$1224.99	122.50%
0.04	$1942.71	−0.06	$942.71	94.27%
0.05	**$1709.06**	**−0.05**	**$709.06**	**70.91%**
0.06	$1514.60	−0.04	$514.60	51.46%
0.07	$1351.83	−0.03	$351.83	35.18%
0.08	$1214.82	−0.02	$214.82	21.48%
0.09	$1098.81	−0.01	$98.81	9.88%
0.10	**$1000.00**	**0.00**	**$0.00**	**0.00%**
0.11	$ 915.34	0.01	−$84.66	−8.47%
0.12	$ 842.38	0.02	−$157.62	−15.76%
0.13	$ 779.13	0.03	−$220.87	−22.09%
0.14	$ 723.99	0.04	−$276.01	−27.60%
0.15	**$ 675.63**	**0.05**	**−$324.37**	**−32.44%**
0.16	$ 633.00	0.06	−$367.00	−36.70%
0.17	$ 595.20	0.07	−$404.80	−40.48%
0.18	$ 561.53	0.08	−$438.47	−43.85%
0.19	**$ 531.38**	**0.09**	**−$468.62**	**−46.86%**
0.20	$ 504.26	0.10	−$495.74	−49.57%

Table B.8   Interest risk exposure, Pn = $1000, coupon rate = 0.00 and yield = 0.10, maturity = 25 years; ry = 1% to 20%

Yield	Zero coupon bond			
	$BP = C[\{1-(1/(1+ry)^n)\}/ry] + Pn(1/(1+ry)^n)$	Yield change from par	BP change from par	BP % change from par
0.01	**$779.29**	**−0.09**	**$692.08**	**793.64%**
0.02	$608.04	−0.08	$520.84	597.26%
0.03	$475.00	−0.07	$387.80	444.71%
0.04	$371.53	−0.06	$284.32	326.05%
0.05	**$290.94**	**−0.05**	**$203.74**	**233.64%**
0.06	$228.11	−0.04	$140.90	161.58%
0.07	$179.05	−0.03	$91.85	105.33%
0.08	$140.71	−0.02	$53.51	61.36%
0.09	$110.71	−0.01	$23.51	26.96%
0.10	**$87.20**	**0.00**	**$0.00**	**0.00%**
0.11	$68.77	0.01	−$18.44	−21.14%
0.12	$54.29	0.02	−$32.92	−37.75%
0.13	$42.91	0.03	−$44.30	−50.80%
0.14	$33.95	0.04	−$53.26	−61.07%
0.15	**$26.89**	**0.05**	**−$60.31**	**−69.17%**
0.16	$21.32	0.06	−$65.88	−75.55%
0.17	$16.92	0.07	−$70.28	−80.59%
0.18	$13.45	0.08	−$73.76	−84.58%
0.19	**$10.70**	**0.09**	**−$76.51**	**−87.73%**
0.20	$8.52	0.10	−$78.69	−90.23%

price increases by 21.48 percent, but only decreases by 15.76 percent for the same 200bps increase in yield.

Bond price volatility also varies by coupon rate and final maturity. In general, the lower the bond's coupon rate, the more volatile the bond. A comparison between Table B.7 and Table B.8 shows that when one holds maturity constant, but changes yields from 5 percent to 10 percent to 15 percent, the percentage change in price is greater on lower coupon bonds than higher coupon bonds. So, if yield increases from 10 percent to 15 percent, the zero-coupon bond price changes by 69.17 percent (shown in Table B.8), whereas the 10 percent coupon bond (shown in Table B.7) only changes by 32.44 percent. Generally, it is considered that zero-coupon bonds are the most volatile securities, for better and for worse.

In terms of final maturity, the percentage change in price for a given change in yield is greater the longer the term to maturity (holding the coupon rate constant). Table B.9 (10 percent coupon for 1-year to 25-year

Table B.9 Interest risk exposure, Pn = $1000, coupon rate and yield = 0.10, maturity = 1 year vs. 25 years

Yield	1-year bond				25-year bond			
	$BP = C[\{1-(1/(1+ry)^n)\}/ry] + Pn(1/(1+ry)^n)$	Yield change from par	BP change from par	BP % change from par	$BP = C[\{1-(1/(1+ry)^n)\}/ry] + Pn(1/(1+ry)^n)$	Yield change from par	BP change from par	BP % change from par
0.01	**$1089.33**	**-0.09**	**$89.33**	**8.93%**	**$2986.43**	**-0.09**	**$1986.43**	**198.64%**
0.02	$1078.82	-0.08	$78.82	7.88%	$2567.84	-0.08	$1567.84	156.78%
0.03	$1068.46	-0.07	$68.46	6.85%	2224.99	-0.07	$1224.99	122.50%
0.04	$1058.25	-0.06	$58.25	5.82%	$1942.71	-0.06	$942.71	94.27%
0.05	**$1048.19**	**-0.05**	**$48.19**	**4.82%**	**$1709.06**	**-0.05**	**$709.06**	**70.91%**
0.06	$1038.27	-0.04	$38.27	3.83%	$1514.60	-0.04	$514.60	51.46%
0.07	$1028.50	-0.03	$28.50	2.85%	$1351.83	-0.03	$351.83	35.18%
0.08	$1018.86	-0.02	$18.86	1.89%	$1214.82	-0.02	$214.82	21.48%
0.09	$1009.36	-0.01	$9.36	0.94%	$1098.81	-0.01	$98.81	9.88%
0.10	**$1000.00**	**0.00**	**$0.00**	**0.00%**	**$1000.00**	**0.00**	**$0.00**	**0.00%**
0.11	$990.77	0.01	-$9.23	-0.92%	$915.34	0.01	-$84.66	-8.47%
0.12	$981.67	0.02	-$18.33	-1.83%	$842.38	0.02	-$157.62	-15.76%
0.13	$972.69	0.03	-$27.31	-2.73%	$779.13	0.03	-$220.87	-22.09%
0.14	$963.84	0.04	-$36.16	-3.62%	$723.99	0.04	-$276.01	-27.60%
0.15	**$955.11**	**0.05**	**-$44.89**	**-4.49%**	**$675.63**	**0.05**	**-$324.37**	**-32.44%**
0.16	$946.50	0.06	-$53.50	-5.35%	$633.00	0.06	-$367.00	-36.70%
0.17	$938.01	0.07	-$61.99	-6.20%	$595.20	0.07	-$404.80	-40.48%
0.18	$929.64	0.08	-$70.36	-7.04%	$561.53	0.08	-$438.47	-43.85%
0.19	**$921.37**	**0.09**	**-$78.63**	**-7.86%**	**$531.38**	**0.09**	**-$468.62**	**-46.86%**
0.20	$913.22	0.10	-$86.78	-8.68%	$504.26	0.10	-$495.74	-49.57%

235

maturities, yield changes from 10 percent to 20 percent) shows that as yield changes, the percentage change in bond price is greater for the 25-year bond (-49.57 percent or +198.64 percent) than the 1-year bond (-8.68 percent or +8.93 percent).

14. DURATION

Duration is a general concept and quantitative measure for: (1) understanding a debt instrument's cash flows; and (2) estimating bond price volatility. Duration is similar to a break-even concept because it is the future point in time when an investor expects to receive exactly half of their investment on a present value basis. Duration measures the weighted average life of the bond's cash flows. The weights are the present values of the cash flows themselves. Duration is a measure of interest rate risk when it is used to measure the volatility or sensitivity of the market value of a bond to changes in interest rates. The duration formula is:

$$D = \frac{\sum_{t=1}^{n} \left[\dfrac{t \times C_t}{(1 + y)^t} + \dfrac{n \times M_n}{(1 + y)^n} \right]}{P} \tag{B.6}$$

The duration calculation is simply a weighted average calculation; the nominal cash flows are weighted for time. Each cash flow is weighted for the present value amount of the cash flow, the timing of the cash flow, and its proportionate contribution to the total present value of the bond. Each nominal cash flow is converted to its present value amount $\left(\frac{C_t}{(1 + y)^t} + \frac{M_n}{(1 + y)^n} \right)$, multiplied by the time period it occurs in $\left(\frac{t \times C_t}{(1 + y)^t} + \frac{n \times M_n}{(1 + y)^n} \right)$, and divided by the price of the bond $\frac{\left[\frac{t \times C_t}{(1 + y)^t} + \frac{n \times M_n}{(1 + y)^n} \right]}{P}$.

Duration has an important relationship with term-to-maturity, coupon rate and yield. Duration is inversely related to a bond's coupon rate of interest, yield and payment frequency and directly related to time to maturity. These duration properties are consistent with the bond price volatility properties discussed earlier.

15. DURATION AND COUPON INTEREST PAYMENTS

A bond's coupon rate and duration are inversely related. Lower (higher) coupon bonds have longer (shorter) durations, all held equal. A lower coupon rate generates lower coupon cash flows in the earlier years relative

Table B.10   *Macaulay and modified durations for a 10-year, 10% required yield; 0% and 4% coupons*

Years	Period (n*2=t)	Present value of $1 at 10%	0% coupon			4% coupon		
			Cash flow	PV of cash flow	t × PV of cash flow	Cash flow	PV of cash flow	t × PV of cash flow
0.5	1	0.9524			0.00	20.00	19.05	19.05
1	2	0.9070			0.00	20.00	18.14	36.28
1.5	3	0.8638			0.00	20.00	17.28	51.83
2	4	0.8227			0.00	20.00	16.45	65.82
2.5	5	0.7835			0.00	20.00	15.67	78.35
3	6	0.7462			0.00	20.00	14.92	89.55
3.5	7	0.7107			0.00	20.00	14.21	99.50
4	8	0.6768			0.00	20.00	13.54	108.29
4.5	9	0.6446			0.00	20.00	12.89	116.03
5	10	0.6139			0.00	20.00	12.28	122.78
5.5	11	0.5847			0.00	20.00	11.69	128.63
6	12	0.5568			0.00	20.00	11.14	133.64
6.5	13	0.5303			0.00	20.00	10.61	137.88
7	14	0.5051			0.00	20.00	10.10	141.42
7.5	15	0.4810			0.00	20.00	9.62	144.31
8	16	0.4581			0.00	20.00	9.16	146.60
8.5	17	0.4363			0.00	20.00	8.73	148.34
9	18	0.4155			0.00	20.00	8.31	149.59
9.5	19	0.3957			0.00	20.00	7.91	150.38
10	20	0.3769	1000.00	376.89	7537.79	1020.00	384.43	7688.55
Σ	**Total**			**$ 376.89**	**7537.79**		**$626.13**	**9756.80**
Macaulay duration (in half years) =					20.00			15.58
Macaulay duration (in years) =					10.00			7.79
Modified duration (in years) =					9.09			7.08

to the price paid for the bond than a higher coupon rate bond. Therefore it takes investors longer to recoup their investment on a low coupon rate bond, and thus, the duration will be necessarily longer. A higher coupon rate results in higher interest cash flows relative to the price paid, thereby decreasing the bond duration, or decreasing the time it takes for investors to recoup their investment.

In the duration formula, higher coupon payments result in earlier payments receiving greater weight than later payments. In Tables B.10 and B.11, for example, the 0 percent coupon bond has a duration of 10 and the 12 percent coupon bond has a duration of 6.31. Lower coupon bonds have more relative weight placed on the last cash flow which includes interest and principal. For a zero-coupon bond, the maturity of the bond is the duration of the bond. Why? There is only one cash flow and it's on the maturity date.

Table B.11   *Macaulay and modified durations for a 10-year, 10% required*
              yield; 8% and 12% coupons

Years	Period $(n*2=t)$	Present value of $1 at 10%	8% coupon			12% coupon		
			Cash flow	PV of cash flow	$t \times PV$ of cash flow	Cash flow	PV of cash flow	$t \times PV$ of cash flow
0.5	1	0.9524	40.00	38.10	38.10	60.00	57.14	57.14
1	2	0.9070	40.00	36.28	72.56	60.00	54.42	108.84
1.5	3	0.8638	40.00	34.55	103.66	60.00	51.83	155.49
2	4	0.8227	40.00	32.91	131.63	60.00	49.36	197.45
2.5	5	0.7835	40.00	31.34	156.71	60.00	47.01	235.06
3	6	0.7462	40.00	29.85	179.09	60.00	44.77	268.64
3.5	7	0.7107	40.00	28.43	198.99	60.00	42.64	298.49
4	8	0.6768	40.00	27.07	216.59	60.00	40.61	324.88
4.5	9	0.6446	40.00	25.78	232.06	60.00	38.68	348.09
5	10	0.6139	40.00	24.56	245.57	60.00	36.83	368.35
5.5	11	0.5847	40.00	23.39	257.26	60.00	35.08	385.89
6	12	0.5568	40.00	22.27	267.28	60.00	33.41	400.92
6.5	13	0.5303	40.00	21.21	275.77	60.00	31.82	413.65
7	14	0.5051	40.00	20.20	282.84	60.00	30.30	424.26
7.5	15	0.4810	40.00	19.24	288.61	60.00	28.86	432.92
8	16	0.4581	40.00	18.32	293.19	60.00	27.49	439.79
8.5	17	0.4363	40.00	17.45	296.68	60.00	26.18	445.02
9	18	0.4155	40.00	16.62	299.17	60.00	24.93	448.76
9.5	19	0.3957	40.00	15.83	300.76	60.00	23.74	451.14
10	20	0.3769	1 040.00	391.97	7 839.30	1 060.00	399.50	7 990.06
Σ	**Total**			**$875.38**	**11975.81**		**$1 124.62**	**14 194.83**
Macaulay duration (in half years) =					13.68			12.62
Macaulay duration (in years) =					6.84			6.31
Modified duration (in years) =					6.22			5.74

16.   DURATION AND YIELD

Duration is inversely related to yield, holding coupon rate and maturity constant. Lower yield levels create longer durations. An increase in
yield increases the weights assigned to early cash flows and decreases the
weights assigned to later cash flows. In Tables B.12 and B.13 we illustrate
the durations for bonds with an 8 percent coupon, 10-year maturity, and
yields from 2 percent to 5 percent to 8 percent to 11 percent. An increase
(decrease) in yield shortens (lengthens) duration.

Furthermore, as yields decline, duration grows at an increasing rate.
Duration increases at an increasing rate the lower the yield environment. This indicates that maturity extensions are increasingly risky in

Table B.12   *Macaulay and modified durations for a 10-year, 8% coupon;*
2% and 5% yield

Years	Period $(n*2=t)$	Cash flow at 8% coupon	2% yield			5% yield		
			Present value of $1	PV of cash flow	$t \times PV$ of cash flow	Present value of $1	PV of cash flow	$t \times PV$ of cash flow
0.5	1	40.00	0.9901	39.60	39.60	0.9756	39.02	39.02
1	2	40.00	0.9803	39.21	78.42	0.9518	38.07	76.15
1.5	3	40.00	0.9706	38.82	116.47	0.9286	37.14	111.43
2	4	40.00	0.9610	38.44	153.76	0.9060	36.24	144.95
2.5	5	40.00	0.9515	38.06	190.29	0.8839	35.35	176.77
3	6	40.00	0.9420	37.68	226.09	0.8623	34.49	206.95
3.5	7	40.00	0.9327	37.31	261.16	0.8413	33.65	235.55
4	8	40.00	0.9235	36.94	295.51	0.8207	32.83	262.64
4.5	9	40.00	0.9143	36.57	329.16	0.8007	32.03	288.26
5	10	40.00	0.9053	36.21	362.11	0.7812	31.25	312.48
5.5	11	40.00	0.8963	35.85	394.38	0.7621	30.49	335.34
6	12	40.00	0.8874	35.50	425.98	0.7436	29.74	356.91
6.5	13	40.00	0.8787	35.15	456.90	0.7254	29.02	377.22
7	14	40.00	0.8700	34.80	487.18	0.7077	28.31	396.33
7.5	15	40.00	0.8613	34.45	516.81	0.6905	27.62	414.28
8	16	40.00	0.8528	34.11	545.81	0.6736	26.94	431.12
8.5	17	40.00	0.8444	33.78	574.18	0.6572	26.29	446.89
9	18	40.00	0.8360	33.44	601.93	0.6412	25.65	461.64
9.5	19	40.00	0.8277	33.11	629.08	0.6255	25.02	475.40
10	20	1 040.00	0.8195	852.33	17 046.52	0.6103	634.68	12 693.64
Σ	**Total**			**$1 541.37**	**23 731.37**		**$1 233.84**	**18 242.97**
Macaulay duration (in half years) =					15.40			14.79
Macaulay duration (in years) =					7.70			7.39
Modified duration (in years) =					7.55			7.04

lower yield environments than in higher yield environments. The inverse relationship between duration and market yield level can be traced to changes in present value factors and the shifting relative cash flow weights.

17.   DURATION AND PAYMENT FREQUENCY

Most bonds pay coupon interest every six months or semi-annually. But payment frequency can be other than semi-annual (quarterly, annual, etc.). The more frequently payments are made, the shorter the duration. The more frequent the coupon payments, the quicker investors recoup their original investments.

Table B.13 Macaulay and modified durations for a 10 year, 8% coupon; 8% and 11% yield

Years	Period (n*2=t)	Cash Flow at 8% coupon	8% Yield			11% Yield		
			Present value of $1	PV of cash flow	t × PV of cash flow	Present value of $1	PV of cash flow	t × PV of cash flow
0.5	1	40.00	0.9615	38.46	38.46	0.9479	37.91	37.91
1	2	40.00	0.9246	36.98	73.96	0.8985	35.94	71.88
1.5	3	40.00	0.8890	35.56	106.68	0.8516	34.06	102.19
2	4	40.00	0.8548	34.19	136.77	0.8072	32.29	129.15
2.5	5	40.00	0.8219	32.88	164.39	0.7651	30.61	153.03
3	6	40.00	0.7903	31.61	189.68	0.7252	29.01	174.06
3.5	7	40.00	0.7599	30.40	212.78	0.6874	27.50	192.48
4	8	40.00	0.7307	29.23	233.82	0.6516	26.06	208.51
4.5	9	40.00	0.7026	28.10	252.93	0.6176	24.71	222.35
5	10	40.00	0.6756	27.02	270.23	0.5854	23.42	234.17
5.5	11	40.00	0.6496	25.98	285.82	0.5549	22.20	244.16
6	12	40.00	0.6246	24.98	299.81	0.5260	21.04	252.47
6.5	13	40.00	0.6006	24.02	312.30	0.4986	19.94	259.25
7	14	40.00	0.5775	23.10	323.39	0.4726	18.90	264.64
7.5	15	40.00	0.5553	22.21	333.16	0.4479	17.92	268.76
8	16	40.00	0.5339	21.36	341.70	0.4246	16.98	271.73
8.5	17	40.00	0.5134	20.53	349.09	0.4024	16.10	273.66
9	18	40.00	0.4936	19.75	355.41	0.3815	15.26	274.66
9.5	19	40.00	0.4746	18.99	360.73	0.3616	14.46	274.80
10	20	1 040.00	0.4564	474.64	9 492.85	0.3427	356.44	7 128.76
Σ	**Total**			**$1 000.00**	**14 133.94**		**$820.74**	**11 038.63**
Macaulay Duration (in half years) =					14.13			13.45
Macaulay Duration (in years) =					**7.07**			**6.72**
Modified Duration (in years) =					6.54			6.06

18. DURATION AND MATURITY

Duration is directly related to term-to-maturity. Longer maturity bonds have higher durations than shorter maturity bonds. In common sense terms, since duration is also a measure of time, the longer the term-to-maturity of a bond, the longer its duration. Zero-coupon bonds have a duration that is the same as the term-to-maturity. Bonds that pay coupon interest have a duration less than the term-to-maturity, and the higher the coupon, the shorter the duration. Tables B.14 and B.15 show durations for varying maturities, all else equal. Longer maturity bonds are more risky than shorter maturity bonds because the principal payment component accounts for most of the recoupment duration. The principal payment

Table B.14 *Macaulay and modified durations for 10% coupon, 10% yield, and 1-year and 3-year maturity*

Years	Period (n*2=t)	Present value of $1 at 10%	1-year maturity			3-year maturity		
			Cash flow	PV of cash flow	t × PV of cash flow	Cash flow	PV of cash flow	t × PV of cash flow
0.5	1	0.9524	50.00	47.62	47.62	50.00	47.62	47.62
1	2	0.9070	1050.00	952.38	1904.76	50.00	45.35	90.70
1.5	3	0.8638				50.00	43.19	129.58
2	4	0.8227				50.00	41.14	164.54
2.5	5	0.7835				50.00	39.18	195.88
3	6	0.7462				1050.00	783.53	4701.16
3.5	7	0.7107						
4	8	0.6768						
4.5	9	0.6446						
5	10	0.6139						
5.5	11	0.5847						
6	12	0.5568						
6.5	13	0.5303						
7	14	0.5051						
7.5	15	0.4810						
8	16	0.4581						
8.5	17	0.4363						
9	18	0.4155						
9.5	19	0.3957						
10	20	0.3769						
Σ	**Total**			**$1000.00**	**1952.38**		**$1000.00**	**5329.48**
Macaulay duration (in half years) =					1.95			5.33
Macaulay duration (in years) =					0.98			2.66
Modified duration (in years) =					0.89			2.42

cash flow weight of longer maturity bonds is significantly higher than shorter maturity bonds. The higher cash flow weight makes the PV weight significantly larger.

19. DURATION AND PRICE VOLATILITY

The duration concept discussed to this point is named after Frederick Macaulay (1938) who is credited for developing the measure. However, in addition to Macaulay duration there is an adjusted version of duration. It is simply called modified duration and is calculated as follows:

Table B.15   Macaulay and modified durations for 10% coupon, 10% yield,
and 5-year and 10-year maturity

Years	Period $(n*2=t)$	Present value of $1 at 10%	5-year maturity			10-year maturity		
			Cash flow	PV of cash flow	$t \times PV$ of cash flow	Cash flow	PV of cash flow	$t \times PV$ of cash flow
0.5	1	0.9524	50.00	47.62	47.62	50.00	47.62	47.62
1	2	0.9070	50.00	45.35	90.70	50.00	45.35	90.70
1.5	3	0.8638	50.00	43.19	129.58	50.00	43.19	129.58
2	4	0.8227	50.00	41.14	164.54	50.00	41.14	164.54
2.5	5	0.7835	50.00	39.18	195.88	50.00	39.18	195.88
3	6	0.7462	50.00	37.31	223.86	50.00	37.31	223.86
3.5	7	0.7107	50.00	35.53	248.74	50.00	35.53	248.74
4	8	0.6768	50.00	33.84	270.74	50.00	33.84	270.74
4.5	9	0.6446	50.00	32.23	290.07	50.00	32.23	290.07
5	10	0.6139	1050.00	644.61	6446.09	50.00	30.70	306.96
5.5	11	0.5847				50.00	29.23	321.57
6	12	0.5568				50.00	27.84	334.10
6.5	13	0.5303				50.00	26.52	344.71
7	14	0.5051				50.00	25.25	353.55
7.5	15	0.4810				50.00	24.05	360.76
8	16	0.4581				50.00	22.91	366.49
8.5	17	0.4363				50.00	21.81	370.85
9	18	0.4155				50.00	20.78	373.97
9.5	19	0.3957				50.00	19.79	375.95
10	20	0.3769				1050.00	395.73	7914.68
Σ	**Total**		**$1000.00**		8107.82		**$1000.00**	13085.32
Macaulay duration (in half years) =					8.11			13.09
Macaulay duration (in years) =					4.05			6.54
Modified duration (in years) =					3.69			5.95

$$Modified\ Duration = \frac{Macaulays\ Duration}{1 + \left(\dfrac{Yield}{N}\right)}$$

$$MD = \frac{D}{1 + \left(\dfrac{Yield}{N}\right)} \tag{B.7}$$

A bond's modified duration is an estimate of price sensitivity or volatility to changes in yield. Higher yield levels and longer bond durations lead to more sizable differences between the two duration formulations. The bond price volatility formula is:

Percent Change in Bond Price = − (Modified Duration) ×

Percentage Basis Point Change in Yield

$$\frac{\Delta P}{P} = -(MD) \times \frac{\Delta Y}{1 + Y} \tag{B.8}$$

For example, from Table B.15, we can estimate bond interest rate risk exposure for the 10-year maturity bond for a 1 percent increase in yield.

$$\frac{\Delta P}{P} = -(MD) \times \frac{\Delta Y}{1 + Y}$$

$$\frac{\Delta P}{\$1000} = -(6.54) \times \frac{0.01}{1 + 0.1}$$

$$\frac{\Delta P}{\$1000} = -0.05946 \text{ or } -5.95\%$$

where:

$\Delta P = -0.0594 \times \$1000$
$\Delta P = -\$59.46$

The modified duration component functions as a multiplier. Modified duration adjustments are more extreme: (1) the larger the change in yield; and (2) the higher the bond's duration. Modified duration is the first derivative of the price/yield function. The first derivative is the slope (the slope of the tangent line) of the price/yield (change in price for a change in yield) curve at a specified point. The price/yield curve is convex to the origin, and the price returns above and beyond those explained by the duration line are called convexity returns.

20. CONVEXITY

Convexity is the second derivative of the price/yield function and graphically consists of the portion of returns between the linear slope line (modified duration) and the curvilinear price/yield curve. Convexity effects are magnified by large changes in yield and by bonds with long durations. Longer maturity bonds exhibit more positive convexity. Convexity enhances price increases and moderates price decreases.

Figure B.6 illustrates the price/yield relationship for a 30-year, 10 percent

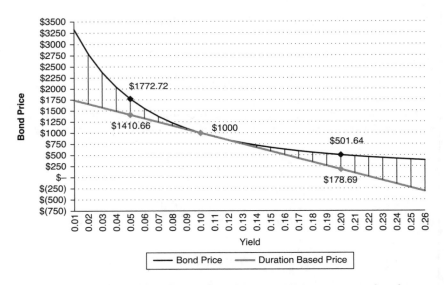

Figure B.6   Yield and bond price for a 30-year, 10% coupon par bond, duration based price and convexity

coupon rate par bond. Notice that the straight line is a measure of bond duration. For smaller yield fluctuations around the initial 10 percent yield, duration is a relatively good tool to assess bond interest rate risk exposure. However, for greater levels of yield shifts, the straight line becomes less accurate. Therefore, it becomes important to correct for the deviations from the straight line for points along the convex line to estimate true gains or losses due to market interest rate risk fluctuations.

Convexity factors are used in conjunction with modified durations to construct price volatility multipliers. The price volatility multiplier is simply the modified duration adjusted for convexity impacts. These price volatility multipliers are better predictors of a bond's price sensitivity than modified durations only. Once again, this is particularly true as prices and yields move away from their current levels farther from the original modified duration slope. However, in stable economies, large year-to-year yield jumps are infrequent. Therefore, duration remains a very useful tool for assessing interest rate risk exposures for bonds, and by extension, bond portfolios.

NOTES

1. For illustration purposes we will use $1000 as par value; today, municipal bonds par value is typically $5000 or $25 000.
2. The yield-to-maturity formula is the general internal rate of return formula applied to bond cash flows.
3. Since a zero-coupon bond has only one cash flow, the YTM on a zero-coupon bond is easier to calculate than the YTM of a bond that pays coupon interest.
4. This yield measure is also sometimes referred to as horizon return. We prefer to use the term realized compound yield (RCY) because the name emphasizes the sensitivity of the reinvestment rate of the coupon cash flows to the total future return.
5. Also, the bond is held to maturity and redeemed at par.
6. Reinvestment return is also called 'interest-on-interest' because coupon interest payments are commonly reinvested in interest-bearing instruments.
7. Bonds may be priced based on RCY expectations. The importance of reinvestment return is fueled by high interest rate (expected or actual) environments, long bond maturities and high coupon rates. The initial attraction of zero-coupon bonds was due to their lower reinvestment rate risk compared to traditional coupon bonds. Also, the expected value of a portfolio with fixed income securities is subject to reinvestment rate risk.

References

PART I

Chapter 1

Government Finance Officers Association (GFOA) (1997). 'Best Practice: Using Variable Rate Debt Instruments'. GFOA, Chicago, IL.

Han, S. and Dan Li (2008). 'Liquidity, Runs, and Security Design: Lessons from the Collapse of the Auction Rate Municipal Bond Market'. Federal Reserve Board, Washington, DC.

Johnson, C.L. (2004). 'The State of the Tobacco Settlement'. *Public Budgeting and Finance*, 24(1): 113–21.

Johnson, C.L. and S.N. Kioko (2005). 'The Use of Derivatives to Hedge Risk – The Case of Tobacco Securitization Bonds'. Unpublished paper.

Johnson, C.L. and M.J. Luby (2009). 'The Birth, Growth and Collapse of the Municipal Auction Rate Securities Market'. Unpublished paper.

Johnson, C.L. and J.L. Mikesell (1994). 'Certificates of Participation and Capital Markets: Lessons from Brevard County and Richmond Unified School District'. *Public Budgeting and Finance*, 14(3): 41–54.

Johnson, C.L. and M. Rubin (1998). 'The Municipal Bond Market: Structure and Changes'. In F. Thompson and M.T. Green (eds), *Handbook of Public Finance*, pp. 483–522. New York: Marcel Dekker.

Johnson, C.L., S.N. Kioko and Y. Abbas (2013). 'Tobacco Securitization and Public Spending'. *Albany Government Law Review*, 6(1): 1–29.

Martell, C.R. and R.S. Kravchuk (2012). 'The Liquidity Crisis: The 2007–2009 Market Impacts on Municipal Securities'. *Public Administration Review*, 72: 668–77.

Mikesell, J.L. (2011). *Fiscal Administration*. Boston, MA: Wadsworth Cengage Learning.

Oates, W.E. (2005). 'Toward a Second-Generation Theory of Fiscal Federalism'. *International Tax and Public Finance*, 12(4): 349–73.

Peng, J. (2003). 'Managing the Risk of Variable-Rate Debt in the Public Sector'. *Municipal Finance Journal*, 23(4): 1–16.

Wallace, A. (2011). 'Managing Municipal Debt in Today's Market'. Paper presented at NASACT Conference, 13–17 August. Burlington, VT.

Chapter 2

Ang, A., V. Bhansali and Y. Xing (2010a). 'Taxes on Tax-Exempt Bonds'. *Journal of Finance*, 65(2): 565–601.

Ang, A., V. Bhansali and Y. Xing (2010b). 'Build America Bonds'. *The National Bureau of Economic Research*. Cambridge, MA.

Atwood, T.J. (2003). 'Implicit Taxes: Evidence from Taxable, Tax-Exempt, AMT State and Local Government Bond Yields'. *The Journal of the American Taxation Association*, 25(1): 1–20.

Congressional Budget Office (2004). *Tax Credit Bonds and the Federal Cost of Financing Public Expenditures*. Congressional Budget Office, Washington, DC.

Congressional Budget Office/Joint Committee on Taxation (2009). *Subsidizing Infrastructure Investment with Tax-Preferred Bonds*. Congressional Budget Office/Joint Committee on Taxation, Washington, DC.

DePaul, J. (2012). 'JCT: $178B for Public Muni Debt'. *The Bond Buyer*. 18 January.

DePaul, J. (2013). 'Issuers Begin Calling BABs Due to Sequestration'. *The Bond Buyer*. Available at: www.bondbuyer.com/issues/122_72.

Johnson, C.L. and M. Rubin (1998). 'The Municipal Bond Market: Structure and Changes'. In F. Thompson and M.T. Green (eds), *Handbook of Public Finance*, pp. 483–522. New York: Marcel Dekker.

Leonard, P. (1998). 'Tax-Induced Segmentation in the Tax Exempt Securities Market'. *Quarterly Journal of Business and Economics*, 37(4): 27–47.

Liu, G. and D. Denison (2010). 'Indirect and Direct Subsidies for Cost of Government Capital: Comparing Yields of Tax-Exempt Bonds and Build America Bonds'. Paper presented at the Association for Public Policy Analysis and Management 2010 Annual Conference. 4–6 November. Boston, MA.

Longstaff, F. (2011). 'Municipal Debt and Marginal Tax Rates: Is There a Tax Premium in Asset Prices?' *Journal of Finance*, 66(3): 721–51.

Luby, M.J. (2012). 'Federal Intervention in the Municipal Bond Market: The Effectiveness of the Build America Bond Program and Its Implications on Federal and Subnational Budgeting'. *Public Budgeting and Finance*, 32(4): 46–70.

Pirinsky, C.A. and Q. Wang (2011). 'Market Segmentation and the Cost of Capital in a Domestic Market: Evidence from Municipal Bonds'. *Financial Management*, 40(2): 455–81.

Poterba, J.M. and A.R. Verdugo (2008). 'Portfolio Substitution and the Revenue Cost of Exempting State and Local Government Interest Payments from Federal Income Tax'. *The National Bureau of Economic Research*. Cambridge, MA.

Seymour, D. (2010). 'New BAB Goal: Revenue Neutrality'. *The Bond Buyer*, 12 October.

US Congress (1909). 'Amendment XVI', passed 2 July 1909, ratified 3 February 1913. Washington, DC: US Congress. Available at: http://www.archives.gov/exhibits/charters/constitution_amendments_11-27.html.

US Congress (1954). 'Internal Revenue Code of 1954. Public Law 591 - Chapter 736'. Washington, DC. Second Session of the Eighty-Third Congress of the United States of America. Available at: http://www.constitution.org/uslaw/sal/068A_itax.pdf.

US Department of the Treasury (2010a). *Treasury Analysis of Build America Bonds and Issuer Net Borrowing Costs*. US Department of the Treasury, Washington, DC.

US Department of the Treasury (2010b). *Build America Bonds are Helping State and Local Governments Finance Infrastructure Projects and Create Jobs While Saving Taxpayer Billions*. US Department of the Treasury, Washington, DC.

US Government Accountability Office (2008). *Tax-Exempt Status of Certain Bonds Merits Reconsideration, and Apparent Noncompliance with Issuance Cost Limitations Should Be Addressed*. (GAO-08-36). February. Government Accountability Office, Alexandria, VA.

Chapter 3

Bayoumi, T., M. Goldstein and G. Woglom (1995). 'Do Credit Markets Discipline Sovereign Borrowers? Evidence from US States'. *Journal of Money, Credit and Banking*, 27(4): 1046–59.

Bergstresser, D. and R. Cohen (2011). 'Why Fears About Municipal Credit are Overblown'. Available at: SSRN: http://ssrn.com/abstract=1836678.

Bunch, B.S. (1991). 'The Effect of Constitutional Debt Limits on State Government Use of Public Authorities'. *Public Choice*, 68(1): 57–69.

Chappatta, B. (2013). 'Detroit's 86-Cent Water Debt Seen Delivering Profit: Muni Credit'. Bloomberg. Available at: www.bloomberg.com/news/print/2013-07-26/detroit-s-86-cent-water-debt-seen-delivering-profit-muni-credit.html.

Clingermayer, J.C. and B.D. Wood (1995). 'Disentangling Patterns of

State Debt Financing'. *American Political Science Review*, 89(1): 108–20.

De Angelis, M. and X. Tian (2013). 'United States: Chapter 9 Municipal Bankruptcy – Utilization, Avoidance, and Impact'. In O. Canuto, L. Lu and K.W. Brown (eds), *Until Debt Do Us Part: Subnational Debt, Insolvency, and Markets*, pp. 311–51. Washington, DC: World Bank.

Denison, D.V., M.M. Hackbart and M. Moody (2006). 'State Debt Limits: How Many are Enough?' *Public Budgeting and Finance*, 26(1): 22–39.

Ellis, M.A. and D.E. Schansberg (1999). 'The Determinants of State Government Debt Financing'. *Public Finance Review*, 27(6): 571–87.

Farnham, Paul (1985). 'Re-examining Local Debt Limits: A Disaggregated Analysis'. *Southern Economics Journal*, 51(4): 1186–201.

Gillette, C.P. (2012). 'Fiscal Federalism, Political Will, and Strategic Use of Municipal Bankruptcy'. *The University of Chicago Law Review*, 79(1): 281–330.

Heins, A.J. (1963). *Constitutional Restrictions against State Debt*, Madison, WI: The University of Wisconsin Press.

Hildreth, W.B. and C.K. Zorn (2005). 'The Evolution of the State and Local Government Municipal Debt Market Over the Past Quarter Century'. *Public Budgeting and Finance*, 25(4): 127–53.

Holcombe, R. (1992). 'Revolving Fund Finance: The Case of Wastewater Treatment'. *Public Budgeting and Finance*, 12(3): 50–65.

Hur, M. (2007). 'Fiscal Limits and State Fiscal Structure: An Analysis of State Revenue Structure and Indebtedness'. *Municipal Finance Journal*, 8(3): 19–35.

Johnson, C.L. (1995). 'Managing Financial Resources to meet the Nation's Environmental Infrastructure Needs: The Case of State Revolving Funds'. *Public Productivity and Management Review*, 18(3): 263–76.

Johnson, C.L. and S.N. Kioko (2009). 'Principal Agent Theory, Fiscal Institutions, and the Supply of Municipal Debt'. Unpublished paper. Bloomington, IN.

Johnson, C.L. and K.A. Kriz (2005). 'Fiscal Institutions, Credit Ratings, and Borrowing Costs'. *Public Budgeting and Finance*, 25(1): 84–103.

Johnson, C.L. and J.Y. Man (eds) (2001). *Tax Increment Finance and Economic Development: Uses, Structure and Impact*, Albany, NY: State University of New York Press.

Johnson, C.L. and M. Rubin (1998). 'The Municipal Bond Market: Structure and Changes'. In F. Thompson and M.T. Green (eds), *Handbook of Public Finance*, pp. 483–522. New York: Marcel Dekker.

Johnson, Craig L. and Robinson & Cole Law Firm (2002). 'Tax Increment Financing'. Washington, DC: National Association of Realtors.

Kerth, B. and P. Baxandall (2011). *Tax Increment Financing: The Need for Increased Transparency and Accountability in Local Economic Development Studies*. Boston, MA: US PIRG Education Fund.

Kiewiet, D.R. and K. Szakaly (1996). 'Constitutional Limitations on Borrowing: An Analysis of State Bonded Indebtedness'. *Journal of Law, Economics and Organization*, 12(1): 62–97.

Kioko, S.N. (2009). *Impact of State Tax and Expenditure Limits on Spending Growth*. Center for Policy Research, Syracuse, NY.

Kioko S.N. (2010). 'The Impact of Property Tax Limits on Local Government Borrowing'. Unpublished paper.

Kioko, S.N. (2011). 'Structure of State-Level Tax and Expenditure Limits'. *Public Budgeting and Finance*, 31(2): 43–78.

Laughlin, A.M. (2005). 'Municipal Insolvencies: An Article on the Treatment of Municipalities Under Chapter 9 of the US Bankruptcy Code'. *Municipal Finance Journal*, 26(2): 37–59.

Lewis, C.W. (1994). 'Municipal Bankruptcy and the States: Authorization to File Under Chapter 9'. *Urban Affairs Quarterly*, 30(1): 3–26.

Lowry, R.C. and J.E. Alt (2001). 'A Visible Hand? Bond Markets, Political Parties, Balanced Budget Laws, and State Government Debt'. *Economics and Politics*, 13(1): 49–72.

Luby, M.J. (2009). 'Reforming State Debt Management Practices: The Case of Illinois, 2004'. *Municipal Finance Journal*, 30(1): 1–36.

Moessinger, M.D., L.P. Feld, A. Kalb and S. Osterloh (2013). 'Sovereign Bond Market Reactions to Fiscal Rules and No-Bailout Clauses. The Swiss Experience'. *Beiträge zur Jahrestagung des Vereins für Socialpolitik. Wettbewerbspolitik und Regulierung in einer globalen Wirtschaftsordnung*. Available at: http://hdl.handle.net/10419/79807, pp. 1–32.

Moldogaziev, T., S.N. Kioko and W.B. Hildreth (2013). 'Bankruptcy Risk Premium in the Municipal Securities Market'. Association for Budgeting and Financial Management Annual Conference 2013. 3–5 October. Washington, DC.

Moody's (2012). *Key Credit Considerations for Municipal Governments in Bankruptcy*. Moody's Investors Service, New York.

National Governors Association/ National Association of State Budget Officers (2012). *The Fiscal Survey of the States*. National Governors Association, National Association of State Budget Officers, Washington, DC.

Nice, D.C. (1991). 'The Impact of State Policies to Limit Debt Financing'. *Publius*, 21(1): 69–82.

Poterba, J.M. and J. von Hagen (1999). *Fiscal Institutions and Fiscal Performance*, Chicago, IL: University of Chicago Press.

Poterba, J.M. and K.S. Rueben (2001). 'Fiscal News, State Budget Rules, and Tax-Exempt Bond Yields'. *Journal of Urban Economics*, 50(3): 537–62.

Robbins, M.D. and D. Kim (2003). 'Do State Bond Banks Have Cost Advantages for Municipal Bond Issuance?' *Public Budgeting and Finance*, 23(3): 92–108.

Spiotto, J.E. (2012). *Primer on Municipal Debt Adjustment*, Chicago, IL: Chapman and Cutler LLP.

Travis, R., J.C. Morris and E.D. Morris (2004). 'State Implementation of Federal Environmental Policy: Explaining Leveraging in the Clean Water State Revolving Fund'. *Policy Studies Journal*, 32(3): 461–80.

US Government Printing Office (2013) 'Title 11, US Bankruptcy Code'. Washington, DC. US Bankruptcy Code and Rules.

Von Hagen, J. (1991). 'A Note on the Empirical Effectiveness of Formal Fiscal Restraints'. *Journal of Public Economics*, 4(2): 199–210.

Wagner, G.A. (2004). 'The Bond Market and Fiscal Institutions: Have Budget Stabilization Funds Reduced State Borrowing Costs?' *National Tax Journal*, 57(4): 785–804.

Wallis, J.J. (2005). 'Constitutions, Corporations, and Corruption: American States and Constitutional Change, 1842 to 1852'. *Journal of Economic History*, 65(1): 211–56.

Wallis, J.J. and B.R. Weingast (2006). 'Dysfunctional or Optimal Institutions? State Debt Limitations, the Structure of State and Local Governments, and the Finance of American Infrastructure'. In E. Garret, E.A. Graddy and H.E. Jackson (eds), *Fiscal Challenges: An Interdisciplinary Approach to Budget Policy*. Cambridge, UK: Cambridge University Press.

Yusuf, J-E. and G. Liu (2008). 'State Infrastructure Banks and Intergovernmental Subsidies for Local Transportation Investment'. *Public Budgeting and Finance*, 28(4): 71–89.

Chapter 4

Johnson, C.L. (2013). 'Understanding Dodd–Frank's Reach into Main Street's Financial Market'. *Journal of Public Budgeting, Accounting & Financial Management*, 25(2): 391–410.

Johnson, C.L. and M. Rubin (1998). 'The Municipal Bond Market: Structure and Changes'. In F. Thompson and M.T. Green (eds), *Handbook of Public Finance*, pp. 483–522. New York: Marcel Dekker.

Kioko, S.N., T. Moldogaziev and C.L. Johnson (2012). 'Financial Information and Pricing of Municipal Bonds in the Secondary Market'. Paper presented at the Association for Budgeting and Financial Management 2012 Annual Conference. 11–13 October. New York.

Moldogaziev, T. (2013). 'The Collapse of the Municipal Bond Insurance Market: How Did We Get Here and is there Life for the Monoline Industry beyond the Great Recession?' *Journal of Public Budgeting, Accounting, and Financial Management*, 25(1): 199–233.

Temel, J.W. (2001). *The Fundamentals of Municipal Bonds*, New York: Wiley.

PART II

Chapter 5

Baumgartner, E., S. Brady and G. Ferguson (2013). 'City of Stockton Case, 2007 Pension Obligation Bond Case Analysis'. Working Paper. Bloomington, IN.

Bifulco, R., B. Bunch, W. Duncombe, M. Robbins and W. Simonsen (2012). 'Debt and Deception: How States Avoid Making Hard Fiscal Decisions'. *Public Administration Review*, 72(5): 659–67.

Hackbart, M. and J. Leigland (1990). 'State Debt Management Policy: A National Survey'. *Public Budgeting and Finance*, 10(1): 37–54.

Jensen, R. (2012). 'Calif. Capital Appreciation Bonds Have Unintended Consequences'. *The Bond Buyer*. 21 September.

Johnson, C.L. (1996). 'Administering Public Debt'. In J. Perry, (ed.), *Handbook of Public Administration*. 2nd edn, pp. 348–71. San Francisco, CA: Jossey-Bass Publishers.

Johnson, C.L. and S.N. Kioko (2009). 'Principal Agent Theory, Fiscal Institutions, and the Supply of Municipal Debt', Unpublished paper. Bloomington, IN.

Johnson, C.L. and J.L. Mikesell (1996). 'The Orange County Debacle: Where Irresponsible Cash and Debt Management Practices Collide'. *Municipal Finance Journal*, 17(2): 1–15.

Johnson, C.L. and M. Rubin (1998), 'The Municipal Bond Market: Structure and Changes'. In F. Thompson and M.T. Green (eds), *Handbook of Public Finance*, pp. 483–522. New York: Marcel Dekker.

Kim, S.K. (2013). *California Senate Analysis of AB 182*. Assembly Committee on Education, Sacramento, CA.

Larkin, R. and J. Joseph (1991). 'Developing Formal Debt Policies'. *Government Finance Review*, 7(2): 11–14.

Lee Jr, R.D. and R.W. Johnson (1998). *Public Budgeting Systems*, Gaithersburg, MD: Aspen Publishers, Inc.

Legislative Counsel's Digest (2013). 'California Assembly Bill No. 182'. 2 October. Sacramento, CA: Legislative Counsel's Digest.

Levine, H. (2011). 'The Impact of Debt Management Policies on the Borrowing Costs Incurred by US State Governments'. *Public Finance and Management*, 11(1): 1–27.

Lovett, I. (2013). 'California Schools Finance Upgrades By Making Next Generation Pay'. *The New York Times*. 10 February.

Luby, M.J. (2009). 'Reforming State Debt Management Practices: The Case of Illinois, 2004'. *Municipal Finance Journal*, 30(1): 1–36.

Luby, M.J. (2014). 'Not All Refinancings are Created Equal: A Framework for Assessing State and Local Government Debt Refinancing Practices'. *State and Local Government Review*, 46(1): 52–62.

Miranda, R., R. Picur and D. Straley (1997). 'Elements of a Comprehensive Local Government Debt Policy'. *Government Finance Review*, 13(5): 9–13.

Petersen, J.E. and T. McLoughlin (1991). 'Debt Policies and Procedures'. In J.E. Petersen and D.R. Strachota (eds), *Local Government Finance: Concept and Practices*, pp. 263–90. Chicago, IL: Government Finance Officers Association.

Robbins, M.D. and C. Dungan (2001). 'Debt Diligence: How States Manage the Borrowing Function'. *Public Budgeting and Finance*, 21(2): 88–105.

Simonsen, W. and W. Kittredge (1998). 'Competitive versus Negotiated Municipal Bond Sales: Why Issuers Choose One Method over the Other'. *Municipal Finance Journal*, 19: 1–29.

Simonsen, W., M. Robbins and B. Kittredge (2001). 'Do Debt Policies Make a Difference in Finance Officers' Perceptions of the Importance of Debt Management Factors?' *Public Budgeting and Finance*, 21(1): 87–102.

Zino, M. (1994). 'The Development of a Planned Debt Policy'. *Municipal Finance Journal*, 15(1): 75–84.

Chapter 6

Allen, A. and D. Dudney (2010). 'Does the Quality of Financial Advice Affect Prices?' *Financial Review*, 45(2): 387–414.

Bifulco, R., B. Bunch, W. Duncombe, M. Robbins and W. Simonsen (2012). 'Debt and Deception: How States Avoid Making Hard Fiscal Decisions'. *Public Administration Review*, 72(5): 659–67.

Briffault, R. (1996). *Balancing Acts: The Reality Behind State Balanced Budget Requirements*, New York: Twentieth Century Fund Press.

Butler, A.W. (2008). 'Distance Still Matters: Evidence from Municipal Bond Underwriting'. *The Review of Financial Studies*, 21(2): 763–84.

Clarke, W. (1997). 'The Interest Cost Implications of the Financial Advisor Turned Underwriter'. *Public Budgeting and Finance*, 17(3): 74–86.

Daniels, K. and J. Vijayakumar (2007). 'Does Underwriter Reputation Matter in the Municipal Bond Market?'. *Journal of Economics and Business*, 59(6): 500–519.

Forbes, R., P. Leonard and C.L. Johnson (1992). 'The Role of Financial Advisors in the Negotiated State of Tax-Exempt Securities'. *Journal of Applied Business Research*, 8(2): 7–14.

Government Finance Officers Association (GFOA) (2010). *Use of Debt-Related Derivative Products and the Development of a Derivatives Policy*. Government Finance Officers Association, Chicago, IL.

Guzman, T. and T. Moldogaziev (2012). 'Which Bonds are More Expensive? The Cost Differentials by Debt Issue Purpose and the Method of Sale: An Empirical Analysis'. *Public Budgeting and Finance*, 32(3): 79–101.

Johnson, C.L. (1994a). 'The Changing Market Structure of the Municipal Financial Advisor Industry'. *Municipal Finance Journal*, 15(1): 1–17.

Johnson, C.L. (1994b). 'An Empirical Investigation of the Pricing of Financial Advisor Services'. *Municipal Finance Journal*, 15(3): 36–52.

Johnson, C.L. (1999). 'State Government Credit Quality – Down, but Not Out!'. *Public Administration Review*, 59(3): 243–9.

Johnson, C.L. and K.A. Kriz (2002). 'Impact of Three Credit Ratings on Interest Costs of State GO Bonds'. *Municipal Finance Journal*, 23(1): 1–16.

Joseph, J.C. (1994). *Debt Issuance and Management: A Guide for Smaller Governments*, Chicago, IL: Government Finance Officers Association.

Kriz, K.A. (2003). 'Comparative Costs of Negotiated Versus Competitive Bond Sales: New Evidence from State General Obligation Bonds'. *The Quarterly Review of Economics and Finance*, 43(1): 191–211.

Leonard, P. (1994). 'Negotiated Versus Competitive Bond Sales: A Review of the Literature'. *Municipal Finance Journal*, 15(2): 12–36.

Leonard, P. (1996). 'An Empirical Analysis of Competitive Bid and Negotiated Offerings of Municipal Bonds'. *Municipal Finance Journal*, 17(1): 37–67.

Luby, M.J. (2010). *Agency Problems in Public Financial Management: Evidence from Debt Refinancing Practices*. Dissertation, Indiana University, Bloomington, IN.

Luby, M.J. (2012). 'Debt and Budget Gimmickry Revisited: The Upfront Bond Refinancing Savings Structure'. *Journal of Public Budgeting, Accounting, and Financial Management*, 24(3): 489–516.

Luby, M.J. and T. Moldogaziev (2013). 'An Empirical Examination of the Determinants of Municipal Bond Underwriter Fees'. *Municipal Finance Journal*, 34(2): 13–50.

Miller, G.J. and J.B. Justice (2012). 'Debt Management Networks'. In G.J. Miller, (ed.), *Government Budgeting and Financial Management in Practice: Logics to Make Sense of Ambiguity*. Boca Raton, FL: Taylor & Francis.

Moyer, M. (2003). 'Current Issues Facing Bond Issuers and Their Financial Advisors'. *Municipal Finance Journal*, 24(2): 17–25.

Municipal Securities Rulemaking Board (2009). *Unregulated Municipal Market Participants: A Case for Reform*. Municipal Securities Rulemaking Board, Alexandria, VA.

Peng, J. and P.F. Brucato, Jr (2003). 'Another Look at the Effect of Method of Sale on the Interest Costs in the Municipal Bond Market – A Certification Model'. *Public Budgeting and Finance*, 23(1): 73–95.

Petersen, J. (2003). 'Changing Red to Black: Deficit Closing Alchemy'. *National Tax Journal*, 56(3): 567–77.

Petersen, J.E. and P. Watt (eds) (1986). *The Price of Advice: Choosing and Using Financial Advisors*, Chicago, IL: Government Finance Officers Association.

Robbins, M.D. (2002). 'Testing the Effects of Sale Method Restrictions in Municipal Bond Issuance: The Case of New Jersey'. *Public Budgeting and Finance*, 22(1): 40–56.

Robbins, M.D. and W. Simonsen (2003). 'Financial Advisor Independence and the Choice of Municipal Bond Sale Type'. *Municipal Finance Journal*, 24(1): 17–57.

Simonsen, W. and L. Hill (1998). 'Municipal Bond Issuance: Is There Evidence of a Principal Agent Problem?' *Public Budgeting and Finance*, 18(4): 71–100.

Simonsen, W. and M.B. Robbins (1996). 'Does it Make Any Difference Anymore? Competitive Versus Negotiated Municipal Bond Issuance'. *Public Administration Review*, 56(1): 57–64.

Vijayakumar, J. and K. Daniels (2006). 'The Role and Impact of Financial Advisors in the Market for Municipal Bonds'. *Journal of Financial Services Research*, 30(1): 43–68.

Wakeman, L.M. (1981). 'The Real Function of Bond Rating Agencies'. *Chase Financial Quarterly*, 1: 18–26.

Wood, W. (2008). 'Municipal Bond Refundings'. In S. Feldstein and F.J. Fabozzi (eds), *The Handbook of Municipal Bonds*. Hoboken, NY: Wiley.

Chapter 7

Johnson, C.L., S.N. Kioko and J.Q. Wang (2010). 'State Government Debt Management: The Forgotten Tool in the Financial Manager Triage Bag'. *Municipal Finance Journal*, 31(1): 21–20.

Standard & Poor's (2007). *Standard & Poor's Public Finance Criteria*. Standard & Poor's, New York.

Chapter 8

Beber, A., M.W. Brandt and K.A. Kavajecz (2009). 'Flight-to-Quality or Flight-to-Liquidity? Evidence from the Euro-Area Bond Market'. *Review of Financial Studies*, 22(3): 925–57.

Brown, D.T. and S. Sirmans (2013). 'Maturity Clienteles in the Municipal Bond Market: Term Premiums and the Muni Puzzle'. Working Paper, pp. 1–29.

Chakravarty, S. and A. Sarkar (2003). 'Trading Costs in Three US Bond Markets'. *Journal of Fixed Income*, 13(1): 39–48.

Chen, Z., A.A. Lookman, N. Schurhoff and D.J. Seppi (2013). 'Rating-Based Investment Norms and Bond Market Segmentation'. Working Paper, pp. 1–59.

Chordia, T., R. Roll and A. Subrahmanyam (2001). 'Order Imbalance, Liquidity, and Market Returns'. *Journal of Financial Economics*, 65(2): 110–30.

Deng, G. and C. McCann (2013). *Using EMMA to Access Municipal Bond Markups*. Securities Litigation and Consulting Group, Inc., Fairfax, VA.

Denison, D.V. (2003). 'An Empirical Examination of the Determinants of Insured Municipal Bond Issues'. *Public Budgeting and Finance*, 23(1): 96–114.

Downing, C. and F. Zhang (2004). 'Trading Activity and Price Volatility in the Municipal Bond Market'. *Journal of Finance*, 59(2): 899–931.

Edwards, A.K., L.E. Harris and M.S. Piwowar (2007). 'Corporate Bond Market Transaction Costs and Transparency'. *Journal of Finance*, 62(3): 1421–51.

Freire, M. and J. Petersen (2004). *Subnational Capital Markets in Developing Countries. From Theory to Practice*, New York: Oxford University Press.

Government Accountability Office (GAO) (2012a). *Municipal Securities: Overview of Market Structure, Pricing, and Regulation*. Government Accountability Office, Washington, DC.

Government Accountability Office (GAO) (2012b). *Options for Improving Continuing Disclosure*. Government Accountability Office, Washington, DC.

Green, R.C., B. Hollifield and N. Schurhoff (2007a). 'Dealer Intermediation and Price Behavior in the Aftermarket for New Bond Issues'. *Journal of Financial Economics*, 86(3): 643–82.

Green, R.C., B. Hollifield and N. Schurhoff (2007b). 'Financial

Intermediation and the Cost of Trading in an Opaque Market'. *Review of Financial Studies*, 20(2): 275–314.

Green, R.C., D. Li and N. Schurhoff (2010). 'Price Discovery in Illiquid Markets: Do Financial Asset Prices Rise Faster than they Fall?' *Journal of Finance*, 65(5): 1669–1702.

Harris, L.E. and M.S. Piwowar (2006). 'Secondary Trading Costs in the Municipal Bond Market'. *Journal of Finance*, 61(3): 1361–97.

Hong, G. and A. Warga (2004). 'An Empirical Study of Bond Market Transactions'. *Financial Analysts Journal*, 56(2): 32–46.

Kalimipalli, M. and A. Warga (2002). 'Bid–Ask Spread, Volatility, and Volume in the Corporate Bond Market'. *Journal of Fixed Income*, 11(4): 31–42.

Kioko, S.N., T. Moldogaziev and C.L. Johnson (2012). 'Financial Information and Pricing of Municipal Bonds in the Secondary Market'. Paper presented at the Association for Budgeting and Financial Management 2012 Annual Conference. 11–13 October. New York.

Kriz, K.A. (2003). 'Comparative Costs of Negotiated Versus Competitive Bond Sales: New Evidence from State General Obligation Bonds'. *The Quarterly Review of Economics and Finance*, 43(1): 191–211.

Lamb, R. (1992). 'The Secondary Market: Trading Municipal Bonds'. In R. Lamb, James Leigland and Stephen Rappaport (eds), *The Handbook of Municipal Bonds and Public Finance,* pp. 39–57. New York: Institute of Finance.

Marlin, M.R. (1994). 'Did Tax Reform Kill Segmentation in the Municipal Bond Market?' *Public Administration Review*, 54(4): 387–90.

Marlowe, J. (2013). 'Structure and Performance in Municipal Debt Management Networks'. Municipal Finance Conference. Boston, MA.

Moldogaziev, T. (2012). *Information Economics in Insurance Markets for Municipal Debt Securities: Monoline Insurance in Primary and Secondary Trades.* Dissertation, Indiana University, Bloomington, IN.

Moldogaziev, T., C.L. Johnson and M.J. Luby (2013). 'Underwriting of Municipal Debt and Placement Risk Premiums in Broker–Dealer Market Transaction Prices'. Paper presented at the Municipal Finance Conference. 1–2 August. Boston, MA.

MSRB (2009). *MSRB Launches the Continuing Disclosure Service of Its Electronic Municipal Market Access System ('EMMA').* Municipal Securities Rulemaking Board, Alexandria, VA.

Pirinsky, C.A. and Q. Wang (2011). 'Market Segmentation and the Cost of Capital in a Domestic Market: Evidence from Municipal Bonds'. *Financial Management*, 40(2): 455–81.

Schultz, P. (2001). 'Corporate Bond Trading Costs: A Peek Behind the Curtain'. *Journal of Finance*, 56(2): 677–98.

Schultz, P. (2012). 'The Market for New Issues of Municipal Bonds: The Roles of Transparency and Limited Access to Retail Investors'. *Journal of Financial Economics*, 106(3): 492–512.

Shields, Y. (2013). 'Illinois Holds its Ground in Big GO Sale'. *The Bond Buyer*. Available at: http://www.bondbuyer.com/issues/122_64/illinois-holds-its-ground-in-big-go-sale-1050294-1.html.

Simonsen, W., M.B. Robbins and B. Jump (2005). 'State Rules About the Use of Net Interest Cost and True Interest Cost for Calculating Municipal Bond Interest Rates'. *Municipal Finance Journal*, 26(1): 1–25.

World Bank/IMF (2001). *Developing Government Bond Markets. A Handbook*, Washington, DC: International Monetary Fund.

PART III

Chapter 9

Bergstresser, D. and R. Cohen (2012). *Jefferson County (Cases A to E)*. Boston, MA: Harvard Business School Publishing.

Bicksler, J. and A. Chen (1986). 'An Economic Analysis of Interest Rate Swaps'. *The Journal of Finance*, 41(3): 645–55.

Government Finance Officers Association (GFOA) (2010). *Use of Debt-Related Derivative Products and the Development of a Derivatives Policy*. Government Finance Officers Association, Chicago, IL.

Javers, E. (2010). 'Debate Tests Members' Financial IQs'. *Politico*. Available at: www.politico.com/news/stories/0410/36059.html.

Luby, M.J. and R. Kravchuk (2013). 'An Historical Analysis of the Use of Debt-Related Derivatives by State Governments in the Context of the Great Recession', *Journal of Public Budgeting, Accounting & Financial Management*. 25(2): 276.

Stewart, L. and C. Cox (2008). 'Debt-Related Derivate Usage by US State and Municipal Governments and Evolving Financial Reporting Standards'. *Journal of Public Budgeting, Accounting & Financial Management*, 20(4): 439.

Chapter 10

Bifulco, R., B. Bunch, W. Duncombe, M. Robbins and W. Simonsen (2012). 'Debt and Deception: How States Avoid Making Hard Fiscal Decisions'. *Public Administration Review*, 72(5): 659–67.

Denison, D. and J.B. Gibson (2013). 'Adjustable Rate Debt Overwhelms

Jefferson County, Alabama Sewer Authority: A Tale of Market Risk, False Hope, and Corruption'. *Journal of Public Budgeting, Accounting & Financial Management*, 25(2).

Kalotay, A. and W. May (1998). 'The Timing of Advance Refunding of Tax Exempt Municipal Bonds'. *Municipal Finance Journal*, 19(3): 1–15.

Kalotay, A., D. Yang and F. Fabozzi (2007). 'Refunding Efficiency: A Generalized Approach'. *Applied Financial Economics Letters*, 3(3): 141–6.

Luby, M.J. (2009). 'Reforming State Debt Management Practices: The Case of Illinois, 2004'. *Municipal Finance Journal*, 30(1): 1–36.

Luby, M.J. (2012a). 'The Use of Financial Derivatives in State and Local Government Bond Refinancings: Playing with Fire or Prudent Debt Management?' *Journal of Public Budgeting, Accounting & Financial Management*, 24(1): 1–31.

Luby, M.J. (2012b). 'Debt and Budget Gimmickry Revisited: The Upfront Bond Refinancing Savings Structure'. *Journal of Public Budgeting, Accounting, and Financial Management*, 24(3): 489–516.

Luby, M.J. (2014). 'Not All Refinancings are Created Equal: A Framework for Assessing State and Local Government Debt Refinancing Practices'. *State and Local Government Review*, 46(1): 52–62.

Miller, G.J. and J.B. Justice (2012). 'Debt Management Networks'. In G.J. Miller (ed.), *Government Budgeting and Financial Management in Practice: Logics to Make Sense of Ambiguity*. Boca Raton, FL: Taylor & Francis.

Petersen, J. (2003). 'Changing Red to Black: Deficit Closing Alchemy'. *National Tax Journal*, 56(3): 567–77.

Wood, W. (2008). 'Municipal Bond Refundings'. In S. Feldstein and F.J. Fabozzi (eds), *The Handbook of Municipal Bonds*. Hoboken, NY: Wiley.

Zhang, W.D. and J. Li (2004). 'The Value of the Advance Refunding Option and the Refunding Efficiency of Tax-Exempt Municipal Bonds'. *Municipal Finance Journal*, 25(1): 17–32.

Chapter 11

Anderson, J. and V. Bajaj (2008). 'New Trouble in Auction-Rate Securities'. *New York Times*, 15 February.

Bergstresser, D., S. Cole and S. Shenai (2011). *UBS and Action Rate Securities (Cases A to C)*. Boston, MA: Harvard Business School Publishing.

California Debt and Investment Advisory Commission (2004). *Auction Rate Securities*. California Debt and Investment Advisory Commission, Sacramento, CA.

Cooke, J. (2008). 'Auction Collapse Quadruples Fee for Bond Alternatives'. *Bloomberg*, 7 April.

Corkery, M. and I.J. Dugan (2011). 'New Hit to Strapped States: Borrowing Costs up as Bond Flops; Refinancing Crunch Nears'. *Wall Street Journal*, 14 January.

D'Silva, A., H. Gregg and D. Marshall (2008). *Explaining the Decline in the Auction Rate Securities Market*. Federal Reserve Bank of Chicago, Chicago, IL.

Government Finance Officers Association (GFOA) (1997). *Best Practice: Using Variable Rate Debt Instruments*. Government Finance Officers Association, Chicago, IL.

Han, S. and D. Li (2008). *Liquidity Runs and Security Design Lessons from the Collapse of the ARS Municipal Bond Market*. Federal Reserve Board, Washington, DC.

Johnson, C.L. and M.J. Luby (2011). 'The Birth, Growth and Collapse of the Municipal Auction Rate Securities Market'. Unpublished paper.

Kardos, D. (2008). 'BofA to Buy Back Auction Securities', *Wall Street Journal*, 10 September.

Lee, S. (2008). *Auction-Rate Securities: Bidder's Remorse?* NERA Consulting, New York.

McConnell, J.J. and A. Saretto (2010). 'Auction Failures and the Market for Auction Rate Securities'. *Journal of Financial Economics*, 97(3): 451–69.

Municipal Securities Rulemaking Board (MSRB) (2010). *Municipal Auction Rate Securities and Variable Rate Demand Obligations: Interest Rate and Trading Trends*. Municipal Securities Rulemaking Board, Alexandria, VA.

Preston, D. (2011). 'Governments Using Swaps Emulate Subprime Victims of Wall Street'. *Bloomberg BusinessWeek*, 14 November.

Quigley, J. (2011). 'SEC, SIFMA Face Off'. *The Bond Buyer*, 21 July.

Securities Industry and Financial Markets Association (2010). *Research Report: Municipal Auction Rate Securities 2010 Update*. Securities Industry and Financial Markets Association, New York.

Seymour, D. (2010a). 'BABs: The Last Pillar Standing'. *The Bond Buyer*, 29 November.

Seymour, D. (2010b). 'New BAB Goal: Revenue Neutrality'. *The Bond Buyer*, 12 October.

Shields, Y. (2008). 'Chicago Schools See Interest Rate on Variable Rate Debt Jump to 9%'. *The Bond Buyer*, 3 March.

US Securities and Exchange Commission (2006). *15 Broker-Dealer Firms Settle SEC Charges Involving Violative Practices in the Auction Rate Securities Market: Firms Ordered to Cease and Desist and to Pay Over*

$13 Million in Penalties. US Securities and Exchange Commission, Washington, DC. Available at: www.sec.gov/news/press/2006/2006-83. htm accessed 19 June 2009.

Wallace, A. (2011). 'Managing Municipal Debt in Today's Market'. Paper presented at the NASACT 2011 Conference. 13–17 August. Burlington, VT.

Ward, A. (2008). 'California: Riverside Shedding its ARS'. *The Bond Buyer*, 18 April.

Wells Capital Management (2008). *An Overview of the Auction Rate Market: Where We've Been and Where We're Going*. Wells Capital Management, San Francisco, CA.

Chapter 12

Acharya, V.V., T. Cooley, M. Richardson and I. Walter (2009). 'Manufacturing Tail Risk: A Perspective on the Financial Crisis of 2007–2009'. *Foundations and Trends in Finance*, 4(4): 247–325.

Bland, R.L. (1987). 'The Interest Cost Savings from Municipal Bond Insurance: The Implications for Privatization'. *Journal of Policy Analysis and Management*, 6(2): 207–19.

Braswell, R.C., E.J. Nosari and M.A. Browning (1982). 'The Effect of Private Municipal Bond Insurance on the Cost to the Issuer'. *Financial Review*, 17(4): 240–51.

Cole, C.W. and D.T. Officer (1981). 'The Interest Cost Effect of Private Municipal Bond Insurance'. *Journal of Risk and Insurance*, 48(3): 435–49.

Cusick, C. (2012). *NLC Sponsors New Mutual Bond Insurer*. National League of Cities, Washington, DC.

Denison, D.V. (2001). 'Bond Insurance Utilization and Yield Spreads in the Municipal Bond Market'. *Public Finance Review*, 29(5): 394–411.

Denison, D.V. (2009). 'What Happens When Municipal Bond Insurance Companies Lose Credit?'. *Municipal Finance Journal*, 29(4): 37–47.

Drake, P.P. and F.R. Neale (2011). 'Financial Guarantee Insurance and the Failures in Risk Management'. *Journal of Insurance Regulation*, 30(2): 24–71.

Feldstein, S.G. (1983). 'Municipal Bond Insurance and Pricing'. In F. Fabozzi, S.G. Feldstein, I.M. Pollack and F.G. Zarb (eds), *The Municipal Bond Handbook*, pp. 404–11. Homewood, IL: Dow Jones-Irwin.

Forbes, R.W. and M.H. Hopewell (1976). 'Private Municipal Bond Insurance'. *Annual Meeting of the Western Economic Association*. San Francisco, CA.

Godfrey, R. and D.L. York (1994). *Higher Bond Yields*, New York: Irwin Professional Publishing.

Green, R.E. and D.P. Smith (2007). *Subprime Exposure is Unlikely to Cause Bond Insurers Major Difficulties*. Standard & Poor's, New York.

Green, R.C., B. Hollifield and N. Schurhoff (2007). 'Dealer Intermediation and Price Behavior in the Aftermarket for New Bond Issues'. *Journal of Financial Economics*, 86(3): 643–82.

Green, R.C., D. Li and N. Schurhoff (2010). 'Price Discovery in Illiquid Markets: Do Financial Asset Prices Rise Faster than they Fall?' *Journal of Finance*, 65(5): 1669–702.

Greenwald, J. (2000). 'Changes Afoot in Coverage for Muni Bonds'. *Business Insurance*. 30 January, available at: www.businessinsurance.com.

Harris, L.E. and M.S. Piwowar (2006). 'Secondary Trading Costs in the Municipal Bond Market'. *Journal of Finance*, 61(3): 1361–97.

Hirtle, B. (1987). 'The Growth of the Financial Guarantee Market'. *Quarterly Review, FRB New York*, 12(1): 10–28.

Hong, G. and A. Warga (2004). 'Municipal Marketability'. *Journal of Fixed Income*, 14(2): 86–95.

Hsueh, L.P. and P.R. Chandy (1989). 'An Examination of the Yield Spread Between Insured and Uninsured Debt'. *Journal of Financial Research*, 12(3): 235–44.

Hsueh, L.P. and Y.A. Liu (1990). 'The Effectiveness of Debt Insurance as a Valid Signal of Bond Quality'. *Journal of Risk and Insurance*, 57(4): 691–700.

Joehnk, M.D. and D. Minge (1976). 'Guaranteed Municipal Bonds – Their Performance and Evaluation'. *Review of Business and Economic Research*, 12(1): 1–18.

Justice, J.B. and S. Simon (2002). 'Municipal Bond Insurance: Trends and Prospects'. *Public Budgeting and Finance*, 22(4): 114–37.

Kidwell, D.S., E.H. Sorensen and J.M. Wachowitz, Jr (1987). 'Estimating the Signaling Benefits of Debt Insurance: The Case of Municipal Bonds'. *Journal of Financial and Quantitative Analysis*, 22(3): 299–313.

Klein, R.W. (2009). 'The Future of Financial Monitoring of Insurance Companies in the US'. *Journal of Insurance Regulation*, 28(1): 73–98.

Kotecha, M.K. (1998). 'The Role of Insurance in Asset-Backed Securities'. In F. Fabozzi (ed.), *Issuer Perspective on Securitization*. Hoboken, NY: Wiley.

Liu, G. (2012). 'Municipal Bond Insurance Premium, Credit Rating, and Underlying Credit Risk'. *Public Budgeting and Finance*, 32(1): 128–56.

Lucas, D.J., L.S. Goodman and F.J. Fabozzi (2004). 'Default Rates on Structured Finance Securities'. *Journal of Fixed Income*, 14(2): 44–53.

Marlowe, J. (2007). 'Method of Sale, Price Volatility, and the Secondary Market for New Issue Municipal Bonds'. Paper presented at the Association of Budgeting and Financial Management Annual Conference. 24 October. Washington, DC.

Moldogaziev, T. (2012). 'Price Formation in Municipal Secondary Trades'. Paper presented at the Western Social Science Association Annual Conference, Houston, pp. 1–48.

Moldogaziev, T. (2013). 'The Collapse of the Municipal Bond Insurance Market: How Did We Get Here and is there Life for the Monoline Industry beyond the Great Recession?' *Journal of Public Budgeting, Accounting, and Financial Management*, 25(1): 199–233.

Moldogaziev, T. and C.L. Johnson (2011). *The Determinants of Bond Insurance Premium*. Indiana University School of Public & Environmental Affairs Research Paper, No. 2011-03-06: 1–28, Bloomington, IN.

Moldogaziev, T., S.N. Kioko and W.B. Hildreth (2013). 'Bankruptcy Risk Premium in the Municipal Securities Market'. Association for Budgeting and Financial Management Annual Conference 2013. 3–5 October, Washington, DC.

Nanda, V. and R. Singh (2004). 'Bond Insurance: What is Special About Munis?' *Journal of Finance*, 59(5): 2253–80.

New York Insurance Department (2008). *Circular Letter No.19, 1-12 'Best Practices' for Financial Guaranty Insurers*. State of New York Insurance Department, New York.

Peng, J. (2002). 'Do Investors Look Beyond Insured Triple-A Rating? An Analysis of Standard & Poor's Underlying Ratings'. *Public Budgeting and Finance*, 22(3): 115–31.

Perkins, M.L. and R. Quinn (2001). 'Financial Guarantee Insurance and Surety Bonds'. In T.C. Kazlow and B.C. King (eds), *The Law of Miscellaneous and Commercial Surety Bonds*. Chicago, IL: American Bar Association.

Rajan, R.G. (2005). 'Has Financial Development Made the World Riskier?' Kansas City, MO, Federal Reserve Bank of Kansas City.

Satz, M.E. and J.R. Perry (1992). 'Municipal Bond Insurance'. In R. Lamb, J. Leigland and S. Rappaport (eds), *The Handbook of Municipal Bonds and Public Finance*, pp. 572–607. New York: New York Institute of Finance.

Smith, S.D. and R.B. Harper (1993). 'Private Insurance of Public Debt: Another Look at the Costs and Benefits of Municipal Insurance'. *Economic Review, FRB of Atlanta*, 78(5): 27–38.

Standard & Poor's (2012a). *Global Structured Finance Default Study, 1978–2011: Credit Quality Fell For The Fifth Consecutive Year In 2011*. Standard & Poor's, New York.

Standard & Poor's (2012b). *The US Bond Insurance Industry is on a Path to Reemergence, But of a Different Profile*. Standard & Poor's, New York.

Thakor, A.V. (1982). 'An Exploration of Competitive Signaling Equilibria with "Third Party" Information Production: The Case of Debt Insurance'. *Journal of Finance*, 37(3): 717–39.

Chapter 13

Bunch, B. (2012). 'Preserving the Public Interest in Highway Public–Private Partnerships: A Case Study of the State of Texas'. *Public Budgeting and Finance*, 32(1): 36–57.

Chicago Infrastructure Trust (2013). 'How it Works'. Chicago, IL, Chicago Infrastructure Trust, http://shapechicago.org/about/how-it-works/.

Luby, M.J. (2009). *The Use of Federal Innovative Finance Techniques in Public–Private Partnerships: The Case of the Capital Beltway*. Government Finance Officers Association, Chicago, IL.

Reason Foundation (2011). *Risks and Rewards for Public–Private Partnerships for Highways*. Reason Foundation, Los Angeles, CA.

Vining, A. and A. Boardman (2008). 'Public–Private Partnerships: Eight Rules for Governments'. *Public Works Management and Policy*, 13(2): 149–61.

Chapter 14

Oates, W.E. (2005). 'Toward a Second-Generation Theory of Fiscal Federalism'. *International Tax and Public Finance*, 12(4): 349–73.

Appendix B

Macaulay, F.R. (1938). 'Some Theoretical Problems Suggested by the Movements of Interest Rates, Bond Yields and Stock Prices in the United States since 1856'. *The National Bureau of Economic Research*. Cambridge, MA.

Index